DATE DUE

THE NORMAN CONQUEST

Critical Issues in History

Consulting Editor: Donald T. Critchlow

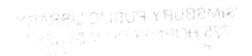

THE NORMAN CONQUEST

England after William the Conqueror

HUGH M. THOMAS

ROWMAN & LITTLEFIELD PUBLISHERS, INC.

Lanham • Boulder • New York • Toronto • Plymouth, UK

ROWMAN & LITTLEFIELD PUBLISHERS, INC.

Published in the United States of America
by Rowman & Littlefield Publishers, Inc.
A wholly owned subsidary of The Rowman & Littlefield Publishing Group, Inc.
4501 Forbes Boulevard, Suite 200, Lanham, Maryland 20706
www.rowmanlittlefield.com

Estover Road, Plymouth PL6 7PY, United Kingdom

Copyright © 2008 by Rowman & Littlefield Publishers, Inc.
All maps by Andrew Lowerre

British Library Cataloging in Publication Information Available

Library of Congress Cataloging-in-Publication Data

Thomas, Hugh M.
  The Norman conquest : England after William the Conqueror / Hugh M.
Thomas.
    p.   cm. — (Critical issues in history)
  Includes bibliographical references and index.
  ISBN-13: 978-0-7425-3839-9 (cloth : alk. paper)
  ISBN-10: 0-7425-3839-7 (cloth : alk. paper)
  ISBN-13: 978-0-7425-3840-5 (pbk. : alk. paper)
  ISBN-10: 0-7425-3840-0 (pbk. : alk. paper)
  1. Great Britain—History—Norman period, 1066–1154. 2. Normans—Great
Britain. 3. Great Britain—History—William I, 1066–1087. 4. William I, King
of England, 1027 or 8–1087. 5. Great Britain—Civilization—French influences.
I. Title.
DA195.T48 2008
942.02'1—dc22

2007020161

Printed in the United States of America

∞™ The paper used in this publication meets the minimum requirements of
American National Standard for Information Sciences—Permanence of Paper for
Printed Library Materials, ANSI/NISO Z39.48-1992.

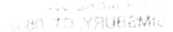

CONTENTS

ILLUSTRATIONS

MAPS

SIMPLIFIED GENEALOGIES

FIGURES

ACKNOWLEDGMENTS

I would like to thank the editors, Donald Critchlow and Susan McEachern, for inviting me to write this volume in their series. I have long wanted to write for a more general audience, and this has given me an opportunity to do so earlier than I expected.

I have incurred a number of other debts as well. The librarians at Richter Library at the University of Miami have continued to help me obtain the needed resources. The following students in my classes have read one or more chapters and provided feedback: Charles Azcuy, Adam Bates, Michelle Benitez, Roland Betancourt, Kristien Mark Boyle, Rachael Burg, Chris Clements, Karina Dearwood, Kate Drescher, Rachelle Durand, Dimitri Gatis, Adam Gibb, Cyrus Girson, Benjamin Gordon, Jane Graham, John Hoyes, Zachary Johnson, Lance Kiss, Sari Lando, Amy Lanham, Bob Larson, Nick Leyden, Theresa Lima, Jason Mannion, Jason Martorella, Natalia Medina, Josh Miller, Retzfellah Mortimer, Yasser Navarrete, Jasmin Nuñez, Freddie Ordoñez, Jacqlyn Pallagi, Darleen Patacchia, Melissa Perez, Nydia Perez, Michael Pitta, Alexis Placencia, Keely Portz, Nick Poulos, Aishwarya Reddy, Katie Reed, Yonner Richert, John Robertson, Cristian Rodriguez, Manelle St. Hilaire, Junko Saito, Therese Savona, Jennifer Scott, Vivian Siu, Greg Speier, Ben Stearns, Elizabeth Tedford, Stephen Treadway, and Wendell Waters. It is both humbling and gratifying to get excellent advice from one's students. Bob Stacey has also provided valuable guidance, and Michael Clanchy has made some useful suggestions. The production staff at Rowman & Littlefield was both helpful and efficient. My children have provided perspective and good cheer throughout the process of writing this book. Needless to say, all remaining shortcomings and errors remain my own.

Map 1. England

Map 2.   Normandy and Surrounding Regions

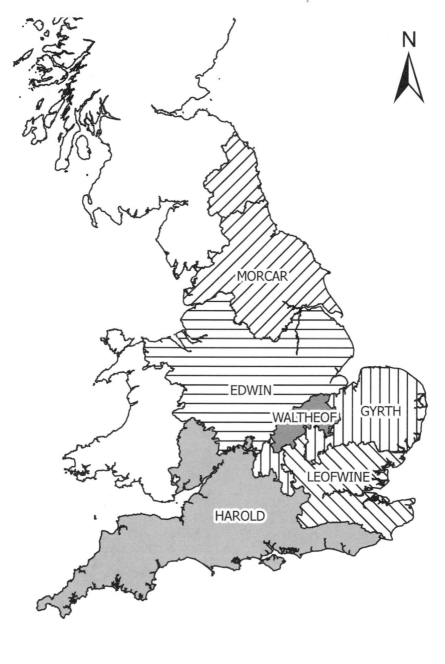

Map 3. English Earldoms at the Death of Edward the Confessor

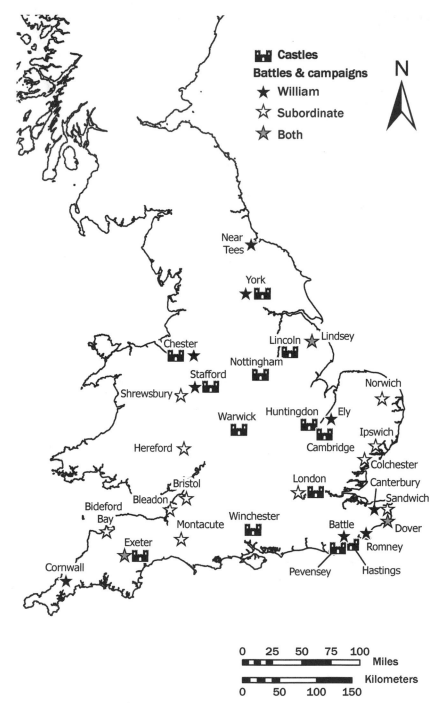

Castles

Battles & campaigns

★ William

☆ Subordinate

★ Both

N

Near Tees

York

Chester

Lincoln Lindsey

Nottingham

Stafford

Shrewsbury

Warwick Huntingdon Ely

Hereford

Cambridge

Norwich

Ipswich

Colchester

Bristol

London Canterbury

Bleadon

Sandwich

Bideford Bay

Montacute Winchester

Dover

Battle

Romney

Exeter

Pevensey Hastings

Cornwall

| 0 | 25 | 50 | 75 | 100 | Miles |

| 0 | 50 | 100 | 150 | Kilometers |

Map 4. William the Conqueror's Castles and Campaigns

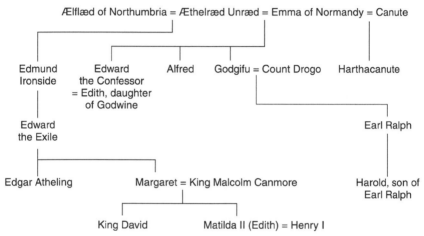

Genealogy 1. Edward the Confessor's Family

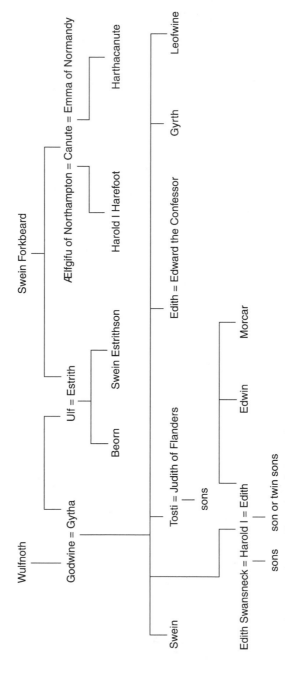

Genealogy 2. The Families of Godwine and Canute

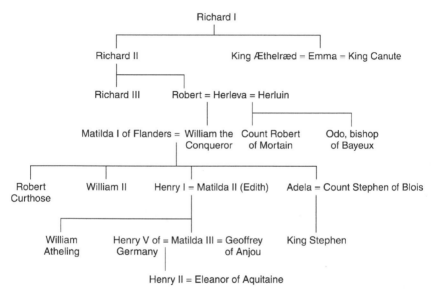

Genealogy 3. **The Family of William the Conqueror**

INTRODUCTION: CONTINGENCY, WARFARE, AND HISTORY

When W. C. Sellar and R. J. Yeatman published *1066 and All That*— their comic history of England— in 1931, they promised to include 103 good things, 5 bad kings, and 2 genuine dates.[1] As the title indicates, one of those dates was 1066, the year in which William the Conqueror seized the English crown. The year 1066 has always been a major date in English history, as famous as 1776 is for the United States, because historians have long considered the Norman Conquest pivotal. This was especially true for earlier generations of historians. For many of them, battles, great men, and political institutions constituted the true stuff of history. The Norman Conquest featured a larger-than-life conqueror, William of Normandy, and the hard-fought and decisive Battle of Hastings. Many historians argued that it introduced what they saw as the central institution of feudalism. Altogether, the Norman Conquest had most of the features that early generations of professional historians believed shaped history. It followed, in their view, that the impact of the conquest must have been profound.

The events of 1066 have also long appealed to more general readers of history, who have been interested in battles and great men at least as long as professional historians have. Even larger-than-life figures can bring the complexities of history down to a comprehensible scale. One can place oneself in the shoes of a figure such as William the Conqueror or the man he defeated, King Harold Godwineson, pondering their actions, wondering what decisions one would make in their places. Warfare still has a strong aura of glory and romance attached to it, despite its brutal costs, and one can wonder how one would perform under its pressures. It is no surprise that military history and biography remain the most popular sorts of history among general readers.

Despite their continuing popularity for general audiences, however, battles and great men have passed out of fashion among professional historians. Even in the nineteenth century, many historians explored other factors, such as economic change, that shaped historical developments. During the twentieth century and especially its later decades, historians cast their nets wider and wider, exploring everything from the history of the department store to the history of pornography. New fields of history, such as the history of gender and sexuality, became mainstream. Though the study of institutions has remained important and there are still many historians working on the history of warfare and of military leaders, the main focus of professional research has passed elsewhere. Military history itself has changed, becoming more comprehensive than the old focus on generals and battles. Military historians themselves are questioning old verities. Stephen Morillo, one of the leading military historians of Anglo-Norman England, rejected the "great man" approach in his introduction to a series of extracts and articles on the Battle of Hastings. Noting that William had benefited from a contrary wind that delayed his attack until Harold Godwineson had been drawn north by a threat from a third claimant, Harald Hardrada of Norway, Morillo invoked the idea of chaos theory, which describes how small, even random, factors can sometimes have a huge effect on larger systems. Drawing on the quip of another scholar, John Gillingham, he wondered if William, who was sometimes called William the Bastard, due to his illegitimate birth, ought really to be known as William the Lucky Bastard.[2]

Naturally, some historians have protested that important individuals and military operations *do* matter and that the shift has gone too far. For me, some of the most interesting attempts to reinvigorate traditional approaches to history have been those of David Hackett Fischer, a specialist in the early history of the United States. In books on Paul Revere and on George Washington's victories at Trenton and Princeton, Fischer has emphasized the idea of contingency.[3] He argues that much historical change is contingent upon— that is, results from—the decisions and actions of individuals, including both ordinary and extraordinary people. On one level, this argument merely states the obvious, but it shifts attention away from impersonal forces in history and refocuses it on the personal. I myself am one of the modern breed of social historians, but I find Fischer's approach intriguing, particularly in relation to the subject of this book. There can be no doubt that the Norman Conquest was contingent upon individual choices and actions, above all, the decision of William the Conqueror to undertake a dangerous expedition in pursuit of a problematic claim to the throne of England. Had William done the sensible thing and remained quietly in Normandy, enjoying the fruits of his considerable accomplishments before 1066, the Norman Conquest would certainly not have happened. The Norman Conquest was also contingent upon military success. The Battle of Hastings was a closely run affair, and had Harold Godwineson, William's English rival, chosen a different military approach, the Norman Conquest might well have failed. The plans Harold did adopt might have worked, had the invasion of Harald Hardrada not pulled him away from southern England and given William a golden opportunity to land in England with little opposition. As Morillo noted, luck played a role here, but so too did the decisions of Harald Hardrada and, as we shall see, Harold Godwineson's brother Tosti. The idea of contingency, with an emphasis on military and political decision making, applies very strongly to the Norman Conquest.

But did the Norman Conquest matter? Obviously, it brought a change of dynasty, but did it affect the lives of ordinary people? Did it bring major changes in the economic and social spheres of English history? For that matter, did it substantially change government? The fact that much work in recent decades stresses historical continuity across the conquest underlines the importance of these questions. Was the Norman Conquest simply a struggle between elites that affected a few thousand families but had little wider impact upon English history? In other words, how much did the decisions of individuals like William the Conqueror and Harold Godwineson influence the broad sweep of English history? It is worth asking such questions explicitly, and now is a good time to do so. Though the Norman Conquest was already being studied in great depth in the nineteenth century, useful works continue to emerge in the twenty-first century. More important, a vast amount of scholarship exists describing various aspects of English society before and after the conquest, making it easier to study how profoundly William's successful invasion changed that country. At this point, one can make a reasonable assessment of whether the Norman Conquest brought widespread and fundamental change, barely affected English history, or had some level of influence between these two extremes.[4]

The first part of this book covers the background and course of the conquest. In it, I seek to explain the motives of the principal actors and how and why the Norman Conquest succeeded. In the second part, I describe the impact of the conquest in a wide range of areas, and I intend to show in what areas the Norman Conquest (and by extension the decisions and actions of William, Harold, and their followers) brought radical change and where it did not. Where this book differs from recent overviews of the Norman Conquest or of the Anglo-Norman period is that in it, I seek to draw out the precise consequences of the conquest on the conquered society.[5] I do not treat the military actions in a vacuum, but neither do I seek to give a comprehensive picture of England in the generations after the conquest. Rather, I focus on the specific changes brought by the conquest. In both sections I draw upon generations of accumulated research as well as my own research and interpretations. I have tried to strike a balance between providing a clear, streamlined narrative and alerting students to the many problems of evidence and the numerous debates between scholars. Instead of discussing every debate over the conquest (and there have been many over the centuries), I have picked a certain number of particularly important or interesting ones as well as ones that uncover the problems medievalists deal with in interpreting difficult and often fragmentary evidence.[6] Overall, I intend to use the Norman Conquest as a case study to explore just how useful traditional ideas about the impact of battles and great individuals remain in the light of recent developments in the study of history.

NOTES

1. W. C. Sellar and R. J. Yeatman, *1066 and All That: A Memorable History of England* (New York, 1931), title page.

2. Stephen Morillo, ed., *The Battle of Hastings* (Woodbridge, 1996), xviii–xx.

3. David Hackett Fischer, *Paul Revere's Ride* (New York, 1994), xiii–xviii; David Hackett Fischer, *Washington's Crossing* (New York, 2004), 364–67.

4. I should note that in focusing on England, I am not following the current trend to write about British rather than English history, relegating to "foreign affairs and geopolitics" the adventures of the Normans in Wales and Scotland. The shift from English to British history has helped bring the fascinating histories of Scotland and Wales to a broader audience and has helped show the interaction among the three lands, but it has as much to do with modern politics as medieval realities. The Normans did have an impact on Scotland and Wales, but it was quite different than the impact on England, on which I have chosen to focus.

5. The book closest to mine is Brian Golding, *Conquest and Colonisation: The Normans in Britain, 1066-1100*, 2nd ed. (New York, 2001). Golding discusses many of the changes brought by the Norman Conquest, but focuses somewhat less than I do on the changes brought by the conquest and somewhat more on describing Anglo-Norman culture. He also concentrates more on the issues I discuss in chapter 3 and less on those I discuss in chapters 4 and 5. Finally, his time frame is shorter than mine.

6. Marjorie Chibnall has done an excellent job of covering the many debates in *The Debate on the Norman Conquest* (Manchester, 1999).

I

CONTEXT AND CONQUEST

Who were William the Conqueror and his rival, Harold Godwine-son? What was their background? How was the Norman Conquest itself fought out? These are the questions that I seek to answer in the first part of this book. Chapter 1 focuses on William, Harold, and the other main actors in the conquest. In it, I describe the claims of William and Harold to the throne of England and the historical background that led to the throne being available to men whose hereditary claims were essentially nonexistent. The dynamics of power that enabled the two men to seize control of England play an important part in this discussion as does the way in which their respective backgrounds shaped them as military and political leaders. An equally important focus of the first chapter is the nature of English and, to a lesser degree, Norman society in the period before the conquest, because an exploration of the extent to which the Norman Conquest reshaped English society requires some description of that society before 1066 and of the culture from which the new elites came.

The second chapter covers the Norman Conquest itself. Naturally, the great Battle of Hastings, in which the Normans decisively defeated the English, forms the centerpiece of the chapter. However, I also discuss the preparations William and Harold made for the invasion and explore their respective goals in the maneuvering leading up to the battle. In addition, I devote a relatively large amount of space to the ways in which William secured his control, militarily and politically, in the years following 1066—partly because I think this period, even more than the campaign of 1066, demonstrates William's qualities as a leader. Obviously, the chapter as a whole contains the key narrative overview of the book, but it also helps set the stage for the book's second part. After all, the manner in which William and the Normans carried out their conquest of England obviously had an impact on the ways in which that conquest affected the country they had conquered.

1

THE BACKGROUND TO
THE CONQUEST

ENGLAND BEFORE THE NORMAN CONQUEST

By the standards of economically developed modern countries, England in 1066 was technologically backward and miserably poor.[1] By the standards of the time, it was a rich land, "most beautiful and fertile," according to one immigrant monk from Flanders, **Goscelin of St. Bertin**. Goscelin went on to describe it as "abundant in farmlands, meadows, pastureland, rivers, and bays, graced with mountains, fields, and woods, rejoicing in towns and crafts and overseas trade, and made famous by a fair people and wealth of goods."[2] When William the Conqueror's biographer described his hero's return with massive plunder, he emphasized the land's wealth in precious metal and grain.[3] To ambitious predators such as William, the Norwegian king Harald Hardrada, and their followers, England seemed a rich prize indeed.

Domesday Book, the great survey commissioned by William twenty years after his victory, reveals why contemporaries thought so highly of England's wealth.[4] The written form of the survey received its distinctive nickname because it went into such detail that people compared it to the accounting of vices and virtues that medieval Christians expected at the Last Judgment, or Doomsday. *Domesday Book* recorded some 269,000 landlords, townspeople, tenants, and slaves, a figure that has produced a wide range of estimates for total population. A sum roughly around two million seems safest, according to current scholarship.[5] Tens of thousands of plows, usually with eight oxen each, prepared millions of acres of land for various crops of grain. Plenty of land remained for pasture: in only eight out of the thirty-odd counties covered by the survey, landlords alone possessed nearly three hundred thousand sheep and much other livestock. The waters in and around

3

England provided an abundant supply of fish. Lords received tens of thousands of herrings per year in rent from coastal fisheries and tens of thousands of eels, a medieval delicacy, from inland fisheries throughout the country.[6]

Though agriculture dominated the economy of eleventh-century England (as in all settled societies before the industrial revolution), a flourishing nonagricultural sector existed.[7] *Domesday Book* lists more than six thousand water mills, relatively high-tech devices in a low-tech society. The survey also records more than one hundred towns, some with populations that may have reached close to ten thousand.[8] London, which was omitted from the survey, probably had even more people. Towns were centers of craft production and of trade; smiths, leather workers, shopkeepers, and merchants all interacted with people transporting goods in from and out to the countryside. The important town of Winchester had streets named for butchers, goldsmiths, shoemakers, shield makers, wood sellers, and tanners, the last of whom turned animal hides into leather.[9] Luxury goods, including wine from France, pepper from Asia, and fine cloth and gems from a variety of places, changed hands in shops, markets, and fairs. Even more trade occurred in ordinary items such as wool, everyday cloth, and pottery. Though much exchange probably took place through barter, England had a partially monetized economy. The only coins were silver pennies, but one recent estimate suggests that about nine million of them circulated at the time of the conquest.[10] Even peasants clearly used coins occasionally, to pay rents or to make major purchases such as a sheep (five silver pennies), a pig (ten silver pennies), or an ox (thirty silver pennies).[11] Money was integral to the lifestyles of the upper classes. Landlords might depend heavily on the produce of their land and on rents paid in foodstuffs for everyday consumption, but they also had to oversee the selling of agricultural surplus so that they could buy military equipment and high-status luxury goods.

From the perspective of the English elites and the Normans who wished to replace them, one delightful aspect of the eleventh-century economy and society was the fact that they were designed to channel wealth upward. *Domesday Book*, which focuses on the resources of lords rather than the economy as a whole, clearly reveals this. For instance, it often records the number of fish that fishermen paid as rent, but not how many they caught. English society was deeply hierarchical, with the king, a handful of earls, and several thousand nobles—called **thanes**—dominating the rest of society. The hierarchy was not rigid: a prosperous, upwardly mobile peasant or a successful merchant could achieve the status of thane, and the bottom ranks of thanes rubbed shoulders with the upper ranks of peasants.[12] Nonetheless, status mattered greatly in late Anglo-Saxon society, and much of the wealth produced by ordinary people passed into the hands of the king, the earls, and the thanes.

The peasantry, like the nobility, was stratified. At the bottom were the slaves, who formed roughly 10 percent of the population and as much as a quarter in some areas.[13] They worked much of the land that lords set aside for themselves. They also served in the households of their masters and mistresses. Comparatively speaking, their lives were probably not as bad as those of plantation slaves under New World slavery, and the freeing of slaves was considered a pious act. Nonetheless, Anglo-Saxon slaves had difficult lives. In one Anglo-Saxon dialogue designed to teach boys Latin, a slave was made to complain about the amount of work given to him because he was unfree.[14] **William of Malmesbury**, a twelfth-century writer, listing the moral shortcomings of the preconquest nobility, described lords impregnating their female slaves and then callously selling them for export abroad.[15]

The mass of the peasantry were generally better off than the slaves, though that is not saying much. They held their own plots of land from their lords, for which they paid rents in produce and sometimes money. Some would work two or three days per week on the lands of their lords, in addition to providing other services such as carting the lord's property around. Above them were a small group of prosperous peasants, freemen and perhaps **sokemen**, who comprised between 5 and 15 percent of the total population and had lighter burdens.[16] Even these peasants supported their superiors in various ways, not just by performing light labor services but by providing hospitality, acting as messengers, helping with hunting (the great pastime of the nobility), and sometimes serving in war. The most important of these figures filled out the circle of followers and flunkies that even the most minor aristocrats needed to provide local muscle, fulfill military obligations, and achieve status.[17]

Lordship over land, slaves, and peasants, along with rents from urban property and miscellaneous sources of income, provided earls and thanes with riches, sometimes in breathtaking quantities.[18] The wealthiest had extraordinarily luxurious lifestyles. In the late Anglo-Saxon period, nobles were building lavish compounds across England, with large wooden halls, private chambers, and stone churches. A number of wills survive from eleventh-century thanes and noblewomen, and among the items listed were weapons inlaid with precious metals, jewelry, gold crucifixes, tapestries, a headband weighted down with gold, and piles of gold and silver.[19] The same dialogue that spoke of the hard work of slaves also described the importation of gems, gold, and silk and other cloth dyed with a notoriously expensive purple tint.[20] It is no wonder that Norman nobles and other continental adventurers found England a tempting target.

Another important recipient of wealth was the church, but ecclesiastical riches only provided another source of appeal to the Normans.[21] Bishops, abbots, abbesses, and their churches collectively acted as landlords to about a quarter of England. Normandy had a clerical elite, closely intertwined with its secular elite, and the English church could provide many opportunities for the more ambitious among them. Norman nobles and knights might also hope to seize land from the church. But the very existence of a well-established and prosperous church would have appealed to the Normans, for they tended to be as pious as they were predatory. I do not mean to downplay the piety of medieval elites, which could be deep and genuine, but in the religious worldview of the time, support for the church served an eminently practical function. Medieval Christians saw God's favor as necessary for success in temporal life, and thus investment in winning divine approval was money well spent, particularly for the nobility. More important, as religious writers and preachers emphasized, was hope for salvation and fear of damnation. After all, the afterlife involved eternity rather than a few measly decades on earth, and the possibilities of unimaginable joy or unbearable pain. Religious thinkers in this time before the crusades saw little hope for the salvation of rich warriors except through the prayers of the religious, especially monks and nuns. The fact that England already had in place a network of well-organized "factories" to produce a continuous output of prayer and worship—which is partly what the great churches were—only made the country more attractive to the thoroughly Christianized warrior elite of Normandy. The church also provided what most contemporaries would have considered crucial aspects of their culture. Great churches were centers for art, music, and, above all, learning. The importance of the church for learning was even truer for Normandy, where all writing was still in Latin, than for England, where the increasing use of English made reading and writing somewhat more accessible for the laity. Thus, the vast amount of wealth channeled to the church made England no less attractive to acquisitive Christian warriors than the wealth left to the laity.

Naturally, the wealthiest and most powerful individual in England was the king. The earliest biographer of King Edward the Confessor, who reigned until 1066, described his richly adorned clothes, loaded with gems, pearls, and gold thread; his gold-covered throne; his precious imported carpets; his walking staff, encrusted with gold and gems; and his saddle and riding gear, covered with gold ornamentation.[22] Conspicuous consumption is not a modern invention. The king was the largest single landholder in the country, but he also headed a government that was very sophisticated for the time, though rudimentary to modern eyes. A large household moved from place to place with the king, though treasure and perhaps some documents remained at Winchester, which was the closest the kingdom had to a capital at the time. The king's household doubled as the central government, but the king also had local representatives. The most important of these were the **earls**, and below them came the **shire reeves**, or sheriffs. In 1066, most of England was already divided into **shires**, or counties (with boundaries that would remain fairly stable until 1974). Shires were divided, in turn, into smaller units called **hundreds**, or **wapentakes.** The king also had estate managers at his individual manors. Finally, since Anglo-Saxon kings firmly controlled the church in their kingdom, bishops and other church officials served partly as royal servants.

Royal government had various responsibilities.[23] A major function was simply to keep the king supplied with the money and goods necessary for his luxurious lifestyle. Beyond this, the only major economic function of the royal government was to produce the standardized coinage that helped England's nascent market economy function. Happily for the king, control of the coinage also brought profit through charges on the minting of coins. More important in medieval eyes was the religious duty of the king. The king benefited from the power and service that control of the church brought him, and also theoretically from the power of prayer. In return he was expected to run the church well, protect it, and support it generously. More broadly, the king was supposed to maintain justice and public morality. A caveat is needed here: medieval people tended to view justice as more of a private or local affair than modern people do. In the early Anglo-Saxon period, if someone killed or injured a person, it was up to the victim's friends and, above all, family to punish the culprits. Not surprisingly, **blood feud** remained an integral part of Anglo-Saxon society.[24] However, during the course of the Middle Ages, justice slowly shifted more into the public, governmental sphere. Anglo-Saxon kings, advised by their bishops and nobles, issued law codes that dealt with both secular and religious matters, though the practical impact of these codes is debatable. More important, a system of shire and hundred courts, overseen by the king's representatives—namely, bishops, earls, and sheriffs—had grown up around England, and the most important cases might be brought to the king himself.

The most crucial duty of the king was to protect the country, ideally by crushing invaders in battle, less ideally by paying them off—a tactic that even King Alfred the Great, a military genius, had resorted to against the

Vikings.[25] Kings normally had a war band as part of their household, recruited through pay and the promise of rewards. In the event of large scale military operations, kings could hire more soldiers, and they expected the greatest nobles to show up with war bands at their summons. Such military practices were common in the Middle Ages, but one of the great achievements of the late Anglo-Saxon kings was to develop a system of units of land, called **hides** (or **carucates** in some areas), through which military burdens could be apportioned. Nominally, each hide had 120 acres of farmland, with attached pasture, meadow, and woodland. The system could be used for various purposes. For instance, when fortifications were being built, the king might allot to each hide in the region the duty of providing workers and defenders.[26] He might expect every five hides to produce a warrior with full armor when he summoned an army.[27] He might levy a certain number of pennies from each hide when the Vikings had to be bought off, though by the end of the Anglo-Saxon period this levy had been turned into a regular tax, the **danegeld**. Eventually, this sophisticated, flexible system would be used for other purposes by local people, such as dividing up village resources. For instance, someone with one hide in a five-hide village could pasture one-fifth of the animals that the village's common pastures could support. However, the system's main purpose was to channel resources to the military efforts of the king.

There is some debate about how sophisticated the Anglo-Saxon state was, and this provides the starting point for our first digression on problems of evidence and interpretation. Most scholars agree that late Anglo-Saxon government was sophisticated for its time (at least within a western-European context), but scholars disagree on whether certain elements existed within the government, and one may ask how sophisticated it was even in comparison to English government in the twelfth century, let alone later periods.[28] Debate must turn ultimately on the weight placed on surviving scraps of evidence and on how much evidence may have been lost. Both questions rest in turn heavily upon the use of English in government.

Anglo-Saxon government, in its use of the native written language, had an advantage most European governments lacked until much later in the Middle Ages. Latin was overwhelmingly the language of writing in western Europe, even where people did not speak a language descended from Latin. Ireland, where written Irish was relatively common, was a major exception, but Ireland did not develop a strong central government during the Middle Ages. During the period of Viking invasions, England became a second exception. The Vikings had inflicted so much damage on English centers of learning that Alfred the Great, ever practical, promoted the use of English in writing as an unfortunate but necessary supplement to Latin. His central concerns were religious, but writing in English also provided many benefits for the government of his successors. The very use of English, however, is one of the factors that makes it hard to judge the level of sophistication of the Anglo-Saxon government, since the Normans shifted back to the use of Latin, rendering earlier government records useless and much more likely to be discarded.

To a large degree, the debate over the sophistication of late Anglo-Saxon government turns on the possible loss of records. A parallel from the twelfth century shows why the question of lost records is so important. From the second half of the twelfth century, we have a nearly unbroken sequence of pipe rolls, yearly accounts of royal revenues. Other regular types of royal records soon joined the pipe rolls, and in each generation that followed, royal records expanded exponentially. These records provide unequivocal evidence of the growing reach and sophistication of government.[29] From another perspective, we can clearly observe that the further one goes back in time, the smaller and less sophisticated the government was. However, it is dangerous to extrapolate too far. Only one pipe roll (dating to 1130) exists from the reign of William the Conqueror's youngest son, **Henry I**, though references in that document reveal that there were once others. If that single roll had not survived, we might imagine that government under Henry I was less developed than it actually was.[30] This should give us pause. Many scholars believe that the financial system that resulted in the pipe rolls was developed under Henry I, but the loss of most of his pipe rolls shows that the lack of evidence for government systems may simply be due to the loss of records rather than to the absence of such systems.

The problem of possible missing evidence becomes even more pressing for the Anglo-Saxon period precisely because records in English were far more likely to be discarded than records in Latin. It is possible that late Anglo-Saxon government was much more sophisticated than the surviving evidence would suggest. There are three main reasons why some scholars think this is the case. First, the effectiveness of the government in such matters as coinage and hidage suggests a sophisticated system of written bureaucracy. Second, odd documents written in English have survived, such as a list of men for coast watch or (from shortly after the conquest) lists of payments of danegeld, which could be remnants of large classes of documents that once existed. Third, two decades after the Norman Conquest, the Normans managed to pull off the Domesday Survey, an impressive feat, but one that would have been easier if they had been able to use much existing documentation. Indeed, one scholar has argued that the Normans were ultimately unable to sustain government at the same level as the Anglo-Saxons.[31]

Though there is merit to these arguments, I remain skeptical about how far they can be taken. As chapter 3 will make clear, the Normans adapted at least one type of English document, the writ, to their own purposes, simply using Latin alone rather than relying on both languages, as the late Anglo-Saxon government had done. There is no reason to think that they could not have done so with other types of documents. Furthermore, I suspect that if the Anglo-Saxon government had possessed as extensive written records as "maximal" scholars argue, more would have survived, though this is only a matter of judgment. Barring the highly unlikely prospect of finding some trove of late Anglo-Saxon government documents, this argument is impossible to resolve with certainty and can serve as an illustration of why scholars can disagree about many aspects of history in the period.

Readers can, however, take away three points. First, Anglo-Saxon government was among the most advanced of its time. Second, by modern standards, this government was fairly rudimentary. Any central government that mostly moved from place to place in a baggage train with the king (and this was true long after 1066) was necessarily limited in its capacity. Moreover, one technique that late Anglo-Saxon kings still used to enforce their will or punish disobedient regions or towns was to send troops to lay waste to lands through plundering and burning. Devastating parts of one's own kingdom could be effective, but it suggests a lack of more sophisticated mechanisms of control. Nonetheless (and this raises the third point), the government worked well enough to make the kings of England enormously wealthy and powerful men by eleventh-century standards.

From 1042 until the first days of 1066, **Edward the Confessor** held that kingly position (for Edward's immediate family, see genealogy 1). He came from the line of the West Saxon kings who had traced themselves back to the Germanic god **Woden** (Odin in Scandinavia) and later, after conversion, from Woden to Noah and then to Adam. **Alfred the Great** was one of Edward's direct ancestors. Alfred's own ancestors had made the West Saxon kings powerful in the south of what became England. Alfred himself strengthened the kingdom in the face of the Viking onslaught and helped prepare the way for a war of expansion against the new Viking elites who had destroyed the other English kingdoms. The expansion itself began under Alfred's son and heir, **Edward the Elder**, and Alfred's daughter, **Æthelflæd**, who together captured the midlands and East Anglia. Æthelflæd had married the ruler of a remnant of the earlier English kingdom of Mercia and ruled it herself after he became senile and then died. Though Æthelflæd proved that a woman could be a very successful war leader even in the Middle Ages, when she died, her brother Edward locked up her daughter and only child in a nunnery and took over her lands. Edward's son **Athelstan** captured most of what is now northern England, though it would be several generations before that region was firmly tied to the rest of the kingdom. Athelstan also participated in a network of international marriage alliances and was even powerful enough to play kingmaker on the continent. Other members of the dynasty claimed imperial titles and asserted, with varying degrees of success, overlordship over other rulers in Britain and Ireland.

Not all of the kings of Alfred's line were destined for greatness. Edward the Confessor's own father, **Æthelræd**, whose name meant "noble counsel," received the nickname Unræd, or un-counsel, from later chroniclers. Though Unræd is often rendered as "the Unready" in modern English, better interpretations might be "the Ill-Counseled," "Bad Counsel" (linked to unrædas, or bad plans), or, to dip into contemporary slang, "the Clueless."[32] He received his unflattering nickname mainly because he lost England to renewed Viking invasions that, in certain respects, foreshadowed the Norman Conquest.

Some scholars have sought to rehabilitate Æthelræd, and their arguments bring up a second kind of problem that will reverberate throughout any history of the Norman Conquest, namely, bias in the sources.[33] During the Norman Conquest itself, bias on the part of chroniclers was a major factor in their positive or negative portrayals of important figures. In Æthelræd's case, the problem is somewhat more subtle. The most important narrative account, from one version of the *Anglo-Saxon Chronicle*, was written in the immediate aftermath of the king's reign. The perspective of the writer may have been shaped by the king's ultimate failure to defeat the Vikings, leading to a distortion of his overall record as a leader.[34] One can point to leaders in the modern world who were intelligent and able in many respects but have ended up with reputations as mere failures because of disasters beyond their control. Perhaps the same was true of Æthelræd, and recent works on the king clearly provide a more nuanced and complicated picture than a simplistic dismissal of Æthelræd "the Unready" or "the Clueless" would provide. Nonetheless, I am skeptical that the rehabilitation should be taken too far.[35] The *Anglo-Saxon Chronicle* was certainly influenced by the final disasters of the reign, but from the distance of centuries, it is not easy to tell the difference between a sloppy, partisan smear job and a thoughtful analysis based on hindsight by an observer who knew far more than we do.

One of the most famous quotes from this account in the *Anglo-Saxon Chronicle* is as follows: "And when [the Vikings] were in the east, then our army was held in the west; and when they were in the south, then our army was in the north. Then all the councilors were summoned to the king, and planned how the land should be held, but no plan stood for one month."[36] Other evidence shows that Æthelræd knew in theory how to successfully fight off the Vikings through practices such as countering the Viking control of the sea by building a fleet; he had learned some of the lessons of his ancestors. Nonetheless, he never quite managed the successful execution of his plans, suggesting that the above quote had some merit and was not simply a diatribe. It is true that with the relatively large Viking armies that came in his day, Æthelræd faced a larger challenge, but he also had greater resources, and historians may make a mistake in too readily dismissing the judgments of writers closer to the events than we are. As the reader will readily observe, getting around biases, or even telling bias from analysis, is a major difficulty for any historian, and we shall face similar problems in discussing key figures in the Norman Conquest. What remains undisputable is the fact that Æthelræd did fail and that Vikings, ultimately led by King **Swein I Forkbeard** of Denmark and then his son **Canute**, took over England (for the family of Swein and Canute, see genealogy 2). King Swein drove out Æthelræd in winter 1013–1014, and though the English called Æthelræd back after Swein's death later in 1014, Swein's son Canute took over the kingdom after the deaths of Æthelræd and his far abler son, **Edmund Ironside**, in 1016. Æthelræd's reign paved the way for the Norman Conquest in two respects. First, Swein and Canute showed that England could be conquered. Second, Æthelræd married **Emma**, a member of the ruling house of Normandy, in 1002. Their two sons, the future Edward the Confessor and Alfred, therefore grew up in exile in the Norman duchy as relatives of the dukes. Meanwhile, Canute ruled England from 1016 to 1035.[37] After ruthlessly eliminating a number of nobles, including many of the most powerful, and establishing a number of his own followers in England, he set about conciliating (but heavily taxing) his subjects. Overall, he managed both conciliation and taxation well, and as a result reigned quite successfully. Surprisingly, Canute married Æthelræd's widow Emma, no doubt to neutralize Norman hostility. He used English wealth to further his Scandinavian ambitions, for he secured his position in Denmark in 1019 and later conquered Norway for a time. England seems to have prospered during his reign, though a recession in church building during the period suggests that it took time to recover from the impact of years of Viking raids and invasions during Æthelræd's reign, and that recovery was slowed by Canute's heavy financial impositions.[38]

After Canute's death in 1035, the succession to the throne became quite confused for seven years, which created tensions that affected the fam-

ily of Harold Godwineson, the king who died at Hastings. Harold Godwineson's earlier namesake, **Harold I**, nicknamed Harefoot, was Canute's
son by an English noblewoman. Harold I moved early on to take power in
England after his father's death. He was opposed by Canute's widow, Emma,
and others, most notably **Godwine**, father of the future Harold II. Emma
and Godwine supported **Harthacanute**, Emma's son with Canute, claiming that he was the legitimate heir to the throne. Harthacanute, however,
focused on securing power in Denmark, which gave Harold I time to consolidate power in England. Harold eventually forced out Emma, made
peace with Godwine, and ruled England until 1040. In that year, Harthacanute came with a Danish fleet to challenge him. Harold died while
Harthacanute was on the way, a happy outcome for everyone but Harold,
since it prevented a likely civil war. Thereafter, Harthacanute ruled for two
years and in that time brought his mother, Emma, back to England and invited over another half brother, none other than Edward the Confessor, a
son of Emma and her first husband, the former Anglo-Saxon ruler Æthelræd.

Bringing Alfred's descendant back to England might have mattered little had Harthacanute enjoyed a long life span and had he borne children.
However, when Harthacanute died without children in 1042, Edward succeeded peacefully.[39] As a result, Alfred's royal line came back to power by a
surprising fluke of fortune that undid most of the consequences of the
Danish Conquest. Edward ruled from 1042 to 1066, and though at first he
had few of the personal relationships with nobles that were so important to
medieval royal power, having grown up in exile, he had a successful though
unspectacular reign. With some exceptions that will be discussed later, Edward's reign was largely peaceful, giving England more time to recover economically. Edward himself undertook few major initiatives, but he did rebuild Westminster Abbey in a new Romanesque style that was becoming
popular on the continent. Overall, the English seem to have had little to
complain of in his reign. Unfortunately, when he died at the beginning of
1066 he had no sons or daughters.

Edward did leave behind two grandnephews in England, **Edgar
Atheling**, who was grandson of Edmund Ironside, and **Harold, son of
Earl Ralph** and grandson of King Æthelræd's daughter **Godgifu** (see genealogy 1).[40] Both, however, were children, and neither had a strong
powerbase. Harold's father had been an earl, but Earl **Ralph the Timid** had
not grown up in England but on the continent with his father's family. Edward brought Ralph to England and made him a powerful figure when he
appointed him earl, but Ralph had limited time to build up a network of

followers and thereby create a secure military following he could pass on to his son. Moreover, Ralph had not had a particularly successful military career. The nickname Ralph the Timid, given to him by one twelfth-century chronicler, was probably not fair, but it may say something about his reputation after his death.[41] Edgar Atheling had perhaps the best claim to the throne as a grandson of Edmund Ironside, and indeed there was an attempt to make him king after Hastings. However, Edgar's father had only arrived in England from exile in 1057, whereupon he promptly died, and as a child, Edgar could not build up support for his claim. Moreover, there were no fixed rules of hereditary succession to the English throne and, as Canute had shown, power could trump legitimacy. In practical terms, succession to Edward the Confessor was wide open upon his death.

THE RISE OF THE GODWINESONS

This brings us to **Harold Godwineson**, the man who first succeeded Edward. To understand why Harold Godwineson rather than Edgar Atheling or Harold, son of Earl Ralph, could take the throne, despite that fact that they had far better claims, one must explore the history of the **Godwinesons**, or **Godwines** (see genealogy 2).[42] Harold's grandfather, **Wulfnoth**, was a powerful thane in the county of Sussex in southeastern England. At one point, he had had enough influence to lead twenty ships of warriors in revolt against King Æthelræd. However, it was Harold's father, Godwine, who truly created the family fortunes by becoming a favorite of King Canute. Canute married him to **Gytha,** who was related to the king by marriage, and made him an earl with responsibility over the old kingdom of **Wessex** in southern England.

After Canute died, Godwine had an uncanny knack for being on the wrong side at the wrong time. Immediately following Canute's death, Godwine backed Harthacanute and his mother Emma, as noted earlier. Harold I Harefoot's success in gaining power instead of Harthacanute might have spelled disaster for Godwine and his family, but Godwine survived by switching sides. How did he do this successfully? Emma, growing desperate in England, had sent messengers to her sons Edward and **Alfred** in Normandy. When Alfred came with a number of Norman followers, Godwine greeted him with open arms and promptly sold him out to Harold Harefoot. Harold tortured and mutilated Alfred and his followers, and Alfred died in prison. As a result, Godwine regained security, at least until 1040, when Harold died and Alfred's half brother Harthacanute showed up with a fleet. Godwine once again stood close to disaster, but with support from fellow earls he successfully avoided punishment by claiming that he was just following Harold Harefoot's orders. Godwine then bought Harthacanute's favor with a gift of a great warship, manned by eighty warriors equipped with fine armor and gold armbands.[43]

Harthacanute died in 1042, leaving the crown to Edward the Confessor, Alfred's full brother. Godwine supported Edward's accession to the throne; presented Edward with an even larger ship, one with purple sails and a prow carved in the shape of a dragon; and arranged for the king to marry his daughter **Edith** in 1045, thus making the king his son-in-law.[44] As a result, the Godwine family continued to prosper despite yet another change of power. Godwine's two eldest sons, **Swein** and the future king Harold, obtained earldoms, as did **Beorn**, nephew of his wife, Gytha. Swein was a political disaster whose subsequent achievements included kidnapping an abbess and treacherously murdering his cousin Earl Beorn. Harold, as it turned out, was far more able. But in the years 1051–1052, the family again teetered on the edge of disaster. Edward had attempted to build a powerbase by bringing in followers from Normandy, and these foreigners increasingly challenged the interests of Godwine and his family. Edith had not yet produced a child, and it is likely that Edward was thinking about putting her aside. It is also likely that Edward had not forgiven Godwine for the death of his brother Alfred. In 1051 a brawl between some continental visitors and some townspeople of Dover escalated into a political crisis when Edward ordered Godwine to lay waste to Dover, and Godwine refused. The earls from outside the family sided with the king, Godwine's support melted away, and the family fled into exile.

Harold and one younger brother escaped to Ireland, and the rest of the family journeyed to Flanders, where yet another brother, **Tosti**, had married into the ruling family. Swein did his family a favor, for a change, by undertaking a pilgrimage to Jerusalem, theoretically regaining divine favor and no doubt recovering some religious credibility for the clan. He did his family an even greater favor by dying on the way home, thus removing his controversial presence from the political scene. In the meantime, Harold and his younger brother **Leofwine** returned from Ireland and plundered southwestern England to demonstrate that the family had military power and the willingness to use it. Godwine returned to southeastern England, where the core of the family's powerbase lay, and rallied support. The king gathered troops, Godwine and Harold recruited followers, and the two forces moved together for a huge anticlimax in which the two sides struck a deal. King Edward restored Godwine and his family to favor and allowed his council to exile many of his Norman followers. Godwine died in 1053, but Harold stepped into his shoes, and the family continued to prosper, with Harold's brothers Tosti, Leofwine, and Gyrth all gaining earldoms.

How did this family manage to flourish despite Godwine's implication in the death of Prince Alfred and the occasional hostility of kings? Except for Swein, they must have had enormous political skills, and all were aided by the preference of most leading nobles of their generation for accommodation and compromise rather than war. Yet they were also relentless in building up their own estates and power. Godwine had accumulated a huge network of estates by the time Canute died, though precisely how large is difficult to say. He and his children gathered land by a variety of means, some of them perfectly legitimate but others dubious: gifts from the king, appropriation from various churches, bequests in wills, and no doubt purchases. By 1065, members of the family (including the queen) collectively held more land than the king, and the yearly income from their estates may have approached 10 percent of what all landlords received from England as a whole. One scholar, Robin Fleming, has estimated that had Godwine's children been willing and able to receive all their rents in money, they would have collected over two million silver pennies a year, or some three tons of silver.[45]

Money alone did not provide power. The Godwines also had a large network of followers. Like the king, Godwine and later his sons attracted household warriors by pay and the promise of reward. They also gained loyalty by the customary method of granting land, and as a result they had various aristocratic tenants throughout England. In addition, Anglo-Saxon England had a system in which fluid networks of influence were created through personal commendation, wherein individuals swore loyalty to a lord, often one from whom they held no land. The account of several counties in *Domesday Book* reveals how every landlord and many free peasants commended themselves to a lord, sometimes the king but often powerful nobles such as Harold and his siblings. Harold and his brothers had hundreds of followers scattered across England. These included wealthy thanes but also humble figures, including one whom *Domesday Book* shows died at Hastings with Harold.[46] It was the support of such commended men, on top of household warriors, that gave Godwine and his family such strong political and military clout, even against the king, and allowed them to recover their powerful position in 1052.

Nonetheless, the exile of 1051 demonstrated the precariousness of the position of Harold and his family. Historians frequently ponder the threat that unusually powerful nobles such as the Godwinesons posed to kings, but rarely consider the threat kings posed to such nobles. Harold was old enough to have seen the dangers his father faced after Canute's death and had experienced the events of 1051–1052 himself. Precisely *because* the family was powerful enough to constrain kings and present a threat to them, they formed a tempting target to any ambitious monarch. It is not surprising that by the end of Edward the Confessor's reign, Harold was planning to eliminate this peril by taking the throne himself.[47]

Ironically, in 1065 Harold's chief rival for power was probably his own brother, Tosti, a favorite of the king and queen. There were two other major families descended from two of Canute's earls, **Siward** (who gained a much later bit part in Shakespeare's *Macbeth* by helping defeat that Scottish king) and **Leofric** (whose wife **Godgifu** later passed into legend as Lady Godiva). But Siward was replaced as earl of Northumbria by Tosti, and in 1065 his young son Waltheof was only a fairly minor political figure. Leofric's grandson, **Edwin**, was a greater figure, but could not match Godwine's sons for power. Both Harold and Tosti were powerful earls, and both had gained prestige in a highly successful campaign in Wales in 1063 that resulted in the death of one of the greatest medieval Welsh kings, Gruffydd ap Llywelyn. Fortunately for Harold, the nobility of Tosti's earldom revolted against the earl in 1065.[48] The rebels slaughtered many of Tosti's followers and called on Earl Edwin's brother, **Morcar**, to be their earl. Tosti claimed Harold had a hand in the plot, but the local nobles had plenty of reasons, from their perspective, to revolt. Tosti was trying to raise taxes and perhaps curb their enthusiasm for unrestrained blood feud. More important, Tosti had arranged for the murder of three important nobles, one of them in his own chamber and another at the royal court through the aid of his sister, Queen Edith. Yet if Harold did not necessarily spark the revolt against Tosti, neither did he firmly stand by his brother. Though King Edward strongly desired to support Tosti, Harold brokered a peace whereby Tosti went into exile and Morcar became earl. It is probably no coincidence that Harold married the sister of Edwin and Morcar either shortly before or shortly after he abandoned his brother. Thus, when King Edward died, almost all of England, as map 3 shows, lay within the earldom of Harold or those of his brothers and brothers-in-law.

Harold obviously had the power to take the throne, but did he have the right? Because there were no fixed rules of succession, this was a highly debatable matter, and unfortunately, we have no record of the debate that led to the crown passing to Harold rather than Edward the Confessor's great nephews. Harold's claim was certainly not hereditary, and he himself clearly based it on a deathbed grant by Edward the Confessor. Several English sources mention such a grant, and William the Conqueror's biographer depicts Harold himself as claiming the throne on this basis.[49] At first glance, it seems surprising that Edward would make such a grant, given his earlier hostility toward Godwine's family and his anger at Tosti's exile. Nonetheless, the claim is almost certainly true. Had Harold's claim been trumped up, there is little doubt that the Normans would have heard of it, since at least three people present at the grant—Queen Edith, Archbishop Stigand, and Edward's foreign follower, Robert fitz Wimarch—made peace with William and would surely have benefited from revealing any subterfuge. It is hard to believe that the Normans would not have made use of such a propaganda coup, even if they learned of it only after the Battle of Hastings. We can only speculate why Edward made such a move. Edward's support for Tosti indicates that his views toward Godwine's children, if not necessarily Godwine himself, could change. Edward may have also felt he had no choice if he wished to spare England turmoil. He had almost certainly hoped that Edgar Atheling's father could succeed him, since he had been responsible for engineering the return of his exiled relatives, just as Harthacanute had engineered his own return. However, since Edgar's father died so soon after reaching England and since Edgar was a child, Edward might have felt that making him king was a recipe for disaster for the kingdom and for Edgar himself. It is also possible that Harold and his allies put strong psychological pressure on the sick and dying king. Whatever the reason, Harold seems to have officially succeeded by the right of Edward's grant.

Harold's accession to power was fairly smooth. Harold might well have expected trouble when King Edward's great-nephews grew older, but at least in 1066 there appears to have been no serious internal challenge to his authority. There was some dissent in the north, but that was apparently smoothed over fairly easily. However, the exiled Tosti did not accept Harold's triumph, and King Edward, for reasons we will see later, had almost certainly earlier granted the succession to yet another figure, Duke William of Normandy, a relative of his mother, Emma. This brings us to the most important figure of the story, **William the Conqueror**.

WILLIAM THE CONQUEROR AND NORMANDY

William was not only a duke but also the head of the Normans, descendants of Vikings who had conquered a part of France and established what was basically an independent state, though the kings of France technically remained overlords over Normandy.[50] In William's time the Norman aris-

Figure 1.1. **William and attendants. Detail from the Bayeux Tapestry, 11th c., Musée de la Tapisserie, Bayeux, France. Erich Lessing/Art Resource, NY**

tocracy remained a warrior elite who valued bravery, military prowess, and hardiness. The Normans liked to hear about Norman successes in battle from clerical historians, and shaved the backs of their heads in a haircut designed to set them apart as warriors and display their toughness (see figure 1.1). Though the Normans used writing, memory was still the chief method through which grants of land were preserved, and to make sure their children remembered specific grants they witnessed, Norman nobles would sometimes beat or whip them. For instance, when **Humphrey de Vieilles**, a powerful noble follower of William the Conqueror's father, made the foundation gift for a monastery, he gave his youngest son a good smack.[51] Their admiration for toughness and military success did not stem simply from their descent from Vikings, for they were much like other medieval elites throughout Europe; indeed, their warrior haircut came from elsewhere in France.[52] Though memory of their Viking ancestry served as an important part of Norman identity and provided part of the glue that held together the Norman aristocrats, by 1066 they had become little different from their neighbors in France. They were Christianized, spoke French, and fought as knights on horseback.

Normandy was simply one of a number of principalities into which France had splintered after royal power became more and more restricted to

Paris and its environs. By William's lifetime, Normandy was one of the more prosperous and well-governed principalities by the low standards of the day. Aside from its smaller size, Normandy was probably as well-off as England, though its government was slightly weaker in institutional terms. For instance, the position of viscount, equivalent to the English sheriff, had become hereditary, which meant the dukes could not hire and fire these important officials as the English kings could. Nonetheless, Norman government was still advanced for the period, and William's own strengths as a leader, at a time when the personal mattered more than the institutional, thoroughly compensated for any Norman institutional weaknesses.

Though the only son of a duke, William had grown up in difficult circumstances, to put it mildly. He was an illegitimate son, and his enemies did not let him forget it (for William's family, see genealogy 3). Moreover, in 1035, when William was seven or eight, his father, Duke **Robert**, left on a pilgrimage to Jerusalem, during the course of which he died. Robert's death, leaving a child to inherit, created a power vacuum and led to a vicious struggle for control. Among the casualties were William's guardian and kinsman, **Gilbert of Brionne**, and another guardian, **Turold**. On one occasion, **William of Montgomery**, a member of a powerful aristocratic family, entered the chamber where William was sleeping with **Osbern**, his steward (or chief household official), and cut Osbern's throat. Osbern's followers soon killed William of Montgomery and his accomplices in retaliation.[53]

Once William was old enough, nineteen or twenty, he had to secure his own grip on power. He faced challenges from rebels, including relatives, within his own duchy and fought various wars with the lords of neighboring principalities. Although King **Henry** of France supported William early in his career, the king eventually came to be a bitter enemy. William spent much of the two decades between his coming of age and the Norman Conquest at war. By 1066, William had crushed all resistance within the duchy, increased ducal power (especially in the western part of his domain), held his neighbors at bay, and dominated the neighboring region of Maine.

William's experiences as a child and young adult shaped him into a seasoned and able warrior. Though Harold Godwineson also had skill in conducting successful warfare, his experience paled beside William's. Year after year of combat gave the duke extensive knowledge of warfare, both offensive and defensive. He learned how to coordinate multipronged campaigns, defeat enemies, and use raiding effectively. He became skilled at building, capturing, and defending castles. The campaign of 1066 reveals that he had gained a mastery of logistics.[54] He had also learned to be politically and militarily ruthless. Among those he pushed out of power were his father's brothers, **William of Arques** and Archbishop **Mauger** of Rouen. In Maine, and no doubt elsewhere, he used the common medieval technique of **wasting**, or devastating, the lands of opponents, not just by plundering but by deliberate destruction, in order to weaken his enemies economically and to spread terror. William used other techniques to inspire terror in his enemies. When the town of Alençon rebelled against him and the defenders of a small fortification outside insulted him as an illegitimate son of a non-noble mother, he captured the fortress, took thirty-two men from it, and cut off their hands and feet. Not surprisingly, Alençon promptly surrendered.[55]

In building his own power, William created a circle of dedicated, loyal, and powerful nobles. Chief among them were his half brothers on his mother's side: **Robert**, who became count of Mortain after a more distant relative was driven into exile, and **Odo**, who became bishop of Bayeux. **William, son of Osbern**, whose father had been murdered in Duke William's childhood, was also a leading follower, but so too was **Roger of Montgomery**, brother of Osbern's murderer. William was more interested in building for the future than revisiting grievances. Many of William's followers were from families that were already powerful, but he increased their power even more. Good lords were expected to be generous lords in the Middle Ages, and land was the gift followers most desired. This presented a dilemma: how did one give away land without weakening one's powerbase? The most expedient solution was to give away other people's land, which was one reason why William was so eager to drive from the duchy those who threatened him, or whom he did not trust, even if they were relatives.

As William's appointment of his half brother Odo to the bishopric of Bayeux demonstrates, the duke also considered the church an instrument of his power. As the previous discussion of England shows, there was nothing unusual about this, although the revitalized papacy of the period was just beginning to raise questions about secular control of the church throughout Europe. Yet William's use of the church to support his dominance did not prevent him from being, to all appearances, a deeply pious man. Of course, William's harsh childhood may have created a kind of ruthless cynicism that led him to pretend piety in the quest for power, but some of his later actions suggest instead that his childhood created in him a deep reliance on religion. To those who view Christianity as a pacifist religion, it may seem contradictory that such a ruthless and able warrior should be pious. The apparent contradiction is highlighted on one occasion when William gave land to a monastery. Donors often handed over some symbol of the land, sometimes a clod of dirt but often a knife, as part of the solemn and hopefully memorable ceremony used to transfer the land. On one occasion, William "jocularly" pretended he was going to plunge a knife into an abbot's hand, saying, "Thus should land be given."[56] No doubt his followers burst into genuine or dutiful laughter while the abbot smiled weakly. Clerics often *were* concerned about the violence of warrior aristocrats, both on practical and religious grounds. On the other hand, eleventh-century Christianity had important models of pious warrior kings, including Charlemagne from a couple of centuries earlier and King David from the Bible. Moreover, religious leaders generally liked strong rulers, such as William, who could maintain order and some semblance of justice. Finally, as we have seen, there was an established practice through which wealthy and powerful nobles might hope to gain salvation, namely generosity to the church.

For William, being a ruthless yet pious warrior would have been a common and acceptable contradiction. His actions as a ruler and warrior brought a very real threat of damnation according to the beliefs of the time, but he might hope to win salvation nonetheless, especially by supporting the church. Moreover, for a believer even practical politics and warfare demanded piety, not only because enthusiastic support from the church was helpful, but also because one wanted God on one's side. William showed his piety partly in entirely conventional ways, such as granting land to existing monasteries and founding new ones. More striking, he appointed reformers to important positions in the Norman church. When William shoved his uncle Mauger out of the archbishopric of Rouen, the chief ecclesiastical position in the duchy, he appointed a reforming monk as his replacement. Later on, the Italian monk, **Lanfranc**, one of the most important theologians of the eleventh century, became the first abbot of the great monastery William founded at Caen.[57] One of Lanfranc's pupils, **Anselm**, was one of the greatest theologians and thinkers of the entire Middle Ages. Under them Normandy became, for a time, one of the most important centers of monastic learning in Europe.[58] William's other appointees varied in quality but on the whole were dedicated ecclesiastics. Under William, the Norman church became more in tune with contemporary intellectual trends and reforming ideology than was the English church under Edward the Confessor and Harold.

William was clearly an able warrior and an able ruler, but what gave him any right to England?[59] Norman writers claimed that Edward had granted the succession to William, an event that apparently happened in 1051, not long before Edward moved against Godwine and his family. No early English source mentions such a grant, and it is possible that William and the Norman writers, who were not beyond using outrageous propaganda on their ruler's behalf, made up this grant of the succession. However, one version of the *Anglo-Saxon Chronicle* also records that William came to England while Godwine was in exile.[60] One of William's principal modern biographers has raised reasonable doubts about this visit on the grounds that William was overwhelmed by fighting in Normandy and that no Norman sources mention it. These arguments are sensible, but such a visit would make sense in terms of a mutual support pact between Edward and William, both of whom faced serious internal opposition. Such a pact could have been guaranteed by a grant of succession to William.[61] Certainly, some hostages—namely, a son and a grandson—that Godwine was forced to give to Edward shortly before being exiled in 1051 ended up in William's hands. Overall, there is good reason to believe that Edward did offer the succession to William, at least pending the absence of any children of his own. It is not at all clear, however, that Edward considered the offer valid in later years. After all, he had probably brought Edgar Atheling's father back to England in 1057 with the thought of making him heir. Thus, it is quite possible that both William and Harold considered that they had valid claims to the throne.

By 1066 there was an added complication, namely, that Harold had sworn one or more oaths to support William's claim to the throne (see figure 1.2). The bare facts of the oath swearing are relatively straightforward but the interpretation is not, and here the problems of propaganda and bias become acute for the historian. At some date not specified in the sources but almost certainly 1064 or 1065, Harold landed in Ponthieu, a region near Normandy, and was captured by the local count. Duke William intervened and Harold ended up at William's court. While with William, Harold served in a campaign by the duke in Brittany. More important, he swore to support William's attempt to gain the English throne, perhaps more than once, since different sources place the oath at different locations, and William may have wanted Harold's allegiance advertised far and wide.

The two earliest Norman sources had a clear explanation for this set of events. Edward had sent Harold to renew the promise and to swear loyalty to William. Harold had been blown off course to Ponthieu, and William obligingly rescued him, whereupon Harold fulfilled King Edward's command. Harold subsequently broke his oath as soon as Edward died, making him guilty of both perjury and usurpation.[62] Unfortunately, contemporary English sources did not mention the event at all (though one probably alluded to Harold's oath[63]). Twelfth-century English sources, however, suggest that different stories circulated in England. According to one story, Harold had gone to gain the release of his brother and nephew, who had been hostages since 1051. Another story was that Harold had been out on a ship, fishing for pleasure, and had been blown by hostile winds to Ponthieu.[64] In both of these

Figure 1.2.   Harold swears fealty to William. Detail from the Bayeux Tapestry, 11th c., Musée de la Tapisserie, Bayeux, France. Erich Lessing/Art Resource, NY

English stories, Harold was then coerced by William into swearing to support him. In such circumstances, Harold would have been justified in repudiating his oath and taking the throne offered to him by the king.

Obviously we will never be certain which of the stories was true. Either William and his supporters or Harold and his followers could have spread a false version to justify their stances. In the momentous clash of English and Normans, truth could have easily fallen victim to rumor fueled by hostility. Both versions raise questions. The Norman version would require that Edward changed his mind several times, turning to William in 1051, to Edgar Atheling's branch of the royal line in 1057, to William in 1064 or 1065, and to Harold at the very end of his life. Such frequent changes of heart must raise eyebrows but are not impossible. It is also possible that Harold, as well as Edward, changed his mind. Faced by a possible rivalry from Tosti and hoping to dominate England under a foreign king bound up with his continental dominions, Harold may originally have been willing to accept William's claim. After coming to know the formidable and dominating duke of Normandy better and after seeing Tosti's powerbase crumble, Harold may have decided to make his own claim, persuading Edward to go along.

The possibility that Edward had turned firmly and permanently away from William after 1052 is also perfectly plausible. However, the English stories have their own problems. If Harold did go to gain release of the hostages, he showed unusual foolishness in placing himself in William's hands, though he may have simply underestimated the unscrupulousness of a figure whose claim had long since ceased to matter in England. As for the alleged fishing expedition, we know much about nobles hunting in the period, but there is little evidence that deep sea fishing was a noble sport. One could multiply arguments for either side, and modern scholars have done so, motivated by differing interpretations of the evidence and sometimes by bias for or against Harold or William. Barring the very unlikely emergence of new evidence, we can only speak of probabilities and possibilities in discussing the rights and wrongs of the two men's claims. Whatever the validity of their claims, however, both Harold and William determined to press them fully.

Harold had the advantage of being on the spot and thus claimed the initial success. At another stage of William's career—when William found himself threatened by enemies in or around Normandy, for example—Harold's swift seizure of the throne might have proved decisive. In 1066, however, with his borders secure, William found himself in an unusually strong position to pursue his claim to England. His former ally and subsequently fierce opponent, King Henry, had died in 1060, being succeeded by a young son. Another powerful foe, Count **Geoffrey Martel** of Anjou, had died the same year. The ruler of Flanders, a powerful principality to the northeast of Normandy, was William's father-in-law, and William had just conducted a successful campaign in Brittany, to the southwest of the duchy. Internally, moreover, his position was now unchallenged. He had developed a strong band of powerful and loyal followers and had earned a name as a good lord to follow and a dangerous man to oppose, a pious man, and a successful ruler. The memory of Harold's oaths was fresh and supported William's propaganda effort. William was in a better position for a bold and risky undertaking than he would be at any other time in his life. Even so, the invasion of England was a breathtaking gamble.

NOTES

1. For good overviews of Anglo-Saxon or late Anglo-Saxon England, on which I have drawn throughout this chapter, see Frank M. Stenton, *Anglo-Saxon England*, 3rd ed. (Oxford, 1971); Henry R. Loyn, *Anglo-Saxon England and the Norman Conquest*

(London, 1962); James Campbell, Eric John, and Patrick Wormald, *The Anglo-Saxons* (London, 1982); Pauline Stafford, *Unification and Conquest: A Political and Social History of England in the Tenth and Eleventh Centuries* (London, 1989); Nicholas J. Higham, *The Death of Anglo-Saxon England* (Stroud, 1997); Wendy Davies, ed., *From the Vikings to the Normans* (Oxford, 2003).

2. Goscelin of St. Bertin, "Historia Minor de Vita S. Augustini Anglorum Apostolici," in *Anglia Sacra*, ed. Henry Wharton (London, 1691), 2:59.

3. William of Poitiers, *Gesta Guillelmi*, ed. R. H. C. Davis and Marjorie Chibnall (Oxford, 1998), 174–75.

4. For a compact translation of *Domesday Book*, see Ann Williams and Geoffrey H. Martin, eds., *Domesday Book: A Complete Translation* (London, 2002). For an accessible introduction, see R. Welldon Finn, Domesday Book: *A Guide* (New York, 1973).

5. For a recent discussion of the issue of population, see John S. Moore, "'Quot Homines?' The Population of Domesday England," *Anglo-Norman Studies* 19 (1997), 307–34.

6. Henry C. Darby, *Domesday England* (Cambridge, 1977), 125–26, 131, 164, 283–86; James Campbell, "Domesday Herrings," in *East Anglia's History: Studies in Honour of Norman Scarfe*, ed. Christopher Harper-Bill, Carole Rawcliffe, and Richard G. Wilson (Woodbridge, 2002), 7–9.

7. One archaeologist even speaks of a "first industrial revolution" in the late Anglo-Saxon period; Richard Hodges, *The Anglo-Saxon Achievement: Archaeology and the Beginnings of English Society* (Ithaca, 1989), 150–66.

8. Darby, *Domesday England*, 361, 364–68.

9. Martin Biddle, ed., *Winchester in the Early Middle Ages: An Edition and Discussion of the Winton Domesday* (Oxford, 1976), 427–28.

10. This is based on a circulation estimate of £37,500 for William the Conqueror's reign; Nicholas Mayhew, "Modelling Medieval Monetisation," in *A Commercialising Economy: England, 1086 to c. 1300*, ed. Richard H. Britnell and Bruce M. S. Campbell (Manchester, 1995), 62.

11. H. E. Hallam, *The Agrarian History of England and Wales*, vol. 2, *1042–1350* (Cambridge, 1988), 716–17.

12. Dorothy Whitelock, ed., *English Historical Documents c. 500–1042* (New York, 1955), 432.

13. David A. E. Pelteret, *Slavery in Early Mediaeval England: From the Reign of Alfred until the Twelfth Century* (Woodbridge, 1995), 233. In addition to Pelteret's excellent overview, see John S. Moore, "Domesday Slavery," *Anglo-Norman Studies* 11 (1989), 191–220.

14. Ælfric's colloquy in Kevin Crossley-Holland, ed., *The Anglo-Saxon World* (Totowa, 1982), 199.

15. William of Malmesbury, *Gesta Regum Anglorum*, ed. Roger A. B. Mynors, Rodney M. Thomson, and Michael Winterbottom (Oxford, 1998), 1:458–59.

16. Darby, *Domesday England*, 337.

17. John Gillingham, *The English in the Twelfth Century: Imperialism, National History and Political Values* (Woodbridge, 2000), 170–77; Rosamond Faith, *The English Peasantry and the Growth of Lordship* (London, 1997), 96–98.

18. Robin Fleming, "The New Wealth, the New Rich and the New Political Style in Late Anglo-Saxon England," *Anglo-Norman Studies* 23 (2001), 1–22. See also Christine Senecal, "Keeping Up with the Godwinesons: In Pursuit of Aristocratic Status in Late Anglo-Saxon England," *Anglo-Norman Studies* 23 (2001), 251–66.

19. Dorothy Whitelock, *Anglo-Saxon Wills* (Cambridge, 1930), 38–39, 46–47, 62–65, 74–75, 80–81, 84–85.

20. Crossley-Holland, *Anglo-Saxon World*, 201–2.

21. Good overviews of the Anglo-Saxon church are Frank Barlow, *The English Church 1000–1066: A Constitutional History* (Hamden, 1963), and John Blair, *The Church in Anglo-Saxon Society* (Oxford, 2005).

22. Frank Barlow, ed., *The Life of King Edward Who Rests at Westminster*, 2nd ed. (Oxford, 1992), 24–25.

23. For an overview of Anglo-Saxon government, see Ann Williams, *Kingship and Government in Pre-Conquest England, c. 500–1066* (New York, 1999).

24. Richard Fletcher, *Bloodfeud: Murder and Revenge in Anglo-Saxon England* (Oxford, 2003); Paul Hyams, *Rancor and Reconciliation in Medieval England* (Ithaca, 2003), 71–110.

25. Richard Abels, *Alfred the Great: War, Kingship and Culture in Anglo-Saxon England* (New York, 1998), 140–41. For a good recent overview of the military organization of the period, see Richard P. Abels, *Lordship and Military Obligation in Anglo-Saxon England* (Berkeley, 1988).

26. Simon Keynes and Michael Lapidge, eds., *Alfred the Great: Asser's Life of King Alfred and Other Contemporary Sources* (Harmondsworth, 1983), 193–94.

27. Williams and Martin, *Domesday Book*, 136.

28. The scholar who has argued most consistently for a quite sophisticated Anglo-Saxon government is John Campbell, who has written a number of articles on the subject, which are contained in two volumes of his collected essays: *Essays in Anglo-Saxon History* (London, 1986) and *The Anglo-Saxon State* (London, 2000). A partial rejoinder, which focuses on the use of documents, is Michael T. Clanchy, *From Memory to Written Record: England, 1066–1307*, 2nd ed. (Oxford, 1993), 26–32.

29. Clanchy, *From Memory to Written Record*, 57–73, 78–80.

30. For Henry's government, see Judith A. Green, *The Government of England under Henry I* (Cambridge, 1986).

31. Wilfrid Lewis Warren, "The Myth of Norman Administrative Efficiency," *Transactions of the Royal Historical Society*, 5th ser., 34 (1984), 113–32.

32. For discussion of the nickname, see Ann Williams, *Æthelred the Unready: The Ill-Counselled King* (London, 2003), 19. Williams should not, however, be blamed for the translation "the Clueless," which is my own coinage. Another, nicely ambiguous, translation is "the ill-advised"; Fletcher, *Bloodfeud*, 64.

33. Simon Keynes laid the foundation for this rehabilitation in *The Diplomas of King Æthelred "The Unready" (978–1016): A Study in Their Use as Historical Evidence* (Cambridge, 1980). See also Williams, *Æthelred the Unready*, and Ryan Lavelle, *Aethelred II: King of the English 978-1016* (Stroud, 2002).

34. Simon Keynes, "The Declining Reputation of King Æthelred the Unready," in *Ethelred the Unready: Papers from the Millenary Conference*, ed. David Hill (Oxford, 1978), 227–53.

35. For a balanced assessment of Æthelræd as a military leader, with both his abilities and failings, see Richard Abels, "From Alfred to Harold II: The Military Failure of the Late Anglo-Saxon State," in *The Normans and their Adversaries at War*, ed. Richard P. Abels and Bernard S. Bachrach (Woodbridge, 2001), 15–30.

36. *Anglo-Saxon Chronicle* E, 1010.

37. A good biography of Canute is Michael K. Lawson, *Cnut: The Danes in England in the Early Eleventh Century* (London, 1993).

38. Richard Gem, "A Recession in English Architecture during the Early Eleventh Century and its Effect on the Development of the Romanesque Style," *The Journal of the British Archaeological Association*, 3rd ser., 38 (1975), 28–49.

39. For Edward and his reign, see Frank Barlow, *Edward the Confessor* (Berkeley, 1970).

40. For Earl Ralph, see Ann Williams, "The King's Nephew: The Family and Career of Ralph, Earl of Hereford," in *Studies in Medieval History Presented to R. Allen Brown*, ed. Christopher Harper-Bill, Christopher J. Holdsworth, and Janet L. Nelson (Woodbridge, 1989), 327–43. For Edgar, see Nicholas Hooper, "Edgar the Ætheling: Anglo-Saxon Prince, Rebel and Crusader," *Anglo-Saxon England* 14 (1985), 197–214.

41. Reginald R. Darlington and P. McGurk, eds., *The Chronicle of John of Worcester*, vol. 2, trans. Jennifer Bray and P. McGurk (Oxford, 1995), 576–77.

42. In the following section, I draw on Ian W. Walker, *Harold: The Last Anglo-Saxon King* (Stroud, 1997); Frank Barlow, *The Godwins: The Rise and Fall of a Noble Dynasty* (Harlow, 2002); Emma Mason, *The House of Godwine: The History of a Dynasty* (London, 2004); Peter Rex, *Harold II* (Stroud, 2005); Kelly Devries, *The Norwegian Invasion of England in 1066* (Woodbridge, 1999), 69–192. For the construction of the Godwineson fortunes, see Robin Fleming, *Kings and Lords in Conquest England* (Cambridge, 1991), 55–103; Robin Fleming, "Domesday Estates of the King and the Godwinesons: A Study in Late Saxon Politics," *Speculum* 58 (1983), 987–1007; Ann Williams, "Land and Power in the Eleventh Century: The Estates of Harold Godwineson," *Anglo-Norman Studies* 3 (1981), 171–87.

43. Darlington and McGurk, *Chronicle of John of Worcester*, 2:530–31.

44. Barlow, *Life of King Edward*, 20–21.

45. Fleming, "The New Wealth," 16–17.

46. Williams and Martin, *Domesday Book*, 1301.

47. After I wrote this chapter, I came across broadly similar arguments in Nicholas J. Higham, "Harold Godwinesson: The Construction of Kingship," in

King Harold II and the Bayeux Tapestry, ed. Gale R. Owen-Crocker (Woodbridge, 2005), 19–34.

48. William E. Kapelle, *The Norman Conquest of the North: The Region and Its Transformation, 1000–1135* (Chapel Hill, 1979), 86–101.

49. *Anglo-Saxon Chronicle* CD, 1065, E 1066; Barlow, *Life of King Edward*, 122–23; William of Poitiers, *Gesta Guillelmi*, 118–19. For discussion of this claim, see Barlow, *Edward the Confessor*, 251–53; Mason, *House of Godwine*, 134–35; Higham, *Death of Anglo-Saxon England*, 173–78; Rex, *Harold II*, 201–6.

50. For the section on Normandy and William the Conqueror, I draw on David Bates, *Normandy before 1066* (Harlow, 1982); Eleanor Searle, *Predatory Kinship and the Creation of Norman Power, 840–1066* (Berkeley, 1988); David C. Douglas, *William the Conqueror: The Norman Impact upon England* (Berkeley, 1964); David Bates, *William the Conqueror* (Stroud, 2001).

51. Emily Zack Tabuteau, *Transfers of Property in Eleventh-Century Norman Law* (Chapel Hill, 1988), 149.

52. Henri Platelle, "Le problème du scandale; les nouvelles modes masculines aux XIe et XIIe siècles," *Revue Belge de Philologie et d'Histoire* 53 (1975), 1073–77.

53. Elisabeth M. C. van Houts, ed., *The Gesta Normannorum Ducum of William of Jumièges, Orderic Vitalis and Robert of Torigni* (Oxford, 1992–1995), 2:92–95.

54. For William as a commander, see John Gillingham, "William the Bastard at War," in *The Battle of Hastings*, ed. Stephen Morillo (Woodbridge, 1996), 96–112.

55. Van Houts, Gesta Normannorum Ducum, 2:124–25.

56. David Bates, *Regesta Regum Anglo-Normannorum: The Acta of William I (1066–1087)* (Oxford, 1998), 725.

57. H. E. J. Cowdrey, *Lanfranc: Scholar, Monk, and Archbishop* (Oxford, 2003), 9–77.

58. For Anselm in Normandy, see Richard W. Southern, *Saint Anselm: A Portrait in a Landscape* (Cambridge, 1990), 14–194.

59. For some recent discussion of the competing claims and Harold's oath taking, see Barlow, *Edward the Confessor*, 214–29, 251–53; Mason, *House of Godwine*, 108–21, 134–35; Michael K. Lawson, *The Battle of Hastings, 1066* (Stroud, 2003), 22–34; Bates, *William the Conqueror*, 72–79; Walker, *Harold*, 91–102; Higham, *Death of Anglo-Saxon England*, 130–36, 152–62, 197–99; Rex, *Harold II*, 125–79, 201–5; George Garnett, "Conquered England, 1066–1215," in *The Oxford Illustrated History of Medieval England*, ed. Nigel Saul (Oxford, 1997), 62–68.

60. *Anglo-Saxon Chronicle* D, 1051.

61. David Douglas, "Edward the Confessor, Duke William of Normandy, and the English Succession," *English Historical Review* 68 (1953), 526–45.

62. William of Poitiers, *Gesta Guillelmi*, 68–71, 76–79; van Houts, Gesta Normannorum Ducum, 2:158–61.

63. Barlow, *Life of King Edward*, 80–81.

64. Eadmer, *Historia Novorum in Anglia*, ed. Martin Rule (London, 1884), 6–8; William of Malmesbury, *Gesta Regum Anglorum* 1:416–19.

2

THE CONQUEST

PRELUDE TO BATTLE

Many of William's leading men objected vociferously to his planned invasion of England, arguing that it was beyond Normandy's resources. They pointed out that procuring a fleet would be difficult, that crossing the channel would be dangerous, and that the English would outnumber them.[1] Their objections were quite reasonable. For all the military prowess of the Normans, the expedition *was* an unfamiliar type of venture for them; they were generations removed from their seafaring Viking predecessors. England's military resources both on land and on sea *were* formidable, and the invaders risked being cut off from escape and destroyed. Loyalty bound the Norman lords to follow William to war within Normandy, but a risky endeavor overseas was a different matter.

Many leaders would have sensibly backed down at this point. William, however, not only rallied support from his own followers but also attracted many adventurers from beyond Normandy, especially from Flanders and Brittany. His reputation as a good lord and fearsome warrior no doubt helped tremendously, and within Normandy many feared to oppose him. Through arm twisting, cajoling, and generous promises, William gathered a formidable force. Without such a resolute leader, the Norman Conquest would never have gotten out of the council chamber.

Having garnered the support of his followers and others, William proved himself a master of the least glamorous of the military arts: logistics. He had many ships built and purchased others, creating a fleet that included vessels capable of carrying the warhorses of his knights. He assembled a huge army, by the standards of the time, and kept it intact for perhaps two months (August and September 1066) before he even crossed to England.

Though Norman sources may exaggerate the orderliness of his forces, he managed to keep them from doing significant damage to his own duchy, a notable achievement at a time when undisciplined armies often created havoc. One prominent military historian has outlined the logistical nightmare his forces created: for instance, tons of grain had to be brought in every day to feed the horses and men, and huge mounds of horse manure and human waste had to be removed to keep the encampments moderately healthy.[2] Why did William wait so long before crossing? The contemporary sources agree that an unfavorable wind delayed him, a plausible explanation given possible meteorological conditions and the sailing technology of the time.[3] Some historians, however, have suggested that William deliberately delayed his crossing because he knew that Harold could not hold his forces together, or because he had news of an impending attack on England by Harald Hardrada. A deliberate delay by William is possible and would certainly fit in with his exceptional abilities as a commander, but I have my doubts. Such a subterfuge would have been hard to hide in the long term, and surely the writers who favored him would have emphasized his cleverness had they known.[4] Moreover, any delay would increase the risk of his force being decimated by disease before it could be brought to bear, as sometimes happened to medieval armies. In either case, he achieved an extraordinary feat in holding an army together for so long without relying on plundering to meet its requirements.

Meanwhile, Harold seems to have taken control of England with little difficulty. One source briefly refers to some trouble in the north, but Harold smoothed that over with the help of one of his bishops.[5] There is no other evidence of rebellion or of dangerous dissent. **Numismatic** evidence reveals that the coinage system operated normally under Harold, suggesting that the government as a whole functioned well during the period of just over nine months that he ruled.[6] Unfortunately, we know little else about his reign, but he must have spent much of it focused on preparing to defend his realm from the outside.

Three threats to Harold's kingdom emerged in the course of 1066. The least important came from the king's disgruntled brother, Tosti. Tosti struck in late spring at the Isle of Wight, then plundered along the coast to Sandwich. As Harold marched toward him, Tosti prudently moved north to the river Humber. There, Harold's brothers-in-law, Edwin and Morcar, inflicted a punishing defeat on Tosti and forced him to flee back into exile. Meanwhile, Harold, calling out men and ships, organized defenses along the southeastern coast against the second threat, Duke William.

Given the ports from which William would sail, he was likely to strike first in the same general area that Tosti began his raiding. Unfortunately, Harold could not predict precisely where William's army would land and would need great luck to intercept William at sea. Harold therefore accepted that William would have the initiative at the beginning of the invasion and stationed forces all along the southeast coast. Because the number of troops at any spot was limited (which reduced logistical difficulties), presumably they would not try to challenge William's army. What the locally stationed troops could have done was prevent the Normans from sending out foraging parties and shadow William's army if it moved. Wars of this period were often wars of attrition in which commanders relied on raiding, skirmishing, and sieges, avoiding major battles unless conditions were favorable or desperate. Thus, Harold could have planned for the local forces to begin English countermeasures on a small scale, hampering William's operations while limiting their own exposure. Meanwhile, Harold and his main fleet waited at the Isle of Wight. From there, in ordinary meteorological conditions, they would have had the wind behind them and could swoop down on William's force wherever it landed. Harold might hope to destroy William's fleet, push for a major battle, or mount a war of attrition from a chosen position, depending on which course of action he believed circumstances favored.[7]

Harold's strategy was a sound one; indeed, the strength of Harold's preparations is one argument in favor of the idea that William purposely delayed his attack. Unfortunately, Harold not only had no way of knowing *where* William would attack, but he also could not know *when* William would attack. Harold seems to have had his forces in place for most of the summer, but the mobilization must have produced tremendous strains on his government and treasury. No doubt the troops became bored and restive, and because he was a new king with problematic claims to the throne, Harold could not afford to risk too much political capital on the difficult task of maintaining a large army in the field. On September 8, 1066, he let his force disband; perhaps having run out of supplies or perhaps hoping that because it was near the end of the sailing season, William would not be able to cross to England that year. Even if William did, as long as Harold stayed in the south with a core force, he could hope to reassemble an army at reasonably short notice. As a result, the danger of disbanding his forces must not have seemed as severe to Harold as it appears in retrospect.

Unfortunately for Harold, the third threat materialized at this point. After Edwin and Morcar drove Tosti from England, Harold's disgruntled brother traveled first to Scotland and then to Norway. There he allied with the Norwegian king, **Harald Hardrada**. Harald was a seasoned warrior with decades of experience behind him.[8] As noted in the first chapter, the Danish conqueror Canute had used English resources to capture Norway for a time. To do so, he defeated King (and later Saint) Olaf, who was Harald's half brother. Harald had therefore fled his native country. He had journeyed first to what is now Ukraine and western Russia. In that region, Viking invaders known as the **Rus** had earlier established themselves as rulers over Slavic peoples. Though the Rus would later merge with the people they had conquered, creating the Russians, they still had strong Scandinavian ties and welcomed adventurers and refugees such as Harald. From the lands of the Rus, Harald traveled south to Constantinople, where he joined the **Varangian guard**, a mercenary force employed by the Byzantine emperors and made up of Scandinavian warriors. Because he came from a royal lineage among the Scandinavians and had considerable personal abilities, Harald quickly rose in imperial service, fighting in such far-flung regions as Sicily and Bulgaria. His career earned him a certain legendary status in Scandinavia. Among the deeds attributed to him was the capture of a city by pretending that he was dead and having his followers request burial in the town's cathedral in return for a generous donation. As the coffin was carried into the church, Harald leapt out, signaling his warriors to start slaughtering everyone in sight. Since the same story is told of other Viking leaders, we may be wise to distrust its truthfulness, but there is no doubting Harald's military ability. His success earned him ample treasure, and eventually he returned with a large following to Norway, where his nephew, Magnus, had reestablished the family on the throne. With the help of his treasure (and perhaps the threat of force), Harald persuaded Magnus to accept him as coruler, and when Magnus died, Harald took over the whole country. If the claims to England of Duke William and Harold Godwineson were weak, Harald's claim was practically nonexistent. But Harald had a powerful army and fleet, England was a rich prize, and that was sufficient motive for Harald.

Like William, Harald moved late in the year.[9] On September 20, he engaged in battle against Earls Edwin and Morcar at Fulford, in northern England, defeating them after horrific slaughter on both sides. Meanwhile, Harold Godwineson learned of the new invasion and marched northward, no doubt gathering troops on the way. One secret to success in medieval warfare was to move with unexpected speed, and Harold seems to have caught his Norwegian namesake by surprise when their forces met at Stamford Bridge on September 25. Harold Godwineson's army suffered heavy casualties but won a decisive victory, slaughtering the vast majority of Harald's warriors on the battlefield or as they fled to their ships. Harald Hardrada and Tosti both perished, but Harold let their sons, along with the remnant of Hardrada's army, return to Norway, since they no longer represented a serious threat.

Harold's victory would have greatly strengthened and solidified his long-term prospects in England had he survived the war against the Normans. Edwin and Morcar's power had been weakened by their loss at Fulford, which would have helped ensure that they remained faithful allies rather than dangerous competitors. More important, the victory at Stamford Bridge would have given Harold tremendous prestige, particularly in the north, where royal power was historically weakest. Internal challenges to Harold would have been much trickier after September 25.

Unfortunately for Harold, his march north allowed William to land largely unopposed in southern England. On September 27 the Norman fleet left St. Valery, and on September 28 the Normans landed in Pevensey. Some of William's ships went astray and landed in Romney, where the English defeated and slaughtered their crews, indicating that Harold did not leave the coast entirely unprotected. Taking no chances, William's forces built a castle at Pevensey, using old Roman fortifications as a basis. The English did not dare to attack William's main force, so he moved without serious incident to Hastings. There his forces built a **motte-and-bailey castle**, which was basically a huge mound of dirt with a wooden tower on top and a courtyard below defended by fences and ditches. Thereafter, William and his men settled down to the standard practice of plundering and ravaging the surrounding area, while still remaining close to their ships (see figure 2.1). Harold, meanwhile, received news of the Norman invasion a few days after William's landing. He moved south with remarkable speed, paused a few days in London to refresh his troops and gather new ones, and then marched south again toward the Normans.

Some sources stated that Harold went south so quickly that he fought the Battle of Hastings with far fewer troops than he might have commanded had he spent more time recruiting during his journey. A twelfth-century story recorded that Harold's mother, Gytha, and brother, **Earl Gyrth**, urged Harold to let Gyrth lead his army against William (since, unlike Harold, he had sworn no oaths to the Norman duke) but that this argument only enraged Harold. The main purpose of the original version of this story was simply to depict Harold as a hardened perjurer and the kind of man who would kick aside his pleading mother. However, a later version had a significant addition: Gyrth urged Harold to adopt a scorched-earth policy (a method of denying supplies to the enemy by devastating the land through

Figure 2.1. Normans burning a home. Detail from the Bayeux Tapestry, 11th c., Musée de la Tapisserie, Bayeux, France. Erich Lessing/Art Resource, NY

which they would march) while he himself confronted William.[10] Many modern historians have agreed with this probably fictional advice, arguing that Harold acted rashly in moving south before he had collected the largest army possible.[11] In retrospect, who can disagree? However, I believe that the negative scholarly judgment of Harold's decision to move quickly fails to consider two important points.

First, the origins of Harold's family lay in Sussex, where the Normans had landed and were busily plundering. Scholars have noted this as a motive for his swift confrontation, suggesting that Harold was concerned about the devastation of family lands. Certainly this must have been a factor, but Harold, as head of the family and as successor to Edward the Confessor, had extensive lands throughout England, and the devastation of the Sussex estates would not have placed him in a dangerous financial situation. Instead, lordship lay at the heart of the matter. As a new king with a dubious claim, Harold had to look beyond the confrontation with William and take measures to maintain his strength against internal challenges, should he remain king. Money no doubt mattered to Harold, as to any sensible ruler, but it was even more important to maintain the network of loyalty described in chapter 1. In 1051, when the family's followers deserted, the Godwines fled into exile. In 1052, when their followers backed them against the king, they recovered their position. Unfortunately, *Domesday Book* does not reveal as much about loyalties in Sussex and Kent as in some other counties, but it is likely that Harold's following there was even stronger than elsewhere, and in 1052 it was thanes from the southeast who had provided the core of Godwine's support. Harold simply could not afford to let so many important followers see their lands ravaged by the Norman army while he waited for troops, especially since he had just acted so promptly and decisively in the defense of northerners who were not traditional family supporters.

Second, Harold may have had several alternatives in mind when he marched south so swiftly. One was obviously the hope that he would catch William by surprise as he had done to Harald. However, Harold did not place all his strategic eggs in one basket, for he also sent ships toward William's fleet, which indicates that a battle on land was not the only approach he was considering. There was no reason for him to think a pitched battle was inevitable if he failed to surprise William. In a study of William's military practices, John Gillingham has suggested that Harold might have reasonably expected William to follow common practice and conduct the kind of war of attrition mentioned earlier. This was the style of war the duke had practiced in Normandy and was practicing in England before the Battle of Hastings.[12] By placing himself with a sizable force near William, Harold might hope to limit Norman ravaging of his own estates and the lands of his followers while continuing to gather reinforcements. By threatening William with both an army and a fleet, Harold might hope to place his enemy in an untenable position and negotiate William's withdrawal from a position of strength. Harold's strategy did not necessarily require him to win a major battle, only to avoid losing one and dying. Of course, that is precisely what happened at the Battle of Hastings, and we must accept that Harold miscalculated. But his strategy was neither rash nor foolish. Harold took a calculated gamble that failed disastrously on the battlefield. Had William reacted more conservatively, Harold's swift march south might have proved an excellent strategy. As it was, Harold met his downfall on the battlefield of Hastings on October 14.

THE BATTLE OF HASTINGS

Our sources provide us with precisely the wrong amount of evidence about the Battle of Hastings. They give us enough information that we cannot resist trying to reconstruct the battle. Historians are even blessed with a near-contemporary pictorial record of the event, the **Bayeux Tapestry**, which was probably commissioned by William the Conqueror's brother, Bishop Odo of Bayeux.[13] Unfortunately, the information our sources provide is sufficiently vague, problematic, and contradictory to prevent any reasonably certain reconstruction. In preparing to write this, I found myself reading and rereading many modern accounts of the battle that impressed me as thoroughly convincing. The only problem was that these modern reconstructions disagreed among themselves about almost every aspect of the battle. They may all be convincing, but they cannot all be correct on all points.[14]

A discussion of what might seem a fairly straightforward issue—namely, the approximate numbers of soldiers on each side—can serve to show the difficulties of reconstructing and understanding the battle and can illustrate why able scholars who have studied every scrap of evidence can come to remarkably different conclusions. For a long time, the scholarly consensus held that both sides had fewer than 10,000 troops, but a recent book by Michael K. Lawson, which I rely on for this discussion, has thoroughly undermined the old view.[15] The primary sources are little help here. One chronicler had a messenger proclaim that Harold's army numbered 1,200,000.[16] Such a figure is impossible, and historians of the Middle Ages long ago realized that huge numbers in medieval writing usually meant nothing more definite than "a whole lot." As a result, the figure for a Norman army of 60,000 by William's biographer, **William of Poitiers**, must be treated with extreme caution, although it is highly improbable rather than completely impossible.[17] Scholars have therefore turned to estimating the size of the forces by indirect evidence. Those who argued for armies numbering in the thousands based their judgment partly on the perceived incapacity to raise and feed larger armies. As Lawson points out, scholars have more recently argued for a more positive view of the governments involved, and thus this approach to the question of numbers only takes us back to the question discussed in chapter 1 of just how sophisticated these governments were. Another approach was to take the rough number of William's ships, for which we *may* have some reasonably good figures, estimate how many soldiers were on each, and thus come up with a broad general figure.[18] However, since estimates of how many soldiers a ship might carry range from seven (based on a simplistic interpretation of the Bayeux Tapestry) to the low hundreds, this method has its own shortcomings. Yet another approach was to use the battlefield itself to estimate the size of Harold's army, which could then be used to suggest the general size of William's army. Lawson, however, provides reasons for thinking that the battlefield extended further than the scholars arguing for small numbers believed, though part of his argument depends on treating the Bayeux Tapestry as a realistic depiction of the battlefield, which is by no means certain. The interested reader is invited to look at Lawson's work and others for this question (and many other scholarly debates over the battle), but Lawson has certainly convinced me that the old consensus for small numbers is weaker than it once appeared, leaving us with no idea whether the armies consisted of thousands or tens of thousands of soldiers. Obviously it makes a huge difference whether there were, to take the reasonable outer limits, five thousand or sixty thousand in each army, but we simply cannot know. What follows, therefore, is a limited and cautious reconstruction of the battle, but the reader should know that even the most cautious reconstruction will necessarily have controversial and problematic aspects.

The Battle of Hastings did not happen at Hastings but several miles away at a spot in the countryside now occupied by the beautiful village of Battle. Neither side managed the kind of decisive surprise attack that Harold had achieved against Harald Hardrada, but at the beginning, Harold did manage to form up his troops in a strong defensive position atop a ridge. According to later sources, the English spent the night before battle drinking and shouting "wassail" while the Normans piously prayed.[19] Given the speed with which the English had traveled to get to the battle, their alleged nightlong drinking bout seems unlikely (for one thing, who carried all the ale?). The praying before battle is more convincing, but overall the contrast is likely an added moralizing detail: "Pray instead of carousing all night before a big battle!" It was also a detail that could theoretically help explain why God favored the pious Norman knights over the hard-drinking and sinful English soldiers. More likely to be somewhat historically accurate are reconstructions of an inspirational speech by William just before the battle, in which he stressed the martial abilities of the Normans and the severe dangers they would face should they not win the battle.

Harold's initial maneuver of seizing the high ground and packing his troops in a dense formation was an important one, because it partially negated one of the chief weapons of the Normans—their heavily armored cavalry. Ideally, such cavalry acted as shock troops, smashing and scattering the enemy, but the slope robbed the horses of their momentum. Placement on the ridge thus helped the dense formation of the English, with their long axes, to drive the Normans off time and again. Harold could afford a draw or even a loss, as long as it was not catastrophic, but William needed to win before Harold got more reinforcements and before the English fleet could threaten his own. By placing William and his army in such a difficult situation, however, Harold gave them a strong incentive to fight more desperately and relentlessly than they might have otherwise, as William had pointed out in his speech just before battle, if later Norman reconstructions

Figure 2.2. Norman charge. Detail from the Bayeux Tapestry, 11th c., Musée de la Tapisserie, Bayeux, France. Erich Lessing/Art Resource, NY

of the speech can be believed. Moreover, he gave William the initiative to choose when and how he would attack. This might have mattered less if William had not possessed two advantages: the mobility of his cavalry (as will become apparent later) and, as far as we can tell, the fact that he had many more archers. William's knights and infantry could attack at will, and while they rested, his archers could, without fear of effective retaliation, wear down the English by killing or wounding some and forcing the rest to remain alert throughout the battle.

The inability to rest was important, because the battle was a long, hard-fought, and very even struggle. It began around nine in the morning and continued until dusk. Norman archery sapped but did not break English strength. Repeated charges by Norman cavalry and infantry failed (see figure 2.2). Both sides fought ferociously: the Bayeux tapestry shows men and horses falling, broken weapons, heads hacked from bodies, and corpses littering the ground (figure 2.3 shows one dramatic scene from the battle). William thrust himself into the midst of the fighting and had either two or three horses slain under him, according to different sources, a clear sign that he was willing to risk even his life on the venture. At one point, indeed, the rumor flew that he had died, and William's army began to flee in panic. A frame in the Bayeux Tapestry shows his brother, Bishop Odo of Bayeux, waving his episcopal staff (which may have doubled nicely as a weapon) and rallying "the boys" as they fled. Another scene shows one of William's chief

Figure 2.3.   Fighting at Hastings. Detail from the Bayeux Tapestry, 11th c., Musée de la Tapisserie, Bayeux, France. Erich Lessing/Art Resource, NY

allies, **Eustace of Boulogne**, pointing the duke's way as William coolly raised his helmet, further risking injury or death to show that he was alive and to calm the panic (see figure 2.4). Even so, William's forces seemed on the verge of defeat.

But this very moment of desperation, according to William's biographer, showed the Normans how they could win.[20] Fleeing cavalry could outride pursuers on foot and regroup. Unless the pursuit was unusually disciplined by medieval standards, the cavalry could then turn and charge again against the now disordered infantry. Apparently, some of Harold's warriors pursued the Normans while others did not, and thus the Normans were able to turn back from their retreat and easily strike down many of their enemies. Indeed, this accidental strategy worked so well that William's men began pretending to flee in order to trap more unwary English fighters and weaken the English still further.[21] Both sides fought hard. As the day wore on, however, the English line grew steadily more vulnerable.

Finally, the Normans began breaking through the English line. Harold's brothers, Earls Gyrth and Leofwine, fell to the Normans' swords, though the Norman chroniclers apparently knew few details about their deaths. The Normans focused their efforts on Harold, his position marked

Figure 2.4.   William shows he is alive. Detail from the Bayeux Tapestry, 11th c., Musée de la Tapisserie, Bayeux, France. Erich Lessing/Art Resource, NY

by a banner. Accounts of Harold's death varied. Perhaps an arrow pierced Harold's eye, perhaps Norman knights struck him down with their swords, or perhaps both occurred (see figure 2.5).[22] In any case, Harold's death assured William of victory. With their leaders dead, the English fled northward, followed closely by the Normans. Even then, the English managed to rally, but William defeated them once again. The fall of night doubtlessly

Figure 2.5. Harold's death. Detail from the Bayeux Tapestry, 11th c., Musée de la Tapisserie, Bayeux, France. Erich Lessing/Art Resource, NY

helped many English escape, but their losses were enormous nonetheless. William's biographer wrote of the battlefield: "Far and wide the earth was covered with the flower of the English nobility and youth, drenched in blood."[23] Harold's body was mutilated almost beyond recognition.

William must be judged to have outgeneraled Harold, given that he gained the victory. He certainly showed extraordinary persistence and bravery in taking a calculated risk, both to his army and to his own safety, and in seeing his gamble through at Hastings. Given the uncertainties in any hard-fought battle, however, the element of chance cannot be ignored. Had William died early in the fighting, as was rumored, his army quite likely would have fallen apart. In those circumstances, he might have gone down in history as William the Rash, and historians might now be writing about Harold's daring and brilliance as a general. Indeed, without slighting William's remarkable achievement at Hastings, I am more impressed by the political and military brilliance he showed in securing and holding on to the crown of England in the weeks, months, and years following Hastings. In my view, it is William's leadership after Hastings that proves his military greatness.

THE STRUGGLE AFTER HASTINGS

The campaign immediately following Hastings was, admittedly, fairly easy for William. After giving his army some time to recover from the battle, William began securing his control in the southeast. He started with some indiscriminate killing in Romney to avenge his followers slaughtered there. He then marched on to secure Canterbury, the chief religious center of the kingdom, and Dover, a key port and stronghold. Outside the area of this march, the English showed little inclination to surrender, and they attempted to rally around Edward the Confessor's young kinsman, Edgar Atheling. Fortunately for William, the surviving English leadership proved more adept at dithering than at organizing resistance, allowing him to march on unimpeded. Moving west, William procured the submission of Archbishop **Stigand** of Canterbury and the surrender of Winchester. William then started on a large loop to the west and north of London, encouraging his troops to lay waste to the land in order to intimidate the Londoners and the English leadership. At this point the trickle of surrenders turned into a flood. Among those who submitted were Earls Edwin and Morcar, the most powerful surviving English nobles; Archbishop **Ealdred of York;** and Edgar Atheling himself. On Christmas Day 1066, Archbishop Ealdred crowned William king in Westminster. Events at William's coronation, however, showed how insecure the Normans felt. At one point in the ceremony, the English dutifully acclaimed William king in their own language, and some nervous Norman guards outside Westminster Abbey thought the shouts in a language they could not understand signaled the beginning of a rebellion. These guards promptly set fire to nearby houses, perhaps trying to set up a barrier of flames to protect their lord out of fear that more English would come to the attack.[24] William's followers clearly knew that his power was far from secure.

Beginning in 1067 and gathering momentum in the following year, the English began a series of dangerous revolts lasting until 1071.[25] Space does not permit a full discussion of the confusing events in those years, but it is worth summarizing the key rebellions to show how many threats William faced and how serious some of those were. The first challenge came in the southeast in 1067, where English rebels who were allied with William's once and future supporter Count Eustace of Boulogne, tried unsuccessfully to seize Dover. In the southwest, the city of Exeter rebelled in 1068, though it soon made terms with the king. King Harold's older sons (born to a mistress or unofficial wife) fled to Ireland but repeated the strategy their father had adopted during the 1051–1052 revolt and attacked twice with Irish help in 1068 and 1069. On both occasions they ravaged parts of southwest England but were driven off. A powerful noble called **Eadric the Wild**, supported by a Welsh alliance, caused problems on the Welsh border in 1067 but eventually submitted to William.

The greatest threat came from the north, where a series of rebellions destroyed two important Norman detachments, at Durham and York, and forced William himself to take the field three times in extended campaigns. Several factors made the northern revolts dangerous. Northern nobles had often resented rule from the south, as the rebellion against Tosti in 1065 indicated, and were accustomed to armed uprisings. In addition, these nobles were able to make Edgar Atheling, who had fled William's court, their leader, giving them strong claims to be supporting the legitimate successor from King Alfred's line. The northern rebels could potentially link up with the rebels under Eadric the Wild in the region of Chester. Edgar himself had made a Scottish alliance through the marriage of his sister to King Malcolm of Scotland, giving him a base in the north and potential military support. Most important, the northerners made a Danish alliance and Danish fleets came to their aid. Given that the Danes had conquered England by themselves early in the century, a combination of Danes and English rebels was a potent threat to William's power. Nonetheless, William defeated the northerners several times and neutralized the Danish threat.

The final major threat came in 1071 when Earls Edwin and Morcar rebelled. Edwin was betrayed and killed by some of his own followers, but Morcar escaped to Ely, where a local thane, **Hereward the Wake**, had established a rebel stronghold in a monastery located on an island within an extensive area of wetlands. William eventually took Ely, and Morcar found himself in prison for the rest of his life, except for a short spell after William's death (William released him, but William's son, William II, quickly put him back in prison). William's capture of Ely in 1071 did not quite mark the end of opposition by English notables. One English earl, **Waltheof**, son of Earl Siward of Northumbria, joined a part English, part Breton earl and a Norman earl in yet another failed revolt in 1075. Moreover, some surviving northern English nobles began an uprising in 1080 after murdering a bishop during a feud. However, William and his supporters crushed these rebellions with relatively little effort, so Norman rule was basically secure by 1071.

William made it look simple. Indeed, he succeeded so well that it is easy to underestimate just what a challenging situation he faced until 1071. It is true that after Hastings William had some important advantages. Many English warriors had died fighting there and at the earlier battles against the

Norwegians. In particular, the war bands of Edwin and Morcar had suffered badly during the Norwegian invasion while the followers of Harold's family must have been decimated at Hastings, leaving Harold's sons with few troops of their own. All of the heirs to the greatest families, including Edwin, Morcar, Harold's sons, Waltheof, and Edgar Atheling, were young and inexperienced, and their interests must often have clashed. Moreover, Edgar Atheling, the most legitimate rival to William, had no more of a personal powerbase in 1067 or 1068 than in 1066, which undermined the advantages his strong claims to the throne gave him. Thus, England suffered from a lack of obvious leadership after Hastings. This leadership vacuum undoubtedly led to the dithering before William was crowned, the apparent lack of coordination in the revolts that followed, and the ability of Hereward the Wake, who was only a minor thane, to become the initial leader of the rebellion at Ely.

Nonetheless, William faced difficult odds even after Hastings. England still had a large reservoir of warriors. Many must have escaped the various battles and many more must not have had the chance to get to any of them, given the speed with which Harold had traveled on campaign. Scottish, Welsh, and Irish interventions provided dangerous distractions, and the Danish fleets represented a threat potentially as great as Harald Hardrada had offered Harold. The English rebellions may have been more coordinated than they seem to modern scholars, since the fullest sources are Norman and we know less than we would wish to about the thoughts and actions of various English leaders. Nonetheless, to the extent that revolts *were* uncoordinated, the very lack of coordination made them harder to predict and to react to quickly. Many of William's troops were mercenaries, which meant that William had to work hard to motivate them to stay in the field when they faced difficult circumstances. Finally, the Normans were fighting in hostile and unfamiliar territory against warriors defending their homes and power. William's eventual victory was far from a foregone conclusion at the end of 1066.

Besides cavalry (the impact of which is difficult to assess for battles and skirmishes after Hastings), William *did* have one important technological advantage: castles. Anglo-Saxon England had extensive experience with fortifying towns, and noble halls may have had some simple fortifications around them. But except for some castles built by Edward the Confessor's French favorites, England lacked the kinds of castles that had been springing up throughout other parts of western Europe in the eleventh century. I shall discuss in the next chapter some arguments over the extent of the "castle revolution" of 1066, but contemporary sources indicate that the English took the military impact of castles seriously. In recounting William's military campaigns after the Norman Conquest, one version of the *Anglo-Saxon Chronicle* noted the many castles William built in his early campaigns and the fighting around them.[26] More explicitly, **Orderic Vitalis**, a twelfth-century writer who grew up in the aftermath of the conquest, wrote that castles were crucial to William's success. Map 4 shows how many castles William is recorded as having built during his early campaigns.[27] He almost certainly built others, as did his followers. Most of these were simple motte-and-bailey castles of the type that William had built at Hastings, but they were nonetheless effective in dominating wealthy English towns, protecting scattered Norman garrisons, and making it harder for rebels to unify their efforts and sweep the invaders out of their country. William's primitive castles alone could not have ensured victory, but they helped, and William was smart enough to exploit this advantage to the fullest.

William's political savvy in handling his enemies was as important as his military abilities and advantages. Once he was crowned, William gained a surprising amount of English support, including military support, which he sometimes used against English rebels. Indeed, one important noble from southwestern England, **Eadnoth the Staller**, died while fighting off the first attack from Harold's sons. Enough nobles remained loyal or at least neutral that William never faced a single revolt from the entire English aristocracy. When nobles did revolt, William often regained their obedience at least temporarily. Thus, Edwin and Morcar first revolted in 1068 but soon submitted, depriving other rebels of key allies. When they revolted again in 1071, they had passed up their best opportunity and it was too late for them to succeed; William soon broke them. Despite the continuing loyalty of some English nobles to 1071 and beyond, William ultimately decided to dismantle the existing power structure. By the time of *Domesday Book*, and probably long before, he had basically destroyed the Anglo-Saxon aristocracy and almost entirely replaced the highest ranks of leadership in the English church.

How did William effectively neutralize and destroy the native elites without provoking a massive and unified rebellion against him and while actually gaining support from some nobles?[28] The most important factor is that William initially gave every appearance of trying to rule with the help of the surviving English aristocracy. William always claimed to act as Edward the Confessor's legitimate successor, and in fact he did respect traditional laws and institutions throughout his reign, as we shall see in the following chapters. Judging from surviving documents, he called many native aristocrats and churchmen to his councils and to his following during the years immediately following 1066. He arranged marriages between English and Norman followers in an attempt to unify the two groups. He even promised to marry one of his daughters to Earl Edwin, and though he broke this promise (thus provoking Edwin's first rebellion), he did marry a kinswoman to Earl Waltheof. According to his Norman biographer, William rewarded English as well as Norman followers, and a study of *Domesday Book* shows this was true. For instance, Earl Waltheof benefited handsomely from the conquest until his implication in the 1075 revolt, and even in 1086 one can find some English landholders who profited from the conquest.[29] Thus, powerful natives initially had good reason to hope that they might survive the conquest by supporting William. Indeed, at some point, William seems to have made it clear that to survive under his rule they *had* to actively support him. They would not be able to keep their lands simply through maintaining a neutral stance during the rebellions.

This initial attempt to rule with widespread cooperation from the native aristocracy was almost certainly not a cynical ploy; William probably did plan to rule in conjunction with the surviving elites, or at least considered it as one possible option. At some point during the rebellions, though, he clearly decided he had to break the leadership of the native elites. In the church, beginning even before the rebellions, he appointed his own followers to key positions as posts came open through the deaths of bishops and abbots. However, William later hurried this replacement process in the church by removing native bishops and abbots for various infractions, some genuine, some pretexts. Most notably, with papal support he replaced Archbishop Stigand of Canterbury in 1070 with one of his own followers, Lanfranc. Well before 1066, Archbishop Stigand had incurred papal hostility by holding two bishoprics at once and by recognizing an antipope, but William kept him on as archbishop until it suited the king (or until William was firmly enough in power) to expel him. By 1073 there were only two native English bishops out of a total of fifteen, and by William's death in 1087 there was only one.[30]

At the same time, William crushed all but the lowest fringes of the Anglo-Saxon aristocracy through systematic dispossession of their land. My own research shows that by the time of *Domesday Book*, landholders who can clearly be identified as English held only 6 percent of the land in England as measured by hides, or carucates, and just over 4 percent of the land as measured by yearly values. These percentages should be increased to account for gaps and problems in the survey, though there is no way to be sure by how much. My own conclusion is that the increase should be small, but this is based on silence in other sources as well as in *Domesday Book* regarding surviving native aristocratic families. Historians are always wary of arguments from silence, and so other scholars may reasonably disagree.[31] However, the invaders continued to seize land from English landholders after 1086, and only a fairly small number of English minor noble families can be shown to have remained in England as nobles. To some degree William was lucky; there was a demand for skilled English warriors throughout many parts of Europe, which meant that many chose exile rather than fighting to the bitter end. After the rebellions, English warriors could be found in Ireland, Scotland, Scandinavia, Russia, and even Constantinople, where English exiles came to dominate the Varangian guard in place of the Scandinavians. No doubt many English nobles falsely hoped that their exile would only be temporary. However, the possibility of exile meant that William was not facing completely desperate opponents during the major revolts and that he could simply drive many out rather than hunt them down and kill them. Moreover, William never dispossessed all the English, which meant that there was always a glimmer of hope for native landholders, even as most were losing their lands. Overall, William must have managed the process carefully, proceeding cautiously until it was too late for the English aristocracy to realize what was happening and rise in a coordinated and universal revolt against him. By virtually destroying the native aristocracy before his death, however, William eliminated any possibility that the Norman Conquest would be reversed.

The flexibility William showed in trying first to co-opt and then to destroy the native aristocracy can be found in other aspects of his leadership. Controlling the territory of Maine, located between Normandy and Anjou, had long been a priority for William, because it provided a buffer zone between his own lands and the lands of the powerful and often hostile counts of Anjou. In 1069, a serious rebellion undermined Norman power in Maine, even as William faced widespread rebellion in England. Faced with crises both in Maine and in England, William resisted the temptation to spread his efforts too thin and instead concentrated on settling the problems in England. In 1073, having settled problems in England, he used English resources, including warriors, to recover his position in Maine.[32] In short, William was willing to temporarily abandon long-term policies when short-term needs demanded it. Similarly, William normally responded to military threats with force, but on one occasion at least he bought off a Danish fleet.[33] This was a tactic reminiscent of the policies of the hapless Æthelræd Unræd, but it deprived William's opponents of key allies, temporarily neutralized the Danish threat, and allowed him to decisively crush English rebels. In the long term, paying off the Danes might have prompted further invasions from the north, but William could get away with this brief show of weakness because he was generally such a powerful leader.

Here, the core of loyal supporters and the reputation as a good lord that he had built up in Normandy before 1066 served him well. Though he did suffer defections and rebellions by some continental followers or allies, most of the men who followed him in 1066 served him steadfastly under difficult circumstances. As map 4 shows, noble subordinates won some important victories for him, including the final destruction of the army of King Harold's sons in 1069.[34] Because he soon had able and loyal followers scattered throughout England, William faced less danger from the sporadic and scattered nature of the English revolts. He in turn cemented his reputation as a good lord by making generous grants of land and treasure in England to his supporters, beginning at an early date. This generosity was one source of friction with the English, since it came at their expense, but it guaranteed William the continuing support of the Normans and others, including mercenaries, in difficult times.

Despite the trust he could place in various noble followers, William's personal leadership was crucial. Although map 4 shows that William relied on his commanders for some victories, it also reveals that whenever possible, he moved rapidly and decisively into danger zones. One reason several incipient rebellions did not spread was that William nipped them in the bud. In other cases he could not arrive quickly enough to prevent the spread of a rebellion, but even then he commanded the army that eventually crushed the rebellion. One moment in the 1069–1070 campaign is particularly telling. Winter campaigning was very difficult in the Middle Ages, and in early 1070 parts of William's army balked at crossing the rugged upland regions between Yorkshire and Cheshire. William led them forward anyway, setting an example and helping others along the way. It is probable that the rebels around Chester were not well prepared for an onslaught in the dead of winter, and William's unexpected march allowed him to end rebellion there more swiftly and easily than had he waited for better weather. He then rewarded his most enthusiastic supporters and punished the more reluctant ones by forcing them to remain in service for a time after the campaign was over.[35]

In addition to leading from the front, William showed a ruthlessness that was unusual even by the standards of the time. His destruction of the old English aristocracy was one example of his ruthlessness, but more striking was his frequent use of devastation of the countryside against his enemies. This was a common tactic in medieval warfare, but William employed it on an unusually large scale. As already noted, it played an important role in his campaign to intimidate and take London. After the northern English aristocrats rebelled once too often, William purposely ravaged the county of Yorkshire and other regions in 1069–1070, sending peasants fleeing to monasteries (if they were lucky) and ordering his men to destroy herds, crops, villages, and everything in their path. *Domesday Book* recorded huge amounts of "waste" in Yorkshire in particular, and though there is debate on this subject (which I will discuss more fully in chapter 4), the traditional association between the wasted lands and William's military operations is almost certainly correct. Even toward the end of his reign, when William prepared for a planned Danish invasion that never got off the ground, he ordered that certain coastal areas of his kingdom be ravaged in order to deny supplies to the Danes when they landed.[36] William's ruthlessness brought him strong criticism even from some writers who otherwise admired him, but it helped crush English rebellions and deterred the natives from rising again.

The Norman Conquest and its success were hardly inevitable but depended on the choices and decisions of individuals. The choice of many Normans and others to accompany William gave him the army he needed to capture and defend England. The decision of Harald Hardrada to invade may have tipped the balance against King Harold. Harold's own decisions before Hastings, though reasonable, led to his death as well as to the deaths of his brothers and many followers. But it was William, above all, who changed history in 1066 and the years that followed. Most leaders in his place would not even have tried to conquer England. Of those with equal daring, many would not have successfully assembled and launched an invasion force. A less able commander might have lost at Hastings or failed to defeat the rebels and their allies. Had William died sometime before 1066, it is almost certain that the Norman Conquest would never have happened.

NOTES

1. William of Poitiers, *Gesta Guillelmi*, ed. R. H. C. Davis and Marjorie Chibnall (Oxford, 1998), 100–101, 106–7. For the campaigns of the Norman Conquest, see Matthew Bennett, *Campaigns of the Norman Conquest* (Oxford, 2001); Edward A. Freeman, *The History of the Norman Conquest of England*, 3rd ed. (Oxford, 1877), vols. 2 and 3; David C. Douglas, *William the Conqueror: The Norman Impact upon England* (Berkeley, 1964), 181–244; R. Allen Brown, *The Normans and the Norman Conquest* (New York, 1968), 141–98; Brian Golding, *Conquest and Colonisation: The Normans in Britain, 1066–1100*, 2nd ed. (New York, 2001), 27–49; David Bates, *William the Conqueror* (Stroud, 2001), 79–109; Ian W. Walker, *Harold: The Last Anglo-Saxon King*

(Stroud, 1997), 144–82; Frank Barlow, *The Godwins:The Rise and Fall of a Noble Dynasty* (Harlow, 2002), 134–55; Emma Mason, *The House of Godwine:The History of a Dynasty* (London, 2004), 141–76; Peter Rex, *Harold II* (Stroud, 2005), 216–52. For books specifically on the battle of Hastings, see n. 14. Richard Abels, "From Alfred to Harold II: The Military Failure of the Late Anglo-Saxon State," in *The Normans and their Adversaries at War*, ed. Richard P. Abels and Bernard S. Bachrach (Woodbridge, 2001), 15–30, points out some of the weaknesses of the late Anglo-Saxon state, but it also had some formidable capabilities.

2. Bernard Bachrach, "Some Observations on the Military Administration of the Norman Conquest," *Anglo-Norman Studies* 8 (1986), 1–25.

3. Christine Grainge and Gerald Grainge, "The Pevensey Expedition: Brilliantly Executed Plan or Near Disaster?" in *The Battle of Hastings*, ed. Stephen Morillo (Woodbridge, 1996), 130–42.

4. The fullest argument that William intentionally waited is in William of Poitiers, *Gesta Guillelmi*, xxiv–xxvi. The editors argue that a story about a shift in the wind would strengthen the idea that William's expedition was blessed with divine favor, but how convincing would such a story have been to the many people that would surely have been aware that it was a lie?

5. William of Malmesbury, *Saints' Lives: Lives of SS. Wulfstan, Dunstan, Patrick, Benignus and Indract*, ed. Michael Winterbottom and Rodney M. Thomson (Oxford, 2002), 56–57.

6. Walker, *Harold*, 138–43; Barlow, *Godwines*, 128–29; Mason, *House of Godwine*, 141.

7. For the meteorological conditions, see Grainge and Grainge, "Pevensey Expedition," 130–42. See also David Howarth, *1066:The Year of the Conquest* (London, 1977), 87.

8. A colorful medieval account of Harald Hardrada can be found in translation in Magnus Magnusson and Hermann Pálsson, trans., *King Harald's Saga: Harald Hardradi of Norway, from Snorri Sturluson's Heimskringla* (Baltimore, 1966). For a modern account of Harald, see Kelly Devries, *The Norwegian Invasion of England in 1066* (Woodbridge, 1999), 23–68.

9. For Harald's invasion, see Devries, *Norwegian Invasion*, 230–96. Devries relies more heavily on later Norse sources than most historians do but makes clear where he uses these sources.

10. Orderic Vitalis, *The Ecclesiastical History of Orderic Vitalis*, ed. Marjorie Chibnall (Oxford, 1969–1980), 2:170–73; Glyn S. Burgess, trans., *The History of the Norman People: Wace's Roman de Rou* (Woodbridge, 2004), 168.

11. Douglas, *William the Conqueror*, 197; R. Allen Brown, "The Battle of Hastings," in Morillo, *Battle of Hastings*, 203; Mason, *House of Godwine*, 156–57.

12. John Gillingham, "William the Bastard at War," in Morillo, *Battle of Hastings*, 109–10.

13. David M. Wilson, *The Bayeux Tapestry: The Complete Tapestry in Color* (New York, 1985). Important recent works on the tapestry include David J. Bernstein,

The Mystery of the Bayeux Tapestry (Chicago, 1987); Richard Gameson, ed., *The Study of the Bayeux Tapestry* (Woodbridge, 1997); Pierre Bouet, Brian Levy, and François Neveux, eds., *The Bayeux Tapestry: Embroidering the Facts of History* (Caen, 2004). For arguments that the Bayeux Tapestry was made outside of England, see Wolfgang Grape, *The Bayeux Tapestry: Monument to a Norman Triumph* (Munich, 1994), 44–54, and George Beech, *Was the Bayeux Tapestry Made in France? The Case for Saint-Florent of Saumur* (New York, 2005).

14. Among the most important books on the battle of Hastings are Morillo, *Battle of Hastings*; Jim Bradbury, *The Battle of Hastings* (Stroud, 1998); and Michael K. Lawson, *The Battle of Hastings, 1066* (Stroud, 2003). See also the works listed in n. 1.

15. Lawson, *Battle of Hastings*, 125–61, 176–86.

16. *The* Carmen de Hastingae Proelio *of Guy, Bishop of Amiens*, Frank Barlow, ed. (Oxford, 1999), 14–15.

17. William of Poitiers, *Gesta Guillelmi*, 116–17.

18. Lawson, *Battle of Hastings*, 181–85; Elisabeth M. C. van Houts, "The Ship List of William the Conqueror," *Anglo-Norman Studies* 10 (1988), 159–83.

19. William of Malmesbury, *Gesta Regum Anglorum*, ed. Roger A. B. Mynors, Rodney M. Thomson, and Michael Winterbottom (Oxford, 1998), 1:452–55; Burgess, *History of the Norman People*, 173.

20. William of Poitiers, *Gesta Guillelmi*, 128–33.

21. Some scholars have doubted that the Normans were capable of such a maneuver, but see Bernard S. Bachrach, "The Feigned Retreat at Hastings," in Morillo, *Battle of Hastings*, 190–93.

22. For the debate over the manner of Harold's death, see Lawson, *Battle of Hastings*, 224–32, 255–66.

23. William of Poitiers, *Gesta Guillelmi*, 138–41.

24. William of Poitiers, *Gesta Guillelmi*, 150–51.

25. The best recent account of the revolts is in Ann Williams, *The English and the Norman Conquest* (Woodbridge, 1995), 24–70.

26. *Anglo-Saxon Chronicle* D, 1066–1067.

27. Orderic Vitalis, *Ecclesiastical History*, 2:218–19. Orderic may have drawn this from his Norman source, William of Poitiers, but since he uses castles to help explain the defeat of the English, to whom he was sympathetic, it is also possible it was his own observation.

28. For the following section, I draw heavily on my article, "The Significance and Fate of the Native English Landholders of 1086," *English Historical Review* 118 (2003), 303–33.

29. William of Poitiers, *Gesta Guillelmi*, 162–63.

30. Frank Barlow, *The English Church, 1066–1154* (New York, 1979), 57.

31. For more optimistic portrayals of survival, see Williams, *English and the Norman Conquest*, 71–125; Christopher P. Lewis, "The Domesday Jurors," *The Haskins Society Journal* 5 (1993), 17–44; Hirokazu Tsurushima, "The Fraternity of Rochester Cathedral Priory about 1100," *Anglo-Norman Studies* 14 (1992), 313–37.

32. Bates, *William the Conqueror*, 104, 109–10.

33. P. McGurk, ed., *The Chronicle of John of Worcester*, vol. 3 (Oxford, 1998), 10–11.

34. Subordinates also experienced some major losses, notably at Durham and York. For fighting at Colchester, which is recorded only in a very late chronicle, see Philip Crummy, *Aspects of Anglo-Saxon and Norman Colchester* (London, 1981), 26–27.

35. Orderic Vitalis, *Ecclesiastical History*, 2:234–37.

36. *Anglo-Saxon Chronicle* E, 1085.

II

CONSEQUENCES:
DID THE CONQUEST MATTER?

So what? The events of the Norman Conquest were exciting, but my earlier question stands: did the conquest matter? It clearly mattered a great deal to the aristocrats on both sides, but was this simply a story of one warlike aristocracy replacing another without broader influence on England's government, economy, and society? The answer to this broad question forms the subject of the second part of the book.

Before turning to the details, however, I wish to address three issues. First, there has been nearly as much debate about certain consequences of the Norman Conquest as about the Battle of Hastings. As noted earlier, I will address only some of these debates. The reader should keep in mind, however, that an enormous amount of scholarly work and a great deal of debate lie behind most of the information and arguments I will provide in the following chapters.

Second, historians have sometimes treated all changes in England in the first fifty years or century after the Norman Conquest as results of the Norman Conquest. The late eleventh and early twelfth centuries, however, were times of great religious, economic, political, and social change throughout Western Europe. Even if Harold Godwineson had sent the Normans fleeing back to their ships, England would have hardly stood still in the fifty or one hundred years that followed. Given the limited sources from the period, it is sometimes hard to tell what changes occurred specifically because of the Norman Conquest, what would have changed anyway, and what changes might have taken a different course had the outcome of Hastings been different. I will focus on changes that directly resulted from or were heavily influenced by the Norman Conquest.

The third issue concerns the chain of causation. In 1144, a young Christian boy—**William of Norwich**—disappeared shortly before Easter, which, of course, was also around the time of Passover. Relatives and later a local monk blamed the local Jewish community, inventing a wild conspiracy theory in which Jews secretly sacrificed Christians in mockery of Easter. The royal sheriff remained skeptical, but a cult grew up around the boy and spawned copycat accusations elsewhere in England and on the Continent.[1] The belief that Jews practiced human sacrifice of Christians became a staple of medieval anti-Semitism. Such beliefs continued in Europe down to the Nazi period and have found a new home among some Islamic fundamentalists.

What does this ugly story have to do with the Norman Conquest? As I will describe in chapter 4, the Normans brought Jews to England. Had Jews not come to England, William of Norwich's story would not have happened, and it is at least possible that such accusations would never have arisen. Even if these arguments are true, however, it is hard to argue that the Norman Conquest caused this story and the strand of anti-Semitism that developed out of it in any meaningful way. Religious fanaticism, the growing intolerance of the period, and the overly active imaginations of a group of individuals were the main causes. In the chapters that follow, I will focus on the direct consequences of the conquest rather than following such tenuous chains of causation. What the story should remind the reader of, however, is just how complex the nature of historical causation can be.

NOTE

1. Gavin I. Langmuir, "Thomas of Monmouth: Detector of Ritual Murder," in *Toward a Definition of Antisemitism*, ed. Gavin I. Langmuir, 209–36 (Berkeley, 1990).

3

LANDOWNERSHIP, GOVERNMENT, WAR, AND LAW

According to the *Anglo-Saxon Chronicle*, when William received the crown, he swore an oath to treat the people as well "as any king before him had done," as long as they were loyal to him. The chronicler followed immediately with a complaint about the heavy taxes William imposed.[1] From the writer's point of view, heavy taxation clearly did not represent good government, but William might have replied that such taxation was a well established tradition by 1066. Moreover, William's stipulation soon gave him an excuse to ignore his oath, for the English were not particularly loyal to him in the years following the coronation. If William could revolutionize anything about English society, it was the government. But did he choose to do so?

In this chapter, I have gathered some of the subjects that would have most concerned King William, his successors, and the new nobility. By seizing the crown of England, William gained direction over the nature of its government. He and his followers (other than churchmen) formed a warrior aristocracy that glorified and relished the practices of war. The acquisition of property had, of course, been the major motive for the invading army, and the distribution of land and the nature of landholding would have mattered greatly to them. The redistribution of land also matters to modern scholars: though the word *feudalism* did not appear in any language spoken by the conquerors or conquered, many modern scholars have attributed to the Normans the introduction of feudalism in England. Finally, kings had oversight of justice, and they, together with the nobility, had the greatest ability to make changes in the nature of the legal system. Thus, one might expect to find the greatest amount of change occurring in landownership, government, war, and law—the areas discussed in this chapter. Will this expectation be met?

Before turning to the answer to this question, it is necessary to discuss the succession to William I in order to introduce some of the other key actors in the politics of the Anglo-Norman period (see genealogy 3).[2] When William died in 1087, he had three surviving sons—Robert Curthose, William Rufus, and Henry. Kings and their heirs often had tense relations in the Middle Ages, with the sons eager to take on more power and the fathers reluctant to let go. William and his eldest son, **Robert Curthose**, were no exception; though Robert was in his thirties when William died, the king had given him little real authority.[3] Robert resented this and rebelled twice. Unfortunately for both father and son, William suffered a mortal injury while putting down the second revolt. As he lay on his deathbed, William decided to disinherit Robert. His advisors managed to convince him not to entirely deprive Robert of his inheritance: William relented and allowed Robert to succeed to Normandy. However, William passed England on to his second son, **William II Rufus**.[4]

Robert felt aggrieved about his father's decision and tried to take England from his brother. William II, who was an able warrior, not only defended his position in England but also took the struggle to Normandy, parts of which he seized from Robert. Peace was restored when Robert joined the First Crusade and mortgaged Normandy to his brother. While Robert journeyed to the Holy Land to do his Christian duty by slaughtering Muslims, William Rufus ably ruled his father's combined realms. He gained a reputation as a chivalric leader, but he also earned the dislike of the church, possibly by being gay and more certainly by milking various bishoprics and abbeys for money. After he died in 1100 in a hunting accident, churchmen considered his death an obvious judgment of God. The collapse of a tower in Winchester Cathedral, where he was buried, only confirmed this view.

Robert Curthose, who was returning from Jerusalem at the time of his brother's death, might reasonably have expected to gain England as well as recover Normandy, but the youngest brother, **Henry I**, moved first.[5] Henry, who was on the spot in England, first seized the royal treasury and then the throne. Robert did recover Normandy without difficulty, and he then tried to dislodge Henry from England. Once again Robert failed, and once again the brother who held England took the war to Normandy. In 1106, six years after he had seized England, Henry captured Robert. In a fine medieval display of traditional family values, Henry held Robert in prison for the rest of his life. Henry, who was probably an even abler monarch than William Rufus, held both Normandy and England until his own death in 1135.

At Henry's death, another succession dispute erupted. Henry left no shortage of children; he had more than twenty that we know of. The problem was that only two of them were legitimate: a son named William and a daughter named Matilda. **William Atheling** had died in a shipwreck in 1120, and Henry had subsequently pressured his nobles to swear to support the succession of **Matilda III**. Afterward, Henry married Matilda to Count **Geoffrey** of Anjou, trying to settle the old rivalry between the dukes of Anjou and the counts of Normandy. Unfortunately, the old tensions resurfaced, and Matilda and Geoffrey were at odds with Henry when Henry died. **Stephen**, a grandson of William the Conqueror (his mother was Henry's sister), followed his Uncle Henry's example and seized power, helped by a claim that Henry had disinherited Matilda on his deathbed. Stephen managed to seize not only England but also Normandy. Geoffrey and Matilda did not take Stephen's actions lying down, and much of Stephen's reign was consumed by civil war. Geoffrey conquered Normandy while Matilda carried on the struggle in England, ultimately achieving a stalemate.[6] The civil war was settled in England only when Stephen's eldest son died in 1153, and Stephen made Henry, the eldest son of Geoffrey and Matilda, his heir. When Stephen died the following year, **Henry II** (1154–1189) succeeded peacefully to England, having already succeeded to his father in Normandy and Anjou. Thus, until 1154 and beyond, England was held by William the Conqueror's direct descendants, but these descendants fought vigorously among themselves for William's lands. Despite their infighting, William's successors maintained firm control of England and its government. How, then, did William the Conqueror and his immediate successors alter the land they controlled?

GOVERNMENT

One might have expected William the Conqueror to change the English government to conform to Norman standards.[7] He did not. Medieval rulers tended to respect tradition, even if it meant that different territories under their rule had different laws and governments.[8] Moreover, English government worked quite well by the standards of the time and was somewhat more sophisticated than Norman government. As long as the government functioned well and provided for the needs of William and his sons, the new rulers saw no need to tamper with it. Thus, William and his sons simply took over the existing system of shires and hundreds. They were more than happy to use the hidage system to collect tax, sometimes at very high rates. It is true that one scholar, Sally Harvey, has argued that the *Domesday Book* inquest was partly designed to create a new system of assessment measured in **ploughlands** rather than hides. If so, the government failed to follow through on the attempted revision, for the old hidage system persisted well into the twelfth century.[9] The coinage system, which produced a better product than Normandy's government did, also remained intact.[10] William and his descendants retained separate governments for Normandy and England and did not try to remake England's government in a Norman image. The essential continuity of English government is why in the United States we can still have county officials called sheriffs, whose title goes back to the shire reeves of Anglo-Saxon England.

William did make some changes, however, the most obvious of which were personnel changes. At first, William kept some of Edward the Confessor's chief administrators (especially ones of foreign birth such as **Regenbald**, head of the royal writing office[11]), but soon Normans dominated the royal administration at its higher ranks, though some English remained in lower positions. The overwhelming majority of sheriffs were immigrants throughout the reigns of William and his sons, and so too were leading members of the royal household.[12] Although the royal government kept the forms and nature of royal documents intact, because of the change in personnel the Normans changed the language in which many documents were written. Until about 1070, William issued many documents in English; thereafter, the government used only Latin, the universal language of educated clerics in western Europe.[13]

Most important, the Normans introduced **forest laws**.[14] Most medieval nobles and rulers were avid hunters, and the new kings of England were no exception. "William," stated the *Anglo-Saxon Chronicle*, "loved the deer as though he were their father," and had those who killed deer in the royal forest blinded.[15] Though earlier laws had protected royal hunting, the new Norman kings set aside large regions as royal forests. These royal forests soon included not just woods and wilderness but also cultivated areas. Successive kings added still more, and by the thirteenth century one-quarter of England, including the entire heavily populated county of Essex, was legally royal forest.[16] From an early period these royal forests had as much to do with revenue collection as with hunting. Inhabitants of the royal forest had to pay fines for all manner of privileges and offenses, including cutting wood, keeping dogs that might be used for hunting, and, of course, hunting. By Henry I's reign, if not before, an administration had been set up to govern the forests, which brought in tidy sums for the kings. If these forests were a blessing for the king (and perhaps for the wildlife), they were a monumental and, in many cases, arbitrary headache and financial drain for those living in the royal forest. The later medieval legends of Robin Hood, who lived in Sherwood Forest and hunted the king's deer, provide an indication of how unpopular these forests were.

Overall, William and his sons maintained the relatively sophisticated government they had seized and built on their inheritance from the Anglo-Saxons. William's desire to push Anglo-Saxon government to new accomplishments can best be seen in the massive survey undertaken at the end of his reign that resulted in *Domesday Book*. William's government relied partly on traditional institutions such as the hundred and the county, and used established methods of gathering information and existing records.[17] Yet the whole process was undertaken on a novel scale, so much so that the Anglo-Saxon chronicler famously complained, "So closely did [the king] have things searched out that not a single hide . . . nor even (it is a shame to say, though he thought it no shame to do), an ox or cow or pig remained that was not written down."[18] Though the Normans built on the existing structure, they did not radically alter government; change under William and his sons was evolutionary rather than revolutionary. Beyond the changes already noted, the need for greater bureaucracy may have been stimulated by the royal family's frequent absences in Normandy. A new accounting system called the **exchequer** (based on the abacus, which had recently been introduced to England) appeared under Henry I. But increasing bureaucracy, literacy, and numeracy were features of the period, and the exchequer owed more to the importation of Arabic (and ultimately Chinese) knowledge of the abacus than to the Norman Conquest.[19] In sum, the impact of the Norman Conquest on government was surprisingly limited.

GEOPOLITICS AND FOREIGN RELATIONS

The Norman Conquest brought more changes to what may be grandly called geopolitics than to the mechanics of government.[20] Within England itself, the Normans incorporated the north more firmly into the kingdom than it had been before. How big an issue northern separatism had been on the eve of the conquest is debatable, but the Norman destruction of northern rebellions and construction of many castles and lordships wiped out any effective separatist feeling. The far northwest was not part of the kingdom at all until William II conquered Carlisle. He and his brother firmly established their control in that region, and Henry eventually created a new bishopric in Carlisle as part of his program to make it part of England.[21]

In aggressively expanding their control in the north, the Norman kings encountered an equally aggressive Scottish dynasty that was expanding in many directions from its base around Edinburgh.[22] Conflict would have almost certainly occurred between English and Scottish rulers without the Norman Conquest. During the late Anglo-Saxon period, the Scots seized Lothian, part of the former English kingdom of Northumbria, and would have been happy to take more territory. But William and his sons dealt with the able monarchs of Scotland effectively, partly by warfare and partly by working out deals. Under King **Malcolm III Canmore**, who married the sister of Edgar Atheling, hostility dominated until the old king died in an ambush during a raid on England in 1093. From then on, Malcolm's sons, who faced internal threats, generally had peaceful relations with the English kings. Malcolm's daughter Edith married Henry I and adopted the Norman name **Matilda** to fit into her new family. Malcolm's youngest son and eventual successor, **David**, had very close relations with Henry. Indeed, David began settling Anglo-Norman lords (including the direct ancestor of Robert Bruce) in Scotland to strengthen his own hand and to help Scotland adopt new military technologies such as the castle and the heavily armored knight. Though David did grab as much of northern England as he could during the civil war between Stephen and Matilda III, his gains were temporary, and the border that was created in the Anglo-Norman period essentially ended up being permanent. Moreover, the peace that Henry I created with Scotland formed the pattern for nearly two centuries, with the two kingdoms mainly remaining harmonious, except when Scottish kings occasionally took advantage of English civil wars to try to recover the lands David had temporarily held or to gain other advantages. Only in the late thirteenth century would the two countries once again become bitter enemies, after **Edward I** tried to seize control of Scotland.

England's pattern of relations with Wales proved quite different from its relations with Scotland.[23] Unlike Scotland, Wales was divided into several small kingdoms. Competition between local rulers left Wales vulnerable to a Norman attack, which was spearheaded by nobles, though the English kings sometimes played a role. The boundary between England and Wales had been broadly stable for centuries, with English kings remaining content with claims of overlordship over Welsh rulers. Harold Godwineson might have changed this situation had he remained king. Earlier, after his victory in Wales, Harold had annexed a small area of it. Because of the conquest, however, it was several Norman lords who truly began the conquest of Wales by seizing lordships for themselves wherever they could in the years after 1066. For the next two centuries, Wales frequently saw war between a bewildering array of Welsh rulers and the English marcher lords who had seized various territories, with occasional interventions by English kings. Early advances into Wales were often reversed, but the Norman period saw the beginning of a process that would eventually snuff out Welsh independence under Edward I. Wales might have suffered English aggression anyway, perhaps under Harold, but the Norman Conquest determined the precise nature of the slow English conquest of that land.

The Norman Conquest also affected relations between England and countries beyond Britain. England had long had close ties to Scandinavia. *Beowulf*, the greatest surviving piece of Anglo-Saxon literature, was about Scandinavians, and not long before 1066, England had been part of Canute's empire, which spanned Denmark and Norway. After 1066, Scandinavian relationships became far less important. Instead, English relations became much closer with France. Indeed, the rulers of England held parts of France until the end of the Hundred Years' War. During that war, they claimed the throne of France itself, a claim that English monarchs maintained well past the Middle Ages.

I have already discussed some of the earliest episodes of English involvement in France. William used English troops and resources to regain control of Maine, and his sons, William Rufus and Henry, used England as a launching pad to attack Normandy. The civil war between Stephen and Matilda was fought on both sides of the channel, and Henry II added Anjou to the territories linked to England. He also added many other regions through his marriage to **Eleanor** of Aquitaine, including Poitou and Gascony. Indeed, Henry held far more of France than the French kings did. Henry II's youngest son, **John** (1199–1216), lost most of these possessions to the French king at the beginning of the thirteenth century, and the French captured Poitou from John's son, **Henry III** (1216–1272). Even so, the English kings continued to control Gascony, source of the fine Bordeaux wines that the English came to favor so much. Their control of Gascony sparked several conflicts with the French kings and was one important cause of the Hundred Years' War, one of the major conflicts of European history. Of course, the chain of causation between the Norman Conquest and the Hundred Years' War was fairly extended, since William I had no control over Gascony. Nonetheless, there is no doubt that the conquest started the long and intimate involvement of rulers of England in French affairs that marked the remainder of the Middle Ages.[24] Overall, the Norman Conquest profoundly affected England's relations with its neighbors.

MILITARY

Not surprisingly, the Normans brought important military innovations to England. The most important of these was the castle. One of the most dynamic current topics in medieval English history is castle history, partly because of the cumulative impact of archaeology, partly because of new techniques such as using Geographic Information Systems to study the placement of castles, and partly because of new intellectual approaches.[25] The new developments have made the Norman impact seem less revolutionary than once thought. For one thing, it is now clear that Anglo-Saxon noble residences could have been at least lightly fortified, and the distinction between such residences and the simplest of castles may not have been too sharp. Second, scholars are emphasizing the nonmilitary roles of castles as residences and centers of administration and lordship. In their nonmilitary functions, castles were not that different from Anglo-Saxon lordly halls, and in some cases at least, castles were built on previous centers of lordship.

Nonetheless, contemporaries were struck by castles in a military context, and it is likely that they brought significant change to the military landscape in post–Norman Conquest England. Setting aside the simplest castles, which may have resembled existing fortified residences, castles provided an intermediate level of fortification between the town walls and the lightly fortified aristocratic residences familiar to the Anglo-Saxons. Though castles served some of the same purposes as older fortifications, they brought new military dynamics. First, the Normans introduced novel designs and technologies in fortification, such as the motte-and-bailey castle, which was described in the previous chapter (see figure 3.1). William the Conqueror and some of his followers also had the first stone keeps built in England, the most famous being the White Tower at the heart of the Tower of London (see figure 3.2).[26] Second, many royal castles were built to dominate fortified towns, which helped the Normans consolidate their conquest and gave later rulers a way to keep firm control of urban areas. Third, the amount of castle building after the conquest meant that England was now fortified in greater depth. Any subsequent invader had to cope not only with towns and lightly fortified residences but also with scores of large castles. Having conquered England, William and his followers made it more difficult for any other foreign army to duplicate their accomplishment. Finally, the new fortifications shifted the balance of warfare away from battles and toward sieges. Control of castles became crucial to military dominance of a region.

Another military change brought by the Normans was the decline of the fleet.[27] From Alfred the Great to Harold Godwineson, sea power had

Figure 3.1. A motte-and-bailey castle. Detail from the Bayeux Tapestry, 11th c., Musée de la Tapisserie, Bayeux, France. Giraudon/Art Resource, NY

been an important tool for Anglo-Saxon kings. Judging from what scraps of information we have, fleets were raised through the hidage system, with groups of hides being designated to provide ships. The Norman kings did not ignore sea power. William the Conqueror himself used a fleet against Scotland. After he died, both William Rufus and Henry I sent out ships against Robert Curthose's attempted invasions, William Rufus with more success than Henry. With these exceptions, however, the use of fleets remained rare and generally improvised for a number of generations after the Norman Conquest. Experience in naval warfare may have declined rapidly with the destruction of the Anglo-Saxon aristocracy, and resources that had gone into ships may have been diverted to castles. Whatever the reason, English naval power declined for a long time because of the Norman Conquest.

The nature of field combat on land also changed, though there were continuities as well.[28] Elite warriors used horses for transportation both before and after the conquest, and the Bayeux Tapestry shows that both sides used similar armor and some of the same weapons, including swords, spears, and bows. The Normans, however, considered the battle axe an English weapon and failed to adopt it. They probably introduced a new missile weapon, namely the crossbow. This was a powerful weapon, with longer range and greater penetration than older bows. It was so powerful that twelfth-century church councils attempted to ban its use against Christians,

Figure 3.2.   The White Tower, Tower of London. Vanni/Art Resource, NY

though by implication they sanctioned its use against Muslims. However, such bows were slow to load and remained most useful in sieges, so they did not revolutionize field warfare as the longbow later did in the Hundred Years' War.

The main change introduced by the Normans will be easy to guess from the account of the Battle of Hastings: the Normans brought heavily armored cavalry to England. Indeed, the reason they did not adopt the battle axe is that it was not a cavalry weapon. One scholar, Stephen Morillo, has recently disputed the impact of the Norman introduction of cavalry, rightly pointing out that Anglo-Norman knights fought dismounted in many of the major battles of the following generations. The Normans recognized that cavalry was not always superior to infantry. Indeed, part of the appeal of cavalry was social rather than military. Mounted warriors were impressive-looking figures, and nobles could set themselves apart as elite mounted warriors, displaying their wealth as well as their martial distinctiveness from lower-class foot soldiers. But cavalry had its military uses as well. It could sweep aside poorly organized infantry and was particularly effective in the pursuit of a defeated enemy, a stage of battle when heavy casualties could most easily be inflicted.[29] Thus, the introduction of cavalry gave Anglo-Norman forces a greater flexibility than their Anglo-Saxon predecessors had possessed, for elite warriors could fight on horseback or on foot as conditions dictated. Because the use of heavy cavalry was so important in most of continental western Europe, this introduction also meant that elite English troops could more easily fight in armies outside England, whether in France or on the Crusades, an important consideration for the Norman kings and their followers. The superiority of the mounted Norman knight to the Anglo-Saxon warrior has sometimes been exaggerated, but there is no doubt that the Normans brought a new way of fighting. Altogether, change in the military sphere, though not as profound as once believed, was nonetheless extensive.

LANDHOLDING

William's biographer described how, after William returned to Normandy for the first time and celebrated Easter, the Normans and their neighbors marveled at the riches he and his followers had brought back: "Indeed as they looked at the clothes of the king and his courtiers, woven and encrusted with gold, they considered whatever they had seen before to be of little worth. Similarly they marveled at the vessels of silver and gold, of whose number and beauty incredible things could truthfully be said."[30] Plunder was highly prized! Land, however, formed the most desirable kind of acquisition in the Middle Ages since agriculture was by far the most important and most stable source of wealth. The general Norman lust for land and William's desire, after c. 1070, to break the back of the native aristocracy meant that the Norman Conquest brought a revolution in landholding. In the previous chapter, I described one aspect of this revolution—the replacement of English landholders by Norman ones. I wish to emphasize two more aspects in this section, although I should note that in the long run, the actual impact of these facets was far less than their potential impact.

The first aspect concerns the balance of landholding within the elites, as revealed by *Domesday Book*. While Edward the Confessor had been the greatest *individual* landholder before the conquest, the *collective* wealth of the Godwine family outstripped that of the king. Other earls also had vast holdings. Below the earls were a few dozen wealthy thanes and then a very large number of minor thanes and other landholders. In addition, the church collectively held about one-quarter of the land in England. The church's share remained largely unchanged, at least in terms of overlordship, but the remainder of the distribution changed drastically. William doubled his share of the lands in England, collecting roughly 17 percent of the revenues recorded in *Domesday Book*. Though he rewarded many of his chief followers richly, none approached Godwine or Harold in landholding. Only the king's brothers came close to having the wealth of Earls Edwin and Morcar and their family. This meant that the balance of landed wealth had shifted drastically between the king and the leading nobles.[31]

Within the aristocracy, the vast majority of the land became focused on about two hundred nobles who held directly from the king. None of these was as rich as the great earls of Edward the Confessor's reign, but most were far wealthier than the average Anglo-Saxon thane. Thus, aristocratic landholding became squeezed into a somewhat narrower spectrum than before. Great variations in wealth remained within the group, and there continued to be many minor landholders. Nonetheless, the kinds of nobles who could challenge the government, as some of the earls had done in Edward the Confessor's reign, disappeared.

These changes, however, were not all permanent. King William may have built up the royal holdings dramatically, but his sons and successors, William II and Henry I, gave out huge amounts of land. Surveys from Henry I's reign for one county and parts of two others reveal that over half of the royal lands had already been alienated in the areas covered.[32] William's massive accumulation of lands into royal hands proved distinctly short-lived, and by 1300, the royal lands accounted for about 2 percent of the landed income from England.[33] The great nobles, however, were also giving out land both before and after *Domesday Book*. The leading immigrant nobles had already granted out much land before 1086, generally more than half their estates.[34] They and their descendants continued to grant much more, a fact that has received insufficient attention from scholars. Many noble families gave out the great majority of the land they had received from the kings in the late eleventh and early twelfth centuries. For instance, the lords of the earldom of Richmond had given away at least 80 percent and probably close to 90 percent of their lands by the late thirteenth century.[35] At first, the knights who received these lands remained closely attached to their benefactors and provided much service in return for the land. As generations passed, for reasons to be discussed later, the knights' descendants became more like independent property holders. Thus, the late Anglo-Saxon phenomenon of a very large lesser aristocracy was effectively re-created over the long term. What did not reappear for several centuries were figures like Godwine, who on their own could challenge royal power. Because magnates were nearly as generous as kings, the greatest nobles could not gain on their rulers despite the relentless generosity of the latter. Moreover, some of the leading *Domesday Book* estates were soon broken up, including those of the king's brothers. Thus, the balance of power did not shift once more against the kings. Only in the later Middle Ages did figures appear whose ambitions threatened kings, and these figures almost invariably came from branches of the royal family.

The distribution of lands after the conquest also restructured the nature of landholding in some areas. Late Anglo-Saxon estates tended to be scattered, in contrast to the more compact lordships common in Normandy and elsewhere on the continent. English lands ended up in Norman hands by four main routes, which had varying impacts on landholding patterns. First, William gave out much land simply by making one of his followers the "heir" of a dispossessed English noble. Second, in militarily sensitive regions, the king gave blocks of properties, sometimes entire counties such as Cheshire, to individual lords. William granted most of these blocks of land in the southeast, the southwest, the borderlands with Wales, and the north. His sons continued the practice in the north to help consolidate Norman control there. Third—as Robin Fleming has demonstrated to the satisfaction of most historians—in some areas, William lumped together all or most of the lands of minor landholders that were "left over" after the redistribution of major estates and gave them to a single Norman lord. Fourth, Norman nobles, particularly sheriffs, also simply grabbed new lands (Fleming has spoken of a kleptocracy). Sometimes they did so by treating ties of personal lordship or commendation as ties of lordship in land (through either genuine or purposeful misunderstanding); sometimes they simply grabbed land. In addition, there were other miscellaneous routes to passing on lands. For instance, William granted some manors individually. There is a considerable debate about how much land was redistributed through the various mechanisms. For instance, some scholars have argued that ties of landlordship or overlordship that existed in 1066 may not always have been recorded in *Domesday Book*. Thus, land that appears to have passed to Normans through the granting of leftover lands or through seizure may in fact have been part of the redistribution through making Normans "heirs" of Anglo-Saxon lords. In the case of the estates of minor thanes, it is also sometimes hard to tell if Norman lords simply seized them or if the king redistributed them in some more formal fashion, thus making the overall lawfulness and orderliness of the procedure hard to estimate. Given the nature of the evidence, it is probably impossible to know definitively what percentages of lands were distributed through the various methods. Nonetheless, there was the possibility that the Norman Conquest could have significantly altered landholding patterns.[36]

The redistribution of land through making Normans the successors to specific Anglo-Saxon landholders would have had very little impact on landholding patterns except when individual Normans became successors to a number of Anglo-Saxon nobles with holdings near to one another. In contrast, the creation of compact lordships in militarily important regions obviously brought radical changes to landholding patterns in some areas. Grants of left-over lands and seizure of lands no doubt had an influence somewhere in between these two. Grants of left-over lands gave lords clumps of estates that were geographically close, though often not contiguous. No doubt lords tended to seize lands near their existing estates, thereby helping to create a clumping pattern. Thus, though redistribution of lands after the Norman Conquest fell far short of overturning the existing pattern in which nobles tended to hold scattered estates, it did create some consolidation. This was particularly true of the compact lordships.

In practice, however, two factors counteracted the long-term results of the Norman changes in the geography of lordship. First, revolts by various nobles caused William and his sons to break up or take over some of the most important compact lordships, such as the earldom of Shrewsbury, which had controlled most of the county of Shropshire. Second, nobles who did not forfeit their lands to the king often broke them up by granting out pieces to various followers. As the descendants of their grantees became more like property owners, the surviving blocks became less important. Lordships, or honors, as they were called, did continue to be more compact and stronger on the **Welsh Marches** and in the north, perhaps helping lords in those regions to have unusual political weight in later periods.[37] Overall, however, the revolution in landholding after the Norman Conquest had less long-term than medium-term consequences for the structure of aristocratic landholding.

FEUDALISM

Scholars have long argued that the Normans introduced feudalism to England, and many believed that the Normans profoundly altered English history by doing so. What this means, however, depends a lot on how one defines *feudalism*. Whenever the subject of feudalism comes up, the wise historian runs for cover, but the very controversy over feudalism makes it a good subject to illustrate the complex debates stemming from the period.[38] Feudalism has long been used as a crucial intellectual framework for understanding the Middle Ages. The problem is that feudalism has many different meanings and is used by historians to discuss very different things. The word is not medieval but was developed by early modern lawyers to discuss certain kinds of land tenure among the nobility. Beginning in the eighteenth century, early social scientists began to use the term. Some of them, including the unlikely pair of Adam Smith and Karl Marx, used feudalism to describe relations between lords and peasants. In this sense, feudalism has come to have a wide comparative use. Medievalists specializing in England, however, have tended to use the term to discuss relations *among* the upper classes. Sometimes these two broad usages have been conflated, leading to the classic depiction of the feudal pyramid ranging from the king at the top to peasants at the bottom. There is a certain broad similarity between how peasants and lords held land; both often held it in return for service. However, the kinds of service and the rules covering elite and peasant landholding tended to be quite distinct. Even if one focuses solely on the elites in discussing feudalism, problems remain, because the term is used to describe different aspects of elite society. For some scholars, following in the footsteps of the lawyers who coined the term, landholding remains an important facet. Linked to this is the study of relations between lords and vassals, involving oaths of fealty, ceremonies of homage, and the granting of land. Another important strand of study focuses on what might be called the privatization of government functions on the continent after the collapse of Charlemagne's empire, with royal functions such as presiding over courts and conducting war passing into the hands of nobles. And the list goes on. Thus, feudalism means many different things to different scholars, and this has led to frustration. One pair of historians, in a book published in 1963, described the terms *feudal* and *feudalism* as "the most regrettable coinages ever put into circulation to debase the language of historians."[39] More recently, historians have discussed the ways in which models of feudalism may distort our reading of the evidence and thus our understanding of medieval societies.[40] Indeed, some scholars urge abolishing the term altogether as a useless construct. I am sympathetic to the desire to purge feudalism from the terminology of historians; it is a bloated concept that conceals as much as it reveals. Nonetheless, I will argue that some of the changes historians have discussed when describing the Normans' introduction of feudalism were indeed real rather than modern constructs, although these changes were less radical and less enduring than once thought.

The "classical" picture of English feudalism after the Norman Conquest, articulated by such historians as Frank Stenton and R. Allen Brown, contains various elements, some common to other scholarly depictions of feudalism, some not.[41] The discussion of lords and peasants never played a significant role in the models of Anglo-Norman feudalism. The idea of political disintegration had only limited importance, since English feudalism was seen as coexisting with and even supporting a powerful royal government. On the other hand, the sorts of military changes mentioned earlier have been part and parcel of discussions of English feudalism but largely absent from discussions of feudalism in other periods and places, mainly because such changes tended to be more gradual elsewhere. Landholding also is crucial to models of English feudalism. Among the changes scholars have argued that the Normans brought were the creation of a feudal pyramid among the landholding classes, a widespread link between landholding and knights' service, and the creation of institutions called **honors**. Honors consisted of the lands held directly by a noble (called the **demesne**) and lands of the noble held by his vassals. The Norman kings assigned a quota of knights to each honor, and the lords of those honors generally assigned quotas to their vassals to make up all or most of the quotas the lords owed the king. Through means of these quotas, the king could raise a feudal host whenever he needed an army. The honor took on nonmilitary functions as well. In particular, lords held courts attended by vassals, and thus a bit of the privatization of government associated with feudalism on the continent appears in England, though never enough to threaten royal government. Landholders did not own land outright but held **fiefs** conditional upon loyal service to their lord.

Indeed, some legal scholars, most notably Samuel Thorne and S. F. C. Milsom, have argued that fiefs were not property but more like tenure at a university.[42] Once a professor receives tenure, she or he has a legal right to a position for life on the condition that the professor actually does the job of teaching classes and so forth. According to this view, once a Norman knight received a fief, he was entitled to hold it for life, assuming he performed the service he owed as a knight, but ultimately a lord and his vassals, in the honor's court, determined the rights and wrongs of individual claims. Just as a professorship is not property and cannot be inherited by a professor's heirs, so too a fief was not property and not heritable by a vassal's heirs, though in Milsom's view there was a very strong customary presumption that the heir would succeed. Again, the honorial court was the final arbiter. According to this view, landholding and land law among the elites in England were overwhelmingly governed by feudal lordship and vassalage until the passage of time (Thorne), or certain legal changes under Henry II (Milsom), turned fiefs into property by giving rights independent of honorial courts. Recent scholarship has undermined in several ways the old view that the Normans introduced a robust feudalism that fundamentally reshaped England. The study of history once concentrated on legal, military, constitutional, and political matters, and feudalism involved all of these to some degree. Thus, feudalism could be placed at the center of historical change. As new areas of history have arisen, however, scholars have seen feudalism as relatively less important in explaining historical change. At the same time, some of the alleged changes discussed previously have come into question. I have already outlined some of the arguments that would lessen the impact of military changes associated with feudalism. Further doubts, which I will address shortly, concern the actual usefulness of the feudal host in war. For reasons that I will also discuss, few scholars have been willing to fully adopt the arguments of Thorne and Milsom. One scholar has challenged the established belief that military quotas emerged only after the Norman Conquest.[43] Finally, I and other scholars have argued that honors declined fairly rapidly in the course of the twelfth century, at least as living institutions.

In the paragraphs that follow, I will outline my own reconstruction of what "feudal" changes the Normans introduced and how they affected English society. In doing so, I will address various points of the historiography outlined already. I must stress, however, that the evidence for the key generations after the conquest is scanty, which is one reason scholarly interpretations can vary sharply. Like others, I will be relying too heavily on a process of working backward from more plentiful later evidence, a necessary and useful but problematic practice.

My starting point is that lordship and patronage were fundamentally important social relationships in the Middle Ages, as in many premodern societies. We have already seen their importance in both England and Normandy before the conquest. Wealthy lords, including kings, relied on followers for social status, various services, and, above all, coercion and military muscle. Followers, in turn, relied on their lords for various kinds of support and in the hope of rewards. Sometimes, both in Normandy and in England before the conquest, followers received land from their lords and held it for various services.

Links of lordship were supposed to be extremely powerful in the Middle Ages. One of the great poems of the late Anglo-Saxon period, "The Battle of Maldon," focused on warriors in a defeated army who chose to die avenging their lord rather than flee.[44] An important aspect of Norman propaganda during the conquest was that Harold had become William's man in Normandy but had then broken his allegiance by taking the English throne. A legal treatise written in England in Henry I's reign stated that anyone who killed his lord should be tormented so badly that hell would seem more merciful, "if such were possible."[45] Lordship was often not as strong in reality as in ideology, but it nonetheless constituted a very important social bond.

Though William the Conqueror relied partly on mercenaries and adventurers in the Norman Conquest, he also relied heavily on lordship. When William called on leading nobles for support, he was not only activating his own patronage network but also asking his leading nobles to call on their own networks. Using these networks, William's nobles raised war bands that accompanied them to England. One Norman nobleman was described as having fought in all the major struggles in the conquest, surrounded by his companions.[46] We know little about the precise makeup of these war bands, and perhaps adventurers and mercenaries joined them. However, ample research has shown that the new Norman tenants of William's great followers in England had often been their tenants or neighbors in Normandy.[47] Perhaps William's chief followers simply handed out land to their old vassals and friends out of the goodness of their hearts, but the overwhelming likelihood is that just as William had rewarded his great lords for their support in the conquest, they too were rewarding the men who had fought by their sides. In essence, England was settled by war bands created by concentric circles of lordship emanating outward from William himself.

On some level, then, William simply replaced the old Anglo-Saxon networks of lordship and patronage with new ones as a byproduct of his destruction of the old aristocracy and his need to entrench Norman power.

On this level, which one might call a macro level, the Norman Conquest brought no structural change whatsoever. Lordship and associated networks of patronage were important before 1066, and they remained important after 1066. This broad continuity across the conquest should not be ignored. Nonetheless, if one focuses in more closely, a number of changes become apparent.

First, in the short term, the conquest probably produced unusually tight networks of patronage, even by medieval standards. The shared experience of war in a hostile land where a different language was spoken must have strengthened bonds between lords and followers and among the followers themselves. The treasures and lands that lords passed out would also strengthen lordship; followers would be in debt to lords for their new fortunes. At the same time, lords owed their followers for the support they had shown in difficult and dangerous circumstances. Thus, one suspects that the bonds of lordship were even stronger than usual in the first generation after the conquest.

Second, as scholars have traditionally argued, lordship, military service, and landholding became very closely tied. Before the conquest, grants of land in return for service were merely one tool in the toolkits of lords trying to build up patronage networks. Moreover, they were an expensive tool, one to be used sparingly. With the seizure of so much land from the English, however, such grants could become the most important means for building lordship for several decades. Most of a lord's tenants after the conquest would naturally be his close followers, and most of his knights could hope to become tenants. Because the lands held by tenants constituted part of a lord's honor, the honor and the war band must have been closely connected in the first generation after the conquest.

Third, most land in England came to be held from a lord; a feudal pyramid of the textbook variety came into being, with knights holding from lords who, in turn, held from kings. Often enough, there were more levels in the hierarchy. Even church lands got brought into the system. The lands of abbeys and bishoprics came to be seen as honors held from the king. Warriors had often held lands from the church in the Anglo-Saxon period, but now churchmen were forced to give land in the form of fiefs to Norman warriors, for reasons that will be revealed in the next paragraph. Though the granting of fiefs was not new, contemporary patterns of landholding, in Normandy and elsewhere in Europe, were normally much more diverse and included allods (lands that were independent holdings, much like modern property) and the holding of land for a monetary rent on short- or long-term leases. In England, the destruction of the old aristocracy allowed William and his followers to create a systematic hierarchy of landholding. Even Susan Reynolds, one of the strongest critics of traditional ideas about feudalism, notes that the land-holding structure in England after the conquest came closest to the "later myths of the origins of feudalism in royal grants."[48]

Fourth, I am reasonably confident that the traditional argument about the creation of quotas after the conquest is correct. Part of the argument for preconquest quotas rests on the silence of the sources regarding the introduction of a quota system after the conquest. However, there is equal silence in the sources for preconquest quotas, whereas there *is* evidence of the hidage system of recruitment. Sir James Holt has convincingly shown that William and his sons, in a process that extended into the first decade of the twelfth century, created the specific quotas that appear in later records.[49] It is possible that the quota system, as opposed to the actual quotas, existed before the conquest, but in view of the lack of evidence for such quotas in the Anglo-Saxon period, it seems preferable to retain the traditional view that the new kings created the system as well as the specific quotas. In this system, each **tenant-in-chief** (to employ the technical term for nobles holding land directly from the king) was required to maintain a war band of a specific size, which the king could call upon in times of need. Bishops and abbots were not exempt, which is why much church property ended up permanently in the hands of knights. Lords did not necessarily have to maintain these war bands by granting out lands, and powerful lords continued to maintain household knights in their followings. In practice, however, most lords did maintain their war bands largely by grants of land or promises of such grants. One advantage of this method was that granting out manors solved problems of administering large collections of estates. Far more important, social pressures required lords to generously reward followers who had accompanied them to England, especially if they wanted to keep the loyalty of those followers. The whole system was probably rough and ready at first. For instance, in one early document, William arranged for a knight to receive a fief from an important abbey in return for serving the abbot with "three or four knights," not a very precise quota.[50] No doubt someone who had a quota of fifty knights might show up with a few less without punishment. Nonetheless, a system did evolve whereby men held their honors in return for military service with set numbers of knights. A century after the conquest, the service of approximately 5,300 knights was owed to the king, and this figure largely reflects quotas set up by William and his sons.[51]

Recent scholarship has tended to argue that the feudal host was not a very effective military force and has emphasized the use by kings of household troops and of mercenaries.[52] I agree with the assessment of the feudal host overall, but would argue that there is one very important exception. In regard to the kinds of wars that kings after William the Conqueror generally had to fight—namely, foreign wars in Scotland, Wales, Ireland, and France—the feudal host was indeed inefficient and fairly ineffective. Troops were expensive to transport, holders of fiefs could be old or incompetent, and the feudal host was not as flexible as household and mercenary troops. But for consolidating the conquest, which was the primary goal of William and his sons, the feudal host was precisely what was needed. First, the feudal host initially developed out of the army that William had brought with him; thus, early on, the host was largely made up of able and experienced warriors. Second, William needed an army of occupation that would keep down any potential rebellion (fear of which lingered long after the rebellions themselves ceased) and drive out any invaders. One important duty of knights was to garrison castles, and some sources show how rotas of knights from various fiefs were established to ensure that royal castles and the castles of great barons were continually staffed.[53] Though these sources are late, it seems likely that the arrangements were made when fear of rebellion was still strong.

Logistically, William could not maintain a huge standing army. Even when he hired large numbers of mercenaries to hold off a threatened Danish invasion in 1085, he had to house them all over England with his nobles rather than at a single location.[54] Creating the feudal host solved such logistical difficulties; lords and their knights supported themselves on the lands they had been given. Having the host scattered throughout England had definite advantages: local lords and knights could respond immediately to local rebellions; because England was relatively small, troops could quickly converge on trouble spots; and, most important, the creation of the feudal hierarchy created an army with very strong interests in preserving the Norman Conquest. Though mercenaries did have to worry about their reputations, nobles and knights who had received grants of land might nonetheless be even more willing to stand fast against rebellion or invasion. The feudal host admirably served its primary purpose, which was to secure the Norman Conquest.

In the long term, however, the feudal host became an awkward and inefficient source of military power for wars after the Norman Conquest itself, especially ones fought in foreign lands. William the Conqueror could reasonably have echoed the adage of the great twentieth-century economist John Maynard Keynes: "In the long run, we're all dead." In the short run, William's strategy helped secure the Norman Conquest, which meant that even the short-term effectiveness of the feudal host had a long-term impact. Nonetheless, the problems of the feudal host meant that feudalism had a relatively limited impact on the military history of England. If kings before and after the conquest relied heavily on household troops and mercenaries, the introduction of feudalism looks less like a crucial turning point in military history than it once did.

The creation of the feudal host, however, had medium- and long-term consequences in other spheres. In the medium term, the Norman settlement institutionalized patronage networks and rooted them in landholding networks. Stenton's discussion of honors as important social, legal, and political institutions is open to attack; his evidence is strong, but not overwhelmingly so.[55] Honors would probably have been strongest in the generations after the Norman Conquest when our records (with the exception of *Domesday Book*) are less plentiful than later. Despite this, Stenton makes a convincing case that honors became crucial in forming networks of power and patronage after the conquest and had important institutional roles for a time. Knights got their English name, *cniht*, from an Anglo-Saxon term referring to retainers, and this is clearly how the natives saw Norman knights even after they had been settled as landholders. Lords did not rely only on followers to whom they had given land to fulfill their military services to the king, but honors continued to be an important recruiting ground even after William I's reign. One early document recording an **enfeoffment** of land clearly refers to service at a lord's side.[56] More broadly, after giving out so much land, lords could not subsequently afford to pay for lots of mercenaries. The rotas of knights performing castle guard for baronial castles strongly indicate that tenants originally served personally in protecting the strongholds of their lords. One interesting set of documents from Pontefract, the center of a northern honor and a new borough founded by its Norman lords, shows feudal tenants holding houses side by side in the town. Perhaps they gained these properties to house their families when they performed castle service at the castle there or to house themselves when they attended their lord's court. Perhaps founding the borough was something of a cooperative effort between lord and men.[57] Clearly, the founding of religious houses was often a cooperative honorial effort—many documents show lords and their men endowing new monasteries together.[58] Honors gained a certain institutional coherence as well—there are early references to various honorial officials, including honorial sheriffs.[59] Finally, honors were given their own courts, a judicial innovation. We know little about these early courts, but they suggest such strong bonds between lords and men that a new jurisdiction was needed. Overall, the Norman

Conquest created a potentially powerful combination of personal patronage, landholding, war bands, and even justice that transformed traditional patronage networks (Norman as well as English) in important ways.

This combination, however, proved fragile over the course of generations. Patronage networks, which depended on personal relations, tended to be far more fluid than landholding structures in societies where land was heritable. This point brings us back to the arguments of Thorne and Milsom. If land was not strictly heritable, then lords, with the assistance of their vassals, could adjust patronage networks as vassals died, at least until the time of Henry II's reforms. Any time a fief became vacant, a lord could place a loyal follower in the fief, whether the individual was the previous vassal's heir or someone else entirely who was closer to the lord or was a better warrior. Heirs would have every incentive to be close and loyal followers of a lord. Of course, even in these circumstances, a strong customary presumption that the heir would succeed to a fief would limit the flexibility of the patronage system. Nonetheless, in such a system, honors could be reasonably flexible instruments of patronage. The question is whether the arguments of Thorne and Milsom are correct.

Research has shown that inheritance of land was already well established in Normandy.[60] But were lands granted out in England property in the modern sense? When powerful magnates abandoned England early in the conquest, William naturally gave their land to other nobles who were willing to stick it out. Nobles undoubtedly did the same in similar circumstances, no doubt with the blessing of other followers, happy to see the backs of those unwilling to share burdens and risks. Clearly, landholding was conditional early on. Moreover, the arguments of Thorne and Milsom help make sense of many aspects of twelfth-century land law, which suggests that such laws were influenced by feudal ideas. However, most scholars believe that the arguments of Thorne and Milsom overstate the case and that inheritance quite soon became well established.[61]

One reason for this is that kings interfered with honorial courts long before Henry II's reign, thus restricting the freedom of lords to do what they wished with the lands of their vassals.[62] Another reason was that tenants as a group had military and political strength—lords had to treat them with care. The English origins of fiefs as rewards for participation in the conquest provide another crucial reason why lands soon became heritable. Lands were partly an alternative form of salary, but they were also rewards for service, and the concept of land as payment for ongoing service clashed with the idea of land as payment for past service. One monastic chronicle described how the abbot of Abingdon gave lands out to much of his war band but ignored a knight who had not yet received land because pirates had cut off his hands while the knight was on royal service. From the abbot's perspective, the knight was no longer any good in helping the abbey fulfill its military quota. However, the king stepped in, after receiving a complaint from the knight, and forced the abbot to give the knight land. After all, the knight had earned it by serving loyally and suffering mutilation.[63] To a large degree, the Norman Conquest was a joint venture by William, his lords, and their patronage networks. The payoff for participation in the venture came in the form of land, and lords could not simply treat the lands they gave as a form of stipend for continuing service, recoverable at their will or at the first available vacancy. This meant that from the beginning, there must have been a certain presumption of permanence to landholding that was independent of a lord's continuing willingness to honor earlier grants. There were undoubtedly competing views on how and when a lord could deprive a tenant or heir, but the evidence shows that by and large, fiefs soon became secure and heritable in practice and increasingly in theory.

With time, patronage networks and landholding structures began to drift apart.[64] Even from the beginning, there were problems and tensions. What about followers who could not perform their service, like the knight who had lost his hands? To whom did knights owe primary loyalty, their immediate lords or the king? The passage of generations exacerbated problems. One problem was that of **subinfeudation**, the process by which tenants gave land to others, who became tenants and gave land to others, who, in turn, became tenants. This was part of the system from the beginning, but as time went on, the system became more and more complex, so much so that several links might exist between the lord of the honor and the holder of a specific manor or property, undermining the personal nature of bonds holding the whole honor together. More generally, the personal aspect of honorial lordship began to fray across the board. Early on, the fear of rebellion must have kept war bands firmly united, but as the fear faded, the urgency to maintain close-knit war bands faded as well. Frequent civil wars, or private wars of the sort common in some areas of the continent, might have kept ties strong had they been common in England. After the crushing of the native English revolts, however, England was mostly peaceful until the civil war between Stephen and Matilda, at least outside of the Welsh borderlands, for the struggles at the beginnings of the reigns of William II and Henry I were very brief. The need for war bands became intermittent.

Study of lords and followers over generations reveals that lords maintained looser patronage networks. They still recruited members from their feudal tenantry, but found themselves having to give new rewards to keep younger generations in their service. Moreover, they might find their tenants less useful, motivated, or congenial than other men, and so they also often recruited new followers. There are indications that these processes began very soon after the conquest. As long as lords rewarded followers by giving them land, patronage networks could be kept within the honorial structure. However, in the course of the twelfth century, lords had to become much stingier about granting out lands, since few new lands were coming into their hands. If lords gave out too much to their tenants, they would eventually become impoverished, as happened to a few minor baronial families. As the twelfth century moved on, lords moved to other means of rewarding followers and maintaining their patronage system.

I should note that the timing and degree of this whole shift is the subject of legitimate debate. Because the evidence for the generations immediately following the conquest is fairly scanty, it is hard to know just how important the honor was early on and, therefore, how much of a change was involved in its decline as a patronage network and how soon the change began. This aspect of the debate will probably remain open indefinitely. The degree of decline before the thirteenth century is another matter. Though I—and other scholars—have argued for the twelfth and perhaps early thirteenth centuries as crucial to the change, one leading scholar of thirteenth-century England, David Carpenter, has argued that honors continued to be a focus of patronage for a longer period.[65] Much of the evidence Carpenter draws upon involves compact honors, where the relative impact of neighborhood and honor may be hard to measure. Since the evidence for the thirteenth century is relatively full, however, a study of patronage networks that systematically compares honor, neighborhood, and other factors can probably settle the question some day. In the meantime, the status of the honor as a focus of patronage in the thirteenth century will remain debatable.

Whatever the timing, the shift of patronage from honors and landholding to other means of reward led to what scholars have called bastard feudalism, which survived in various forms through the Middle Ages and beyond.[66] The term suggests that this kind of feudalism was a bastardized form of some longstanding, stable, and "real" feudalism. Based on my assessment of the honor as a relatively fragile focus of patronage, I would suggest that this is a problematic perception. Patronage networks in which grants of land were only one, fairly infrequent, method of rewarding people represented the norm throughout the Middle Ages in England. The real anomaly was the situation in the two generations immediately following the conquest, in which patronage networks could be closely linked to land-holding structures simply because of the land bonanza created by the Norman Conquest. In the long term, this close link was not sustainable because of the contrast between the relatively rigid structure of landholding and the fluid nature of personal relations and, therefore, of patronage networks.

Nonetheless, the system created after the conquest did have some long-term effects, which helped create the perception that the feudalism of William the Conqueror's time was the norm rather than the anomaly. What were these long-term consequences? First, there was a theoretical shift in how troops were recruited within England. Before 1066, hidage had been the notional basis in determining the rough size of forces that lords brought with them. Afterward, quotas were the key. In the actual raising of armies, the difference between the two systems may not have mattered that much. I have already noted the use of royal household troops and mercenaries. For raising troops from the aristocracy, both Anglo-Saxon and Norman kings probably had to rely on what Stephen Morillo has called the "Let's go, boys" rule; lords were expected to show up, when summoned, with as large a war band as they could gather in a reasonable amount of time.[67] As I have emphasized before, this was a world in which the personal mattered as much as the institutional, and as long as lords made good-faith efforts, kings probably did not place too much emphasis on precise numbers. This change, therefore, was not particularly revolutionary in military terms. What it did do, however, was weaken the hidage system by removing one of its functions.[68]

William's system also created certain long-term rights of lords over their tenants and tenants' lands. Some of these are rightly called feudal incidents because they were originally incidental or subordinate to the main purpose of the honor, which was to endow and maintain a war band.[69] For example, say a loyal knight died, leaving an underage son who could not fight. The lord would gain guardianship (or **wardship**) over the boy in order to raise him as a loyal follower. Until the boy could fight, the lord collected the income of the boy's land in order to pay for a substitute warrior or warriors. Say a knight died leaving only daughters or a widow with rights in the land. The lord had the right to arrange the marriage of such girls or women to loyal followers who could fulfill the service of the dead lord. Say a knight died without heirs—the lord recovered the land to grant out again or keep in his own possession.

Other rights were strictly financial from the beginning. From an early date, lords sometimes paid money to the king in wartime instead of bringing knights; perhaps they were unable to attend, or perhaps the money was more useful in a foreign campaign. Such payments were called **scutage**, from a Latin term for shield. Presumably knights unable to serve lords due to old age or sickness could likewise pay instead. Tenants were expected to help their lords financially outside of war as well, including granting money on specific occasions, such as when a lord married off his eldest daughter, knighted his eldest son, or needed to be ransomed. Tenants paid a kind of inheritance tax as well. All of these rights and payments could survive even after the patronage networks and landholding structures drifted apart, for they did not depend on maintaining close ties of personal loyalty and lordship, as raising an effective war band did. Indeed, as personal ties of lords and tenants faded, these rights of lordship slowly became more carefully defined, more purely financial in nature, and, eventually, the main reason for the survival of honors. It is true that marriage and wardship must sometimes have restored close ties between lords and tenant families when the lord married an heiress off to a loyal follower or gained the admiration of a boy in wardship. On the whole, however, the rights became a source of funds rather than followers—indeed, the kings, who were the greatest lords of all, sometimes essentially sold off widows and heiresses to the highest bidder. Kings also came to rely more and more on scutage payments as time went on, and in the latter half of the twelfth century, such payments replaced the hidage system as the main conduit for taxation. In the thirteenth century, feudal taxation was in turn replaced. However, fiscal feudalism, as the financial exploitation of feudal incidents is often called, had a very long life indeed. In fact, certain royal feudal rights survived into the seventeenth century and played a role in provoking the revolt against King Charles I, which led to the English Civil War.

The system created by William and his sons may also have had a long-term impact by serving as a model throughout Catholic lands, though this suggestion is offered here merely as a hypothesis. Most of the elements of what scholars call feudalism already existed in England and in many areas of the continent, but one can argue that the Norman kings first turned these elements into a national system and that others subsequently followed them. There were two ways in which the Norman system in England could have served as a model. First, it may have influenced the creation of similar feudal systems after other conquests. The likely impact of William's system on the Anglo-Norman conquerors of Wales and much of Ireland is obvious, since the latter were descended from William and his followers. The system also appeared in Norman Sicily, where the potential links will be evident, and in the crusader states, where many figures familiar with the Norman Conquest gained positions of power. Second, William's model may have encouraged the attempts of kings and lawyers to move toward a similar system in areas in which conquest was not a factor. Several scholars have argued that feudalism only became systematized in Normandy after England provided a model.[70] Susan Reynolds has argued that in France and elsewhere, lawyers in some sense created feudal systems.[71] Lawyers did so by trying to systematize the complexities of earlier lordship into a comprehensible legal system and by emphasizing what nobles owed their kings. Such lawyers could draw on local roots, but England, where kings long continued to derive income from feudal taxation and fiscal feudalism, would have been an obvious model. This hypothesis is tentative and probably impossible to prove. Nonetheless, it is possible that the Norman Conquest proved more important in the history of what later scholars have characterized as the feudal system than has generally been recognized.

LAW AND THE LEGAL SYSTEM

Because Anglo-Saxon law seems so different from the common law of England that began emerging in the twelfth century, it is easy to imagine that the Normans must have radically changed the legal system. The Normans themselves claimed otherwise. William I and his son Henry both promised to maintain the "Law of Edward," their name for the laws that were in practice when Edward the Confessor died. Sources from after the conquest reveal the Normans consulting with English experts on law. For instance, William himself had **Aegelric**, an aged bishop "wise in the law of the land," brought by wagon to testify in an important lawsuit between Archbishop Lanfranc and the king's half brother, Bishop Odo of Bayeux.[72] Moreover, many Anglo-Saxon law codes were copied and studied after 1066, and a compilation describing the laws in practice under Henry I, containing much Anglo-Saxon law, was written by an anonymous French-speaking student of Anglo-Saxon law.[73]

Only recently has law under the early Norman kings received particularly close scrutiny, and the consensus that seems to be emerging is that the Norman kings did maintain a great deal of continuity and that change was evolutionary rather than revolutionary.[74] Some of the changes that slowly took place, moreover, were caused by a continuing increase in royal power or by changing intellectual currents in western Europe, which might have affected English law anyway. Continuity may be illustrated in a number of ways. The existing public court structure of shire and hundred courts remained in place after the conquest. Much of what we would call criminal law remained the same. Landholding by peasants seems to have continued to follow traditional rules. Even practices of feuding, though already in decline, may have survived the conquest.[75]

Nonetheless, the Norman Conquest did bring some alterations. One small collection of laws notes a number of specific decrees attributed to William himself.[76] Some of these simply repeated earlier English royal laws, but some did bring changes. One set of changes concerned the practice of **ordeals**. During the Middle Ages people had an acute awareness of the limitations of human justice. Then, as now, judges could be corrupt or incompetent, people could lie or simply make a muddle of things, and no one could be certain about the motives of another. God, by traditional Christian definition, had none of these faults or deficiencies. Therefore, in cases of doubt, medieval people often left matters up to God through religious rituals called ordeals. One form of ordeal common in England was to heat up an iron, place it in a person's hands, bandage the wounds, wait three days, and see if the wound was healing or not, which would theoretically reveal God's judgment. Both Normans and English used ordeals; only in the late twelfth century did intellectuals begin to doubt these methods, mainly because they felt it unseemly to expect God to perform miracles on demand. But the Normans had a form of ordeal unknown to the English—trial by battle. William, therefore, had to issue a decree working out how this was to apply in cases between English and Normans.

Another change was a revival and adaptation of a law from Canute's time concerning **murdrum**, whereby if a Norman were murdered and the perpetrator escaped, the local villages would be heavily fined.[77] Obviously, this was a weapon against guerrilla warfare, but it survived the early rebellions and became a steady source of income for English kings long after English and Normans had ceased to be distinct peoples; anyone who was free was counted as Norman. In a separate decree, which survives in the original form, William helped along a process that was widespread in Europe under the reforming papacy in which church courts became separate from secular courts.[78] Other changes under the Normans that are not specifically attributed to a royal decree were the introduction of their forest laws and the introduction of feudal or honorial courts, both noted already. Collectively, these innovations represented a fair amount of change, but no revolution.

The Norman Conquest also influenced the type of evolutionary change mentioned earlier. Even if change would have happened anyway, the course of evolution would have been different under a native dynasty. Evolutionary change was aided by the fluid nature of law in this period. Though much English law was written, it is not clear that written law was very important in the actual running of courts. To a large degree this was still an oral culture, and English law consisted less of what was written than of what was remembered and what was practiced. Even today, when written law is more powerful, law evolves under the pressure of changing opinions and practices, and this was even truer in the Middle Ages. Thus, the Normans could easily change the Law of Edward even while they thought they were maintaining it.

The Norman Conquest helped shape various evolutionary changes. One scholar has argued that William was more inclined to interfere with local courts proactively than reactively. This was partly because of the very disorder brought on by the conquest and the competing claims to land that resulted and partly because of William's need to keep a reasonable amount of harmony among his followers in the face of potential rebellion or invasion.[79] William's tendency to interfere more frequently provided a boost to the trend toward royal control of justice that had begun long before the conquest and continued long afterward. The Normans might also have been subtly influenced in England by their own practices in Normandy. One legal change that scholars can spot over the long term is the decline in the payment of compensation to relatives of victims and the increase in fines, generally to the royal government. Since there are no signs of the payment of compensation in Normandy, the Norman Conquest might have played an important role in this change.

Long-term evolutionary change was most apparent in laws concerning aristocratic landholding, and here the Norman Conquest almost certainly played a key role. I have already noted that feudal ideas played a role in land laws, and to some degree these must owe their origin to the Norman Conquest. In the next chapter, I shall discuss a shift in aristocratic inheritance patterns and, therefore, inheritance law. Briefly, in Anglo-Saxon society the dispersion of estates to a variety of heirs was common, but under the Normans, **primogeniture**, by which the oldest son inherited the lot, became the norm. Together, narrower inheritance patterns and feudalism made much existing aristocratic land law obsolete. What seems to have taken its place were new customs and rules, many of which were influenced by practices in Normandy and northern France, though others developed independently in England.[80] Although aristocratic land law was only one area of law, it was particularly important to the elites who ran England. When later kings began systematically making innovations in the conduct of law, which led to the construction of the English common law, many of the changes emerged in the area of land law.

Thus, the Normans brought changes to legal practices in England despite a commitment to continuity. Eventually the changes made by the

Normans, the evolution of law after the conquest, and the reshaping of it by later kings made the Law of Edward obsolete, and Anglo-Saxon law became unimportant to practitioners of the common law. This should not be allowed to obscure (as it sometimes has) the great legal continuity across the conquest. A moderate tone should be set here. The Norman Conquest did not revolutionize English law but did change it and helped lead the way to the decline and disappearance of Anglo-Saxon law.

The Normans brought varying amounts of change to the areas that mattered most to the new elites. They hardly changed government at all, except for the language of writing, since the existing government suited them well. They consciously maintained the legal system with minor adjustments, but their new landholding system and inheritance practices brought greater legal changes than they originally intended. The replacement of the old aristocracy with a new one brought other important changes. Landholding became concentrated at what before the conquest would have been a middle to upper level of the aristocracy, and powerful links were created between landholding and patronage networks. Over the long haul, these changes proved ephemeral, except for fiscal feudalism, which lasted until the seventeenth century. The changes in military practices also had long-term effects, and the Norman Conquest had an impact on the English role in wider politics that would last beyond the Middle Ages, since the Normans created a new acquisitive drive within Britain and a lasting link with French politics. Overall, this chapter shows that the Normans were capable of bringing great change to England, but normally did so only when it suited their interests.

NOTES

1. *Anglo-Saxon Chronicle D*, 1066.

2. For the political history of the period, see Marjorie Chibnall, *Anglo-Norman England, 1066–1166* (Oxford, 1986), 54–101; Barbara Harvey, ed., *The Short Oxford History of the British Isles: The Twelfth and Thirteenth Centuries, 1066–c. 1280* (Oxford, 2001), 84–91; David Carpenter, *The Struggle for Mastery: Britain 1066–1284* (Oxford, 2003), 125–90; and Christopher Daniell, *From Norman Conquest to Magna Carta: England, 1066–1215* (London, 2003), 33–44. See also the biographies cited in other notes.

3. For Robert, see Judith A. Green, "Robert Curthose Reassessed," *Anglo-Norman Studies* 22 (2000), 95–116.

4. For William, see Frank Barlow, *William Rufus* (New Haven, 2000); Emma Mason, *William Rufus, the Red King* (Stroud, 2005).

5. For Henry, see C. Warren Hollister, *Henry I* (New Haven, 2001); Judith A. Green, *Henry I: King of England and Duke of Normandy* (Cambridge, 2006).

6. For Matilda, Stephen, and their civil war, see Marjorie Chibnall, *The Empress Matilda: Queen Consort, Queen Mother and Lady of the English* (Oxford, 1991); Jim Bradbury, *Stephen and Matilda: The Civil War of 1139–53* (Stroud, 1996); David Crouch, *The Reign of King Stephen, 1135–1154* (Harlow, 2000); and Donald Matthew, *King Stephen* (London, 2002).

7. For government in the postconquest period, see Henry G. Richardson and George O. Sayles, *The Governance of Mediaeval England from the Conquest to Magna Carta* (Edinburgh, 1963); Michael T. Clanchy, *England and Its Rulers, 1066–1307*, 3rd ed. (Oxford, 2006), 53–59; Robert Bartlett, *England under the Norman and Angevin Kings, 1075–1225* (Oxford, 2000), 121–201; Brian Golding, *Conquest and Colonisation: The Normans in Britain, 1066–1100*, 2nd ed. (New York, 2001), 86–118; Chibnall, *Anglo-Norman England*, 105–34; Daniell, *Norman Conquest to Magna Carta*, 108–24; Judith A. Green, *The Government of England under Henry I* (Cambridge, 1986).

8. John Le Patourel, *The Norman Empire* (Oxford, 1976), argues for a fair amount of unity. See however, David Bates, "Normandy and England after 1066," *English Historical Review* 104 (1989), 851–80; Judith A. Green, "Unity and Disunity in the Anglo-Norman State," *Historical Research* 62 (1989), 115–34.

9. Sally P. J. Harvey, "Taxation and the Ploughland in *Domesday Book*," in *Domesday Book: A Reassessment*, ed. Peter Sawyer (London, 1985), 86–103.

10. Michael Dolley, *The Norman Conquest and the English Coinage* (London, 1966).

11. For Regenbald, see Simon Keynes, "Regenbald the Chancellor (sic)," *Anglo-Norman Studies* 10 (1988), 185–222.

12. A few instances of English sheriffs can be found, however. For the background of sheriffs, see Judith A. Green, "The Sheriffs of the Conqueror," *Anglo-Norman Studies* 5 (1983), 131–32; Green, *Government of England*, 145–46.

13. David Bates, *Regesta Regum Anglo-Normannorum: The Acta of William I (1066–1087)* (Oxford, 1998), 107.

14. For the history of royal forests, see Charles R. Young, *The Royal Forests of Medieval England* (Philadelphia, 1979).

15. *Anglo-Saxon Chronicle* E, 1086.

16. Young, *Royal Forests*, 5.

17. Sally P. J. Harvey, "*Domesday Book* and its Predecessors," *English Historical Review* 86 (1971), 753–73; Sally P. J. Harvey, "*Domesday Book* and Anglo-Norman Governance," *Transactions of the Royal Historical Society*, 5th ser., 25 (1975), 175–93.

18. *Anglo-Saxon Chronicle* E, 1085.

19. The exchequer is discussed in many of the works in n. 7 above. See also Richard fitz Nigel, *Dialogus de Scaccario*, ed. Charles Johnson, F. E. L. Carter, and Diana E. Greenway, rev. ed. (Oxford, 1983).

20. Bartlett, *England under the Norman and Angevin Kings*, 68–120; Golding, *Conquest and Colonisation*, 49–60; Chibnall, *Anglo-Norman England*, 44–53; Le Patourel,

Norman Empire, 52–88; Carpenter, *Struggle for Mastery*, 106–90; B. Harvey, *Short Oxford History*, 31–66.

21. William E. Kapelle, *The Norman Conquest of the North: The Region and Its Transformation, 1000–1135* (Chapel Hill, 1979), 120–230; William M. Aird, *St Cuthbert and the Normans: The Church of Durham, 1071–1153* (Woodbridge, 1998); Paul Dalton, *Conquest, Anarchy, and Lordship: Yorkshire, 1066–1154* (Cambridge, 1994), 19–112; Paul Dalton, "The Governmental Integration of the Far North, 1066–1199," in *Government, Religion and Society in Northern England, 1000–1700*, ed. John C. Appleby and Paul Dalton (Stroud, 1997), 14–26.

22. For Scotland and Anglo-Scottish relations, see G. W. S. Barrow, *Kingship and Unity: Scotland, 1000–1306*, 2nd ed. (Edinburgh, 2003); Judith A. Green, "Anglo-Scottish Relations, 1066–1174," in *England and Her Neighbours, 1066–1453*, ed. Michael Jones and Malcolm Vale (London, 1989), 53–72.

23. R. R. Davies, *The Age of Conquest: Wales 1063–1415* (Oxford, 1991), 24–55, 82–107.

24. For a recent overview of relations until 1300, see Donald Matthew, *Britain and the Continent, 1000–1300* (London, 2005). See also, B. Harvey, *Short Oxford History*, 91–98.

25. More traditional works include R. Allen Brown, *English Castles* (London, 1970), and Norman J. G. Pounds, *The Medieval Castle in England and Wales: A Social and Political History* (Cambridge, 1990). Innovative recent work includes Robert Liddiard, *Landscapes of Lordship: Norman Castles and the Countryside in Medieval Norfolk, 1066–1200* (Oxford, 2000); Charles L. H. Coulson, *Castles in Medieval Society: Fortresses in England, France, and Ireland in the Central Middle Ages* (Oxford, 2003); and Andrew Lowerre, *Placing Castles in the Conquest: Landscape, Lordship, and Local Politics in the South-Eastern Midlands, 1066–1100* (Oxford, 2005). See also Stephen Morillo, *Warfare under the Anglo-Norman Kings, 1066–1135* (Woodbridge, 1994), 94–97, 136–44; Matthew Strickland, "Military Technology and Conquest: the Anomaly of England," *Anglo-Norman Studies* 19 (1997), 369–72; and the essays in Robert Liddiard, ed., *Anglo-Norman Castles* (Woodbridge, 2003).

26. See, however, Derek Renn, "Burhgeat and Gonfanon: Two Sidelights from the Bayeux Tapestry," in Liddiard, *Anglo-Norman Castles*, 69–90.

27. Nicholas Hooper, "Some Observations on the Navy in Late Anglo-Saxon England," in *Studies in Medieval History Presented to R. Allen Brown*, ed. Christopher Harper-Bill, Christopher Holdsworth, and Janet L. Nelson (Woodbridge, 1989), 203–13; Strickland, "Military Technology and Conquest," 373–80; N. A. M. Rodger, *The Safeguard of the Sea: A Naval History of Britain, 660–1649* (New York, 1997), 18–49.

28. Morillo, *Warfare under the Anglo-Norman Kings*, 97–119, 144–74; Strickland, "Military Technology and Conquest," 355–69.

29. Morillo, *Warfare under the Anglo-Norman Kings*, 150–60. See also Matthew Bennett, "The Myth of the Military Supremacy of Knightly Cavalry," in *Armies, Chivalry and Warfare in Medieval Britain and France*, ed. Matthew Strickland (Stamford, 1998), 304–16.

30. William of Poitiers, *Gesta Guillelmi*, ed. R. H. C. Davis and Marjorie Chibnall (Oxford, 1998), 180–81.

31. Robin Fleming, *Kings and Lords in Conquest England* (Cambridge, 1991), 215–31.

32. Robert S. Hoyt, *The Royal Demesne in English Constitutional History: 1066–1272* (Ithaca, 1950; reprint New York, 1968), 89–90. See Judith A. Green, "William Rufus, Henry I and the Royal Demesne," *History* 64 (1979), 337–52, for a very careful analysis of alienation by William the Conqueror's two sons.

33. Christopher Dyer, *Making a Living in the Middle Ages: The People of Britain, 850–1520* (New Haven, 2002), 115.

34. Fleming, *Kings and Lords*, 216.

35. Hugh M. Thomas, "Subinfeudation and Alienation of Land, Economic Development, and the Wealth of Nobles on the Honor of Richmond, 1066 to c. 1300," *Albion* 26 (1994), 402–3.

36. The most important recent work on tenurial shifts is Fleming, *Kings and Lords*, 107–214, which discusses various ways in which land changed hands. For the chief challenges to her work, see Peter Sawyer, "1066–1086: A Tenurial Revolution," in Sawyer, Domesday Book: *A Reassessment*, 71–85; David Roffe, *Domesday: The Inquest and the Book* (Oxford, 2000), 17–48. Richard Abels, in "Sheriffs, Lord-Seeking and the Norman Settlement of the South-East Midlands," *Anglo-Norman Studies* 19 (1997), 19–50, joins Fleming in stressing the relatively lawless and chaotic nature of the transfer. In contrast, Judith A. Green, *The Aristocracy of Norman England* (Cambridge, 1997), 48–99, argues that the process was more orderly.

37. For a detailed investigation of one such lordship on the Welsh Marches, see Frederick C. Suppe, *Military Institutions on the Welsh Marches: Shropshire, A.D. 1066–1300* (Woodbridge, 1994), 34–62.

38. For some recent discussion of feudalism with respect to England, see David Crouch, *The Birth of the Nobility: Constructing Aristocracy in England and France, 900–1300* (Harlow, 2005), 261–302; Susan Reynolds, *Fiefs and Vassals: The Medieval Evidence Reinterpreted* (Oxford, 1994), 323–95; Marjorie Chibnall, *The Debate on the Norman Conquest* (Manchester, 1999), 79–85; Morillo, *Warfare under the Anglo-Norman Kings*, 24–28; Clanchy, *England and Its Rulers*, 59–62; Golding, *Conquest and Colonisation*, 135–41; J. O. Prestwich, *The Place of War in English History, 1066–1214* (Woodbridge, 2004), 83–103. See also the works cited in the following notes.

39. Richardson and Sayles, *Governance of Mediaeval England*, 30.

40. Elizabeth A. R. Brown, "The Tyranny of a Construct: Feudalism and Historians of Medieval Europe," *American Historical Review* 79 (1974), 1063–88; Reynolds, *Fiefs and Vassals*.

41. Frank Stenton, *The First Century of English Feudalism, 1066–1166*, 2nd ed. (Oxford, 1961); R. Allen Brown, *Origins of English Feudalism* (London, 1973).

42. Samuel E. Thorne, "English Feudalism and Estates in Land," *Cambridge Law Journal* (1959), 193–209; S. F. C. Milsom, *The Legal Framework of English Feudalism* (Cambridge, 1976).

43. John Gillingham, *The English in the Twelfth Century: Imperialism, National History and Political Values* (Woodbridge, 2000), 187–208.

44. Elliot van Kirk Dobbie, *The Anglo-Saxon Minor Poems* (New York, 1942), 7–16. Translations of this poem may be found in various anthologies, including Kevin Crossley-Holland and Bruce Mitchell, eds., *The Battle of Maldon and Other Old English Poems* (New York, 1966).

45. L. J. Downer, ed., *Leges Henrici Primi* (Oxford, 1972), 232–33.

46. Orderic Vitalis, *The Ecclesiastical History of Orderic Vitalis*, ed. Marjorie Chibnall (Oxford, 1969–1980), 3:254–55.

47. Green, *Aristocracy of Norman England*, 45–46, 163; Katharine S. B. Keats-Rohan, *Domesday People: A Prosopography of Persons Occurring in English Documents, 1066–1166*, vol. 1, *Domesday Book* (Woodbridge, 1999), 16; Le Patourel, *Norman Empire*, 32–35, 311; Lewis C. Loyd, *The Origins of Some Anglo-Norman Families* (Leeds, 1951), throughout.

48. Reynolds, *Fiefs and Vassals*, 345.

49. James C. Holt, *Colonial England, 1066–1215* (London, 1997), 81–101.

50. David C. Douglas, "A Charter of Enfeoffment under William the Conqueror," *English Historical Review* 42 (1927), 245–47. For a different interpretation of this document, see Holt, *Colonial England*, 220–21.

51. Thomas K. Keefe, *Feudal Assessments and the Political Community under Henry II and His Sons* (Berkeley, 1983), 82–86.

52. Marjorie Chibnall, "Mercenaries and the *Familia Regis* under Henry I," *History* 62 (1977), 15–23; J. O. Prestwich, "The Military Household of the Norman Kings," *English Historical Review* 96 (1981), 1–35; Prestwich, *Place of War in English History*, 83–130; Morillo, *Warfare under the Anglo-Norman Kings*, 49–57, 60–74.

53. Pounds, *Medieval Castle in England and Wales*, 44–50.

54. *Anglo-Saxon Chronicle* E, 1085.

55. Stenton, *First Century of English Feudalism*.

56. Stenton, *First Century of English Feudalism*, 171.

57. Hugh M. Thomas, *Vassals, Heiresses, Crusaders, and Thugs: The Gentry of Angevin Yorkshire, 1154–1216* (Philadelphia, 1993), 36–37.

58. Emma Cownie, *Religious Patronage in Anglo-Norman England, 1066–1135* (Woodbridge, 1998), 172–80.

59. Stenton, *First Century of English Feudalism*, 67–68

60. Holt, *Colonial England*, 202–13; Emily Zack Tabuteau, *Transfers of Property in Eleventh-Century Norman Law* (Chapel Hill, 1988), 98–102.

61. For nuanced discussions of the subject, see Holt, *Colonial England*, 113–59, 197–221; John Hudson, *Land, Law, and Lordship in Anglo-Norman England* (Oxford, 1994), 65–106.

62. Hudson, *Land, Law, and Lordship*, 133–40, 279–80.

63. John Hudson, ed., *Historia Ecclesie Abbendonensis: The History of the Church of Abingdon* (Oxford, 2002), 2:8–9.

64. For these developments, see Thomas, *Vassals, Heiresses, Crusaders, and Thugs*, 14–58; Dalton, *Conquest, Anarchy, and Lordship*, 249–97; David Crouch, David A. Carpenter, and Peter R. Coss, "Debate: Bastard Feudalism Revised," *Past and Present* 131 (1991), 165–203; Crouch, *Birth of the Nobility*, 280–97.

65. David A. Carpenter, "The Second Century of English Feudalism," *Past and Present* 168 (2000), 30–71. For debate, focusing on the importance of neighborhood and lordship, see Crouch, *Birth of the Nobility*, 289–97.

66. For an overview of bastard feudalism, see Michael Hicks, *Bastard Feudalism* (Harlow, 1995).

67. Morillo, *Warfare under the Anglo-Norman Kings*, 72.

68. However, Richard Abels cautions against seeing the hidage system in the Anglo-Saxon period as being necessarily pervasive in recruitment; Richard P. Abels, *Lordship and Military Obligation in Anglo-Saxon England* (Berkeley, 1988), 97–184.

69. Despite using the term *incidental* I do accept Carpenter's point that the fiscal aspects of the honor were important early on; Carpenter, "Second Century of English Feudalism," 44–47.

70. Marjorie Chibnall, "Military Service in Normandy before 1066," *Anglo-Norman Studies* 5 (1983), 66.

71. Reynolds, *Fiefs and Vassals*, 215–322.

72. David C. Douglas and George W. Greenaway, eds., *English Historical Documents*, 2nd ed. (London, 1981), 2:482–83.

73. Downer, *Leges Henrici Primi*, 42–43.

74. For an overview of legal developments after the conquest, see John Hudson, *The Formation of the English Common Law: Law and Society in England from the Norman Conquest to Magna Carta* (London, 1996). For Anglo-Saxon law after the conquest, see Patrick Wormald, *The Making of English Law: King Alfred to the Twelfth Century*, vol. 1, *Legislation and Its Limits* (Oxford, 1999), and Bruce R. O'Brien, *God's Peace and the King's Peace: The Laws of Edward the Confessor* (Philadelphia, 1999).

75. Paul Hyams, *Rancor and Reconciliation in Medieval England* (Ithaca, 2003), 111–54.

76. Douglas and Greenaway, *English Historical Documents*, 2:431–32

77. For a recent account of the origins of murdrum, see Bruce R. O'Brien, "From Morðor to Murdrum: The Preconquest Origin and Norman Revival of the Murder Fine," *Speculum* 71 (1996), 321–57.

78. Douglas and Greenaway, *English Historical Documents*, 2:647–48.

79. Robin Fleming, Domesday Book *and the Law: Society and Legal Custom in Early Medieval England* (Cambridge, 1998), 28–34.

80. Paul Hyams, "The Common Law and the French Connection," *Proceedings of the Battle Conference on Anglo-Norman Studies* 4 (1982), 77–92.

4

ECONOMIC AND
SOCIAL CONSEQUENCES

English writers who looked back on the conquest in later decades lamented its effects not just on the nobility but also on the country as a whole.[1] How justified were their laments? More generally, how broadly did the Norman Conquest affect English society? This chapter looks at the influence of the Norman Conquest on broader economic and social trends. Did the conquest strengthen or weaken the economy? Did it alter relations between social classes or drastically change the standing or structure of specific classes? How did it influence gender relations? What about ethnic or national identity? The previous chapter focused on matters of particular concern to the most traditional historiography, areas in which one would expect a major conquest to matter. This chapter concerns some of the social issues that have most interested recent generations of historians.

THE ECONOMY

Before discussing the impact of the conquest on the economy, I need to briefly describe some general economic trends in England and in western Europe as a whole during the central Middle Ages, roughly 1000–1300. The period saw impressive economic growth by premodern standards.[2] One important component was population growth, which both fueled and resulted from the expanding economy. The growing population was accompanied by the expansion of farmland, as peasants and lords drained wetlands and cleared woodlands. Agricultural productivity grew as well, though it remained terrible in comparison to the results of modern farming. A striking aspect of the evolving economy was the growth of towns and markets as society slowly became more commercialized. The agricultural segment remained dominant throughout the period (and indeed until the Industrial Revolution), but crafts, the use of money, and trade all grew. Though miserably poor by the standards of developed modern nations, England and its neighbors were growing richer.

Overall, the Norman Conquest had a decidedly negative but surprisingly short-lived impact on the English economy.[3] Various chronicles describe the devastation brought by William's armies, and their accounts seem to be amply confirmed by *Domesday Book*.[4] That survey reveals that war, fire, and disruption of trade reduced the population of many towns. In addition, the Normans knocked down hundreds of urban homes in order to build castles within town walls.[5] Devastation was also severe in the countryside. *Domesday Book* records the value of manors to their lords not just in 1066 and 1086 but also, in ten southeastern counties, at a time shortly after the conquest. Total values dropped in all ten counties, with the drops ranging from 15 percent in Kent to 40 percent in Sussex (where William had landed) and Middlesex (London's county).[6] In the northern and northwestern counties where William had most fully used devastation as a military tactic, *Domesday Book* lists hundreds of settlements as fully or partially "wasted."

The term *waste* brings us to another controversy among historians and provides an illustration of yet more reasons why historians often disagree: differing interpretation of past terminology and differing views of the past more broadly. Traditionally, scholars viewed these "waste" entries as reflecting the intentional wasting, or devastation, of lands in war. This is simply common sense, but common sense does not always lead to historical accuracy, and in the past several decades, a number of historians have challenged this interpretation.[7] In the process they have downplayed the level of devastation that traditional interpretations indicate the conquest caused. This seems to be part of a more general, uncoordinated trend to argue for a "kinder, gentler" Middle Ages, as historians have questioned the level of violence and suffering caused by such events as the collapse of the western Roman Empire, the disintegration of the Carolingian empire, or the civil war in England between King Stephen and the Empress Matilda.[8] Important motives lie behind this trend: the duty of scholars to question previous assumptions and received traditions, the desire of medievalists to modify the simplistic stereotype of the "Dark Ages," and a healthy concern for how closely the rhetoric of medieval chroniclers reflected reality. However, though this recent work has often raised important questions and made important points, I am concerned that it has tended to create an overly antiseptic picture of the Middle Ages. As for the more specific question of

Domesday waste, I believe that a recent article by John Palmer has largely countered those who would downplay the link between war and waste entries in *Domesday Book*.[9]

What are the arguments for and against downplaying the impact of military devastation and of interpreting entries on wasted lands as reflecting military actions, particularly in the north? Some scholars have pointed out that the most contemporary accounts of the "harrying" of the north are also the shortest, and that greater detail and condemnation is found in twelfth-century works. This is true, but that probably stems from the nature of the earlier works. In particular, the *Anglo-Saxon Chronicle* tended to be brief. The later writers were more likely to inject moral commentary, but that does not mean that the events they described were false. After all, because of oral traditions, they were in a much better position to know about eleventh-century events than we are. Moreover, even the *Anglo-Saxon Chronicle* was fairly definite, despite its brevity. In one version, William marched into Yorkshire and "completely devastated it." In another, he "completely harried and wasted" the county.[10] Another objection is that the term *waste* was sometimes flexible. For instance, land was sometimes described as wasted even though there was clearly some economic activity going on. However, as Palmer has shown, the instances in which this was true were few. In other cases, waste might have been a term of bureaucratic convenience for lands from which no revenue could be gained for whatever reason, but again Palmer has shown that the evidence for such use is limited and anecdotal. A further doubt has been whether a small army could have caused such devastation in a relatively brief time, but we have already seen that traditional ideas about the small size of armies in the period are questionable. Moreover, because William had achieved surprise and driven the rebels from Yorkshire, his army could split up, and small bands of soldiers employing fire could efficiently devastate wide areas. Some scholars have argued that the "waste" lands were not where one might expect from the sparse records of William's movements, but this ignores the likelihood that William's army fanned out and the possibility of later resettlement of displaced peasants for the convenience of their new lords (see later discussion) or in their own search for a better situation. As Palmer has shown, even in the Yorkshire holdings that were not counted as waste, values fell by 60 percent between 1066 and 1086. Is it not more likely that there was more waste recorded in Yorkshire because the devastation was worse there? Finally, I would note that recent work on military history argues that devastation designed to economically weaken one's foe and to spread terror was a standard part of warfare in the period.[11]

There is no way to prove beyond a shadow of a doubt the traditional view that William's armies brought widespread devastation in their trail. The analysis here is necessarily brief, and the interested reader would need to go to the relevant scholarship to fully evaluate the question. Certainly, the scholars with whom I am disagreeing have shown that not every piece of evidence for devastation can be taken at face value and that individually the various types of evidence all have their problems. Nonetheless, the cumulative evidence of the chronicles, the fall in values in many areas, and the widespread entries for waste, combined with the growing realization that medieval warfare tended to bring devastation, argue that the Norman Conquest delivered a major blow to the English economy.

Yet the English economy bounced back surprisingly quickly. Perhaps a society that had to be able to cope with frequent natural disasters such as crop failures, plagues, and fires was well equipped to deal with manmade disasters as well. Peasants, in particular, had to be resilient simply to survive in medieval conditions. The ten counties noted above had all seen at least a partial recovery in rents by 1086, and some of them—Kent, Surrey, and Hampshire—recorded higher rents overall than in 1066.[12] Part of this recovery came from squeezing the peasants more, as I shall discuss later, but clearly the economy was making a swift recovery. The *Domesday Book* entries for waste in the north indicate that progress in that region was slower. Indeed, one English monk reported that the effects of William's devastation could still be seen there in the early twelfth century.[13] Even in the north, however, no long-term negative economic effects can be detected. There are no comparable figures that would allow one to measure the speed of recovery in the region, but certainly the overall impression provided by the sources is of robust recovery and growth in the generations after 1086. Information on medieval economies and their overall performance will always remain problematic, given the limited statistical data available in the sources, but England's long-term trajectory looks little different from those of other western European countries. The Norman Conquest seems to have been no more than a major bump in the slow road to prosperity, but in the Middle Ages, that road was normally fairly rough anyway.

The recovery probably owed something to the Normans themselves; after devastating the economy, they helped rebuild it. Though they damaged the old towns, they founded many new ones, often next to castles. The leading modern scholar on new towns indicates that the Normans founded twenty-one new towns between 1066 and 1100, and another nineteen before 1130.[14] Townspeople immigrated into England from France, and ports opposite Normandy flourished even before 1086. The Normans almost certainly created stronger links with the thriving economy of northern France, though these links may have come at the expense of economic ties with Scandinavia.[15]

Several scholars have suggested that the Normans stimulated the economy as consumers, particularly with their massive building projects, including castles and churches (see the next chapter for Norman church building). By squeezing more money from the peasantry and perhaps by melting down accumulated English treasures for their projects, they may have put more money into circulation.[16] This hypothesis ignores the probable reduction of peasant spending and the likelihood that Norman aristocrats changed aristocratic spending habits rather than simply increasing them. However, it is certainly possible that by demanding higher rents and services from peasants, the Normans forced them to work harder, at least temporarily and perhaps permanently increasing productivity. The greatest help the Normans provided to economic growth, however, was stability. Though William and his sons all faced occasional baronial revolts, England was a relatively peaceful place between 1071 and Henry I's death in 1135. This long and largely peaceful stretch gave the economy time to recover and flourish.

In the short term, therefore, the Norman Conquest damaged the economy fairly severely, though some Norman actions had mildly positive impacts. In the long run, the Norman Conquest seems to have barely dented the overall growth of the English economy, and England followed the slow upward trajectory of prosperity common to western Europe in the period. England's ability to recover swiftly from the Norman Conquest is testimony to the economic resilience of medieval societies in the face of the many disasters of natural and human origin that they suffered.

COMMONERS AND CLASS RELATIONS

In the short run, the impact of the Norman Conquest on ordinary people varied widely. Those in the path of Norman armies probably experienced plundering at the very least. Women were raped and men no doubt suffered casual violence. Where the Normans deliberately devastated lands, peasants fled and faced the loss of their livelihoods. Many suffered starvation; one monastic chronicle reveals how refugees suffered so badly that they continued to die after they reached the safety of the monastery.[17] Peasants outside of the areas of combat suffered far less. A few may have been evicted from their lands to make way for royal forests. Many more had to shoulder the inconveniences and costs that came with the introduction of Norman forest law. Most must have felt the increased burden of taxation, either directly or indirectly. But for many, the main immediate consequence of the Norman Conquest was simply that their Anglo-Saxon lord was replaced by a Norman lord. Moreover, once the fighting ended, even the surviving peasants who suffered the most could begin rebuilding their lives.

There are indications, however, that the Normans put into effect some changes that had longer-term effects on the peasantry. I have already referred several times to increased burdens on them.[18] One way to extract more money from them was simply to raise rents. The *Anglo-Saxon Chronicle* refers to William the Conqueror doing this as a matter of policy, and *Domesday Book* contains intermittent complaints about the level of exactions on specific manors in royal and aristocratic hands.[19] There are clear indications that at least some Norman lords actively sought to build up **demesnes** on their estates. These were the parts of manors set aside to produce grain and other products directly for the lord's table or for the lord to sell. Further study is needed to reveal how widespread a phenomenon this was, but potentially it may have affected many peasants. Evidence from northern England suggests that the Normans had a particularly free hand in areas they had devastated.[20]

In order to increase their revenues and obtain the labor they needed for their demesnes, the Normans, who were backed by raw military power and unencumbered by local traditions, sometimes ran roughshod over the rights of local peasants. In particular, Norman lords reduced the standing of many relatively high-status peasants, the freemen and **sokemen**. Together, freemen and sokemen made up about 14 percent of the recorded population in *Domesday Book*, but their numbers dropped—markedly, in some areas— between 1066 and 1086.[21] There is no way of knowing how dramatically the peasantry suffered overall. Moreover, many of the negative effects of the conquest for peasants may have been counteracted by the growing prosperity of succeeding generations. Nonetheless, it is clear that the conquest had bad long-term consequences for at least some segments of the peasantry.

In contrast, the Norman Conquest helped the worst-off group in society: slaves. At the time of *Domesday Book*, slaves remained a significant minority in England. In late Anglo-Saxon England, as throughout western Europe, chattel slavery was slowly declining, though the decline was slower in England than elsewhere. The Norman Conquest hastened its demise in England. For most counties, *Domesday Book* does not reveal the number of slaves for both 1066 and 1086, but it does for Essex. There, the number fell by 25 percent, with the drop being higher on the estates of many Norman lords than on the more conservatively managed church lands.[22] The causes of the decline may have been partly moral. Christian thinkers in this period often had mild qualms about slavery, and Lanfranc, William's appointee as archbishop of Canterbury, joined a native bishop in opposing the export of slaves.[23] Economic reasons probably played a larger role, as indicated by the swifter decline of slavery on lay estates versus church estates. What Norman lords seem to have been doing was freeing slaves and giving them small plots of land in return for large amounts of labor, thus making their estates more closely fit the norms of northern France and gaining more motivated workers, at least in the short run. The Norman Conquest did not end slavery in England right away—it lingered several decades into the twelfth century. Nonetheless, the leading historian of Anglo-Saxon slavery has described the conquest as a "shock" to the slaveholding system that hastened its end.[24]

Even this highly positive development for the most oppressed group in English society had its negative consequences. Freedom in eleventh-century England was a matter of degrees, and the bulk of the peasantry lay between the freemen at the top and the slaves at the bottom. In the twelfth century, a new line developed between free peasants and **serfs**, or **villeins**, as they were often called in English sources. Unlike slaves, serfs or villeins generally held plots of land, but they were considered the property of lords and faced many legal disadvantages. They also faced social disadvantages; the fact that our modern term *villain* comes from "villein" indicates the contempt and hostility lords felt toward them. The largest category of peasants in *Domesday Book*, including many prosperous ones, were labeled **villani**. As the similarity of terms suggests, many of the descendants of the *Domesday Book* villani, as well as the descendants of slaves and other minor peasants, ended up as villeins.

One scholar, Rosamond Faith, has argued that the Norman Conquest brought new attitudes and traditions from the continent that caused the Normans to suppress the bulk of the peasantry into the category of serfs.[25] The more common argument is that the new line between free peasants and unfree serfs emerged as a result of legal reforms and the great expansion of royal justice in the late twelfth century. Only free people were entitled to exercise many rights in royal courts, and the royal justices had to therefore determine which peasants were free and which were not. As a result, the royal courts developed a series of tests that made a stronger single divide than had hitherto existed between free peasants and those peasants who were lower on the social scale.[26] Even if this development was independent from the Norman Conquest, however, the earlier disappearance of slavery probably influenced it. Without slaves around, other peasants may have looked less free, and thus the line between free peasants and serfs may have ended up in a different place than it otherwise would have, subjecting more peasants to the stigma and burdens of serfdom. This argument, however, is speculative, and on the whole it is hard to argue that the disappearance of slavery was not a positive development in English history. In any case, it is clear that the Norman Conquest led directly and indirectly to a reshuffling of the categorizations of rural commoners.

Once the fighting was over and the conquest secured, the Normans treated townspeople fairly well. Indeed, one of the earliest documents William issued in England guaranteed Londoners their traditional rights.[27] Besides the introduction of castles and the probable shift in trade links, both noted earlier, the main long-term impact of the conquest came from the introduction of new groups of townspeople. Though the new French inhabitants of towns started merging with the local population quite quickly, they nonetheless helped introduce French influence over the long haul. This is witnessed by the eventual English adoption of such French institutions as the position of mayor and by the title of Cinque Ports given to five (later more) ports that provided kings with ships in times of war.[28]

The Normans also changed towns, and, indeed, England as a whole, by introducing a Jewish community.[29] Jews first appeared in London and later spread to other towns. It is surprising that no Jews appear to have settled in Anglo-Saxon England; perhaps the kings prohibited them from immigrating to protect local merchants from competition. There was, however, a Jewish community in Rouen in Normandy before 1066 and one in London by the end of the century. Whether the initiative for Jewish immigration came from William or from the Jews themselves remains unknown, but according to one twelfth-century historian, William transferred a group from Rouen to London.[30] In return for their protection, subsequent English kings profited from heavily taxing the Jews.

It took time for the Jews to become a powerful economic force in England. Only in the middle of the twelfth century did they start moving beyond London. Not until late in that century did they become the leading moneylenders. They achieved this dominance partly because of church sanctions against Christian moneylenders, partly because of their own business acumen, and partly because of their business networks, which spread across Europe and beyond. During their years of greatest success in medieval England, some individual Jews were among the richest people in the country, and they established a flourishing culture. Unfortunately, their very success, along with deep-rooted and growing Christian anti-Semitism, created a backlash. In the thirteenth century, King Henry III, motivated by religious hostility as well as financial necessity, taxed the Jews into penury. In

1290, his son Edward I, motivated partly by baronial demands, expelled the Jews, eliminating any substantial Jewish settlement from England until the middle of the seventeenth century. Nonetheless, the Norman introduction of the Jews to England did lead to two centuries of Jewish presence in medieval England.

Given the limited Norman impact on the economy, the effects of the Norman Conquest on rural and urban commoners, and on the rural and urban social structures, were surprisingly high. Many of the most direct impacts, such as plundering and violence, happened only in the immediate aftermath of the conquest. In the longer term, however, the Norman Conquest led to a marked change in the social and legal structure of the English peasantry and brought a large amount of French influence to the towns. The Normans also introduced a new religious minority to England. Thus, the Norman Conquest made a big difference to the common people of England.

ARISTOCRACY

The aristocracy was naturally the segment of society to which the Norman Conquest brought the greatest change.[31] Much of this change has been discussed earlier: the overwhelming transformation in membership, shifts in landholding structures, and alterations in military practice. Some cultural changes in which the aristocracy had an important role will be described in the next chapter. However, three crucial developments will be discussed here.

The first two developments, which are related, involved shifts in family structures and inheritance patterns. The last is more certain. Preconquest Anglo-Saxon wills reveal an inheritance pattern of dispersing estates among many relatives.[32] Closer relatives may have been favored, but cousins and others might also receive lands. Estates, therefore, were built up and then dispersed with each generation. After the conquest, the system of primogeniture developed in which the eldest son received all the inherited land, which he held as a unified fief from the lord.[33] Theoretically, therefore, unified estates remained intact and passed whole from generation to generation.

The shift, however, was not as dramatic as might first appear. First, the new system did not emerge full-blown in 1066. Second, in the decades after the conquest, the new land held by the conquerors was all acquired rather than inherited, and under the new system, fathers had freer disposition of lands they had acquired than ones they had inherited. Third, though initially one daughter often inherited the bulk of the estates in the absence of sons, after a ruling by Henry I, estates were generally divided equally among daughters. This new practice cut against the grain of preserving estates intact.[34] Finally, even after the system of primogeniture came fully into play, Anglo-Norman aristocrats often granted parts of their estates as fiefs to their younger sons or brothers. They also generally gave out land in marriage with their daughters. I have argued elsewhere that aristocratic families probably tried, as a rule, to provide for all their children, though the provisions got progressively smaller for younger children and daughters as fathers favored the older siblings and the sons.[35] For these reasons, the shift to primogeniture was partial and, to some degree, simply brought technical changes in the mechanisms by which people passed on lands. Nonetheless, primogeniture frequently led families to pass on the bulk of their estate to one heir from generation to generation. The shift to primogeniture thus represents a broader trend that scholars have traced elsewhere on the continent in which families tried to restrict inheritance in order to preserve the unity of a family's estates from one generation to the next.

In recent decades, scholars have argued that these shifts in inheritance formed part of a larger shift in kinship structure, from aristocratic clans to lineages.[36] In the clan structure, many different ties of kinship had importance for individuals, and therefore aristocratic estates were distributed among different relatives at the death of a landholder. In the lineage system, estates, which often centered on castles, were preserved from one generation to the next through a variety of methods that restricted who could inherit. According to this school of scholarship, the new inheritance patterns accompanied a narrowing focus of kinship ties from broad kinship groups to restricted lineages in which the relationship between fathers and male heirs was particularly important. Often this shift was accompanied by the adoption of family surnames, frequently taken from the chief manor or castle of the estate. More generally, vertical ties across time mattered more than horizontal ties between relatives.

One leading scholar, Sir James Holt, has argued that the Normans brought this change in kinship structure to England, having recently made the shift in Normandy.[37] Certainly, the Normans brought family or lineage names.[38] The Anglo-Saxons did not have family names; this is why modern scholars have to use anachronistic inventions such as the Godwines or Godwinesons to identify Anglo-Saxon families. In contrast, powerful Norman families had already begun the gradual adoption of surnames. Occasionally these developed out of nicknames; one minor aristocratic family that settled in England was the Golden Testicle family, whose males were no doubt noted for their modesty in every sense of the word.[39] It was more common for Norman families to adopt their surnames from particular castles or estates in Normandy or in England.[40] More important, the shift to primogeniture formed a key part of the shift from clan to lineage in this model.

Recently, however, the view that there was a sharp shift from clan to lineage has faced justifiable criticism. Most of the criticism has concerned the supposed change from clan to lineage on the continent, but clearly, if the change did not occur in France, the Normans were unlikely to have brought it to England.[41] Moreover, lineages, which emphasized vertical ties of kinship over time, evidently played an important role in earlier medieval thinking; one has only to consider the Anglo-Saxon royal genealogies tracing rulers back in a succession of sons and fathers stretching to Woden and ultimately to Adam. Likewise, ties between siblings, cousins, and other relatives continued to matter after the theoretical shift to a lineage structure. As I previously noted, the shift in inheritance patterns was certainly not as radical as the change in rules made it seem. Even if a shift did occur, one scholar has recently argued that it began in late Anglo-Saxon England.[42] Clearly, there will continue to be debate on this point. In the interim, I would point out that after the Norman Conquest, there certainly was a shift toward focusing inheritance on the eldest son, and this inevitably reflected or caused a change in emphasis from broader kinship networks to narrower lineages. Family structures were complex *throughout* the central Middle Ages and could differ *within* a given society according to particular needs and individual circumstances. I would argue, nonetheless, that there was a shift of emphasis within the complex and varied kinship structures of the period that both resulted from and led to a narrowing of inheritance. The Normans brought the latter of these changes to England, and I believe that they therefore at least accelerated the former process.

In addition to shifts in family structures and inheritance patterns, the Norman Conquest brought a third major development: it opened England to the slowly developing ethos of **chivalry**. The adoption of heavy cavalry meant that English nobles were more likely to participate in cultural as well as military practices common on the continent; after all, the very term *chivalry* comes from "cheval," French for horse. The degree of change should not be exaggerated. The Anglo-Saxons already had an aristocratic warrior ethos and valued loyalty, courage, and other attributes prized in chivalry. Moreover, many aspects of chivalry, such as **heraldry**, had yet to develop. Nonetheless, the Norman Conquest brought two important changes in the rules of war that came to be associated with chivalry. Slaughter of the defeated after battle was frequently practiced in Anglo-Saxon England up to the eve of the conquest. The Normans did not follow this practice, and they introduced a very different treatment of aristocratic prisoners, following a pattern that was gradually developing on the continent. Normans of William's generation killed and mutilated their enemies far less often than their fathers or their English contemporaries. William himself normally imprisoned even dangerous rivals such as the English rebel Earl Morcar. An important new chivalric practice was the ransoming of aristocratic prisoners, and though William himself rarely followed this practice, the Normans in general introduced it to England. In these respects, the Normans brought chivalry to England.[43]

Besides these three major developments, there were other changes in aristocratic lifestyle. Robert Liddiard has recently emphasized the degree to which Anglo-Norman castles formed part of planned landscapes that included elements such as deer parks, fishponds, gardens, and planned settlements. Though centers of lordship existed in the Anglo-Saxon period, the introduction of castles no doubt radically changed the style of aristocratic residences and the landscapes that surrounded them.[44] The Normans also brought changes to the traditional aristocratic sport of hunting. Naomi Sykes's work on animal bones at archaeological sites indicates that the Normans introduced a new breed of deer, the fallow deer, from Sicily, and tended to hunt the red deer more than the roe deer. The latter shift may have reflected certain changes in hunting practices as well as prey. The Normans also introduced a new way of butchering deer that had various ceremonial elements, reflecting the general growth of practices designed to set the nobility apart from others. In falconry, the Normans tended to pursue the heron more than their Anglo-Saxon predecessors, and they also introduced peafowl (peacocks and peahens) as a new type of prey as well as a new item on the aristocratic menu.[45]

The changes described here, along with changes discussed in other chapters, show that the Norman Conquest brought a great deal of change to aristocratic culture. This is what one might expect, given the replacement of the Anglo-Saxon aristocracy with a Norman one. The fact that change among aristocrats is unsurprising should not cause us to underestimate its importance, however. Because medieval societies placed so much power and influence in aristocratic hands, changes at the aristocratic level reshaped society as a whole, even though such changes involved only a small percentage of the population.

GENDER

Scholars once looked back to the Anglo-Saxon period as a golden age for women.[46] Indeed, some early examples of what today would be called feminist scholarship discussed women's property rights and their decline after the conquest.[47] For such scholars, the Norman Conquest represented a serious blow to the position of women in England. At first glance, surviving wills of aristocratic Anglo-Saxon women doling out large amounts of property strongly support such notions, particularly in contrast to the lack of such wills in Norman society.[48] However, scholars today are less sanguine about the position of women in Anglo-Saxon England. Though noble women could have power, wealth, and influence in the Anglo-Saxon period, particularly if they were widows or had unusually forceful characters, *Domesday Book* reveals that women held only a small percentage of land before the conquest, and much of this was held by women from the families of Earls Godwine and Leofric. Overall, Anglo-Saxon society was as sexist as most known premodern societies. After the conquest, noble women could also have great influence and power, at least as widows, so the change was fairly limited. In fact, the disappearance of wills had more to do with the changing inheritance patterns discussed earlier than with any decline in the position of women, for such wills disappeared for men as well as for women. Changes in property law did affect women, but overall the evidence does not suggest that their position declined significantly after 1066, mainly because it was not that wonderful before 1066. Further research is needed to provide a more nuanced picture of the effects of the conquest on women in English society. Nonetheless, it is likely that the current picture of limited impact will remain largely unchanged.

IDENTITY, ETHNICITY, AND ASSIMILATION

One area in which the Norman Conquest naturally did have a great deal of impact was on ethnic or national identity and on ethnic relations within England.[49] Whether one should describe Englishness and **Normanitas** as national or ethnic identities is arguable, but I will use ethnicity here since both identities were operating within a single state in the period covered by this book. By 1066, a strong sense of English identity already existed, at least among the elites. The English were "a celebrated people," according to one monastic reformer. Another writer described them as a "glorious and splendid people."[50] Genetically, most English people were probably descended from the **Romano-British** and ultimately from earlier peoples.[51] Moreover, the **Angli** who gave them their identity were only one people among the Germanic invaders who took over England after the collapse of the Roman Empire in the west. How did the English become English?[52]

The great eighth-century historian **Bede** helped popularize the concept of Englishness within the various kingdoms dominated by the Germanic invaders and their cultural descendants, but it was Alfred and his descendants who created a unified English state. Through its documents, coinage, and the oaths that it required free males to swear, this state helped solidify Englishness by making people aware that they were part of an English kingdom. Royal control over the church also solidified Englishness. Though the English church was one branch of an international institution, writers spoke of it as an *English* church and often associated native saints not just with their particular shrines but also with the country as a whole. Alfred and his descendants built the English state through military operations against the Vikings, and continuing wars against Scandinavian invaders helped establish an ideal of defending the homeland; indeed, monks described defending the homeland as the chief duty of warriors. "The Battle of Maldon," one of the greatest of the Old English poems, described a doomed English noble telling a Viking messenger that he would stand with his followers to defend the homeland of King Æthelræd.[53] A supporter of King Harold II's family improbably tried to put Earl Godwine's actions in a patriotic light in his description of the events of 1051–1052. According to the *Anglo-Saxon Chronicle*, when the collected nobles forced a settlement on a reluctant king in 1052, they stated that they wished to prevent a battle because both sides were largely English and because they wanted to avoid exposing the country to invaders. They also agreed to blame the whole affair on French advisors of Edward the Confessor, whom they promptly exiled.[54] Englishness in the eleventh century was a far cry from modern nationalism, but English identity was already strong enough to play an important theoretical role in politics.

Norman identity was also strong.[55] One of William the Conqueror's major followers, Roger of Montgomery, described himself in one document as "Normannus ex Normannis," which might be translated as "a Norman among Normans."[56] Though culturally very similar to the French around them, the Normans preserved a strong memory of their Danish ancestry, that is, the Danish ancestry of much of the nobility. In the early eleventh century, a French historian hired by Duke William's ancestors went one better by inventing a prestigious Trojan ancestry for the Danes.

More concretely, political hostility between the Normans and their French neighbors helped the Normans to regard themselves as distinct, and growing confidence in their own military prowess also strengthened Norman identity. William's biographer had William remind his followers of their homeland, noble deeds, and great reputation before the Battle of Hastings.[57] In following generations, the Norman occupation of England and Norman military successes in southern Italy, the Holy Land, and elsewhere caused the Normans to see themselves as uniquely warlike. Thus, conquerors and conquered both had a strong sense of themselves as distinct and proud peoples.

Not surprisingly, the violence of the conquest created hatred between the two peoples. William's biographer wrote that the English of Kent hated the Normans.[58] Another chronicler wrote that an abbot was deposed in 1085 because "he was English and hateful to the Normans."[59] This hatred was mainly based on political differences and the experience of war, since the two peoples were not far apart culturally. The major cultural difference, in fact, was language. But in the heated emotional conditions following the conquest, even minor cultural differences such as haircuts or clothing could become a source of conflict. Though the two peoples shared a common religion, even minor points of religion could divide them. For instance, the status of many English saints became a matter of debate because some Normans doubted their sanctity. The sources may exaggerate the Normans' hostility toward English saints, but they probably reflect English anxieties about what Norman hostility did exist.[60] Worse, the attempts of the first Norman abbot of Glastonbury to introduce continental elements to the prayers and services practiced at that monastery led to a riot by his English monks in 1083. The abbot's soldiers put down the riot forcefully. The *Anglo-Saxon Chronicle* describes the soldiers' actions as follows: "What more can we find to say except to add that [the Norman archers] showered arrows, and their companions broke down the doors to force an entrance, and struck down and killed some of the monks, wounding many, so that their blood ran down from the altar onto the steps and from the steps onto the floor."[61] So strong was the hostility after the Norman Conquest that even the details of religious services could prompt bloodshed.

Despite the initial enmity, the English and Normans assimilated relatively quickly, so that the kinds of ethnic divides that have scarred so many societies did not become a long-term problem in England. Hostility did linger through the reigns of William the Conqueror's sons, William II and Henry I. A prophecy attributed to Edward the Confessor was interpreted by writers in Henry I's reign and even at the beginning of Stephen's reign to indicate that the English were still being oppressed. In the early 1160s, however, during the reign of William's great-grandson, Henry II, a monk of English descent named **Ailred of Rievaulx** wrote that the prophecy had been fulfilled through intermarriage at all levels of society.[62] Though hints of a lingering ethnic divide appeared in Henry II's reign, they had disappeared by its end in 1189.

Why could the English and Normans overcome their early enmity with such relative speed and assimilate into one people, when so many other hostile peoples have remained antagonistic for centuries on end? One important factor was the absence of major cultural differences, particularly religious ones; in the Middle Ages, religious divides were by far the greatest barriers to amity. Other factors contributed as well. William claimed the throne as the rightful successor to Edward the Confessor and proclaimed that he would treat his new subjects well as long as they remained loyal. Obviously, his actions often diverged from his propaganda, but the propaganda mattered and created a presumption of legal equality between English and Normans. The law concerning murdrum might have created legal divides, except that after the end of the rebellions it became largely a source of revenue and became linked to class rather than ethnicity. The related link between being English and being unfree that appears in some legal documents was also a threat to ethnic harmony, but the number of free English people meant that the connection was tenuous. Otherwise, the Normans did not create laws to set themselves apart from the English, except on some technical points. Though Norman writers sometimes denigrated English valor and treated the English as religiously backward, they never made an attempt to base the legality of the conquest on Norman cultural superiority. In contrast, the English later created legal divides and claimed cultural superiority in Wales and Ireland in ways that reinforced strong ethnic divisions.

The Normans also lacked mechanisms to link class and ethnic boundaries as some cultures have done. Though Normans, like other medieval peoples, were very insistent that some people were of a higher class than others, they lacked the kinds of specific categories of nobles and nonnobles, or lords, knights, **squires**, and gentlemen, which developed later in France and England.[63] Therefore, though most aristocrats were Norman and most commoners were English, class and ethnicity never became fused. Another factor was that William crushed English resistance so effectively that there were no rebellions after his day; indeed, chroniclers described how the English supported his sons against baronial rebels. This meant that the hatred created by the early violence could disappear in subsequent generations and that ethnic hostility did not remain on a slow boil. Shared religion, despite the initial problems, did ultimately help create ethnic peace. Even in the first generation, Norman and English churchmen (and probably nuns) were forging bonds that helped calm the hatreds stirred by the violent conquest. Ultimately, of course, the intermarriage noted by Ailred of Rievaulx ensured the merging of the two peoples into one, but intermarriage was as much a result as a cause of the growing harmony between the English and the Normans.

That the Normans should become English rather than the English becoming Normans is often taken for granted.[64] It should not be. Norman identity remained strong among the upper classes well into Henry II's reign, and thereafter anybody who was anybody tended to claim that their ancestors came to England with William the Conqueror. This is true even in some cases where the claim was demonstrably false. Generally, scholars have assumed that the fact that Norman immigration outside the aristocracy was limited and that the bulk of the population remained English in ancestry automatically brought the triumph of English identity. The imbalance of population was obviously an important factor, but conquerors have often imposed their identities on the conquered. After all, in 1066 only a small proportion of the genetic material in the English population likely went back to the Germanic invaders who entered Britain after Rome's withdrawal, let alone to the specific tribe known as the Angli who gave their name to the English. The Norman Conquest created a real threat to English identity, and one writer in the early twelfth century, who considered himself English, wrote that God used the Normans to destroy the English people for their sins and that it was shameful to be called English.[65]

How did the Normans become English? People often assume that identity comes from ancestry, but ancestry obviously cannot explain how the Normans adopted an English identity. Intermarriage was only part of the explanation, since people with both Norman and English ancestry could and often did choose to emphasize their Norman rather than English heritage. What factors, then, helped the Normans to think of themselves as English? One surprising aspect is that the adage "the winners write the history" was not particularly true in the case of the Norman Conquest. Much of its history was written by churchmen who identified with the English. Though acknowledging that the English had angered God through religious and other shortcomings immediately before 1066 (in their view, why else had God allowed William to win?), they argued for the earlier and innate worthiness of the English people, extolling their bravery, loyalty, learning, piety, and glorious past. They helped, in short, to make Englishness an honorable and therefore acceptable identity.

This was only a first step, making it possible but not certain that the Normans would become English. Other factors are harder to trace, because matters of identity are often very subtle. Comparison of the English and Normans with other groups helped bring them together by emphasizing what they had in common. For instance, the introduction of a Jewish community underlined the shared Christianity of the two groups. Cultural differences with the Scots, Welsh, and Irish, and an increasing tendency to label these peoples as barbaric, helped the "civilized" English and Normans focus on what unified them. Warfare with these other peoples of Britain and Ireland also reinforced unity between English and Normans. This was especially true of reactions to invasions from Scotland, but the Anglo-Norman invasions of Wales and Ireland also knit together the English and Normans. The wars between the kings of England and France led the English to adopt the existing Norman hostility toward the French, and this newly shared antagonism served to negate the strong influence of French culture on England, particularly among the aristocracy. The adoption of spoken English language by the descendants of the invaders no doubt helped, though language probably mattered less to identity than it would in the modern period.[66]

A more important factor is that William kept the two lands and two governments separate. England thus retained its independent identity. People who lived in England, owed allegiance to the king of the English, served in the English government or church, used English coinage, and began giving allegiance to English saints slowly came to think of themselves as English. A geographic identity may have served as a transition; people may have thought of themselves as the Normans of England. Eventually, however, allegiance to England led to adoption of an English identity.

The shift from Norman to English identity was eased along by an intermediate stage in which people adopted dual identities, thinking of themselves as both English and Norman. The tendency for continental people to think of the Normans of England as English also helped the latter embrace Englishness. This was partly because external labels often influence the way people view themselves. Labeling the conquerors as English also mattered because the descendants of the Normans were being lumped into stereotypes concerning the English, even though some of these characterizations were ridiculous.

Favorable stereotypes depicted the English as generous and intelligent people who knew how to eat and drink well. Negative stereotypes were more common; the English were gluttons and drunks who, shockingly enough, preferred ale to wine. They were spendthrifts. Strangest of all, a belief developed after the conquest that the English had tails. This belief was based on the misreading or distortion of a miracle story concerning St. **Augustine of Canterbury**, the first missionary to the English. Though clearly nonsensical, the slur became a surprisingly popular way to taunt the English.[67] Obviously, positive stereotypes could make Englishness attractive. One might think that negative stereotypes would discourage people from adopting an English identity, and no doubt they sometimes did. But negative stereotypes could also create solidarity among people who suffered from them, prompting defiance or a backlash. Sometimes exchanges concerning ethnic stereotypes were good natured and humorous. For instance, a letter by a French immigrant in the late twelfth century extolling the virtues of wine over ale refers to a lost work by an Englishman who sought to defend his homeland but ended up (the immigrant sarcastically wrote) focusing on a defense of ale.[68] On a more serious note, an early-thirteenth-century archbishop of Canterbury, **Stephen Langton**, used the stereotypes of gluttony and drunkenness to call the English to a nationwide reform.[69] In doing so, he was addressing an elite audience, showing how stereotypes about the English had come to encompass the descendants of Normans, whether they liked it or not.

A range of factors, no doubt including many that cannot be traced, helped the Normans learn to think of themselves as English. By the early thirteenth century, Englishness had even returned to elite politics. In the revolt that led to the **Magna Carta** in 1215, as in the events of 1051–1052, both rebels and royalists used what might be called protonationalist arguments, appealing to the good of England and the English. Overall, the Norman Conquest had a profound influence on ethnic relations and ethnic or national identity, but only for a time. By the end of the twelfth century, this influence had disappeared because of the assimilation of the two peoples and the surprising adoption of English identity by the descendants of those proud Normans who had conquered the country in 1066.

The Norman Conquest had less impact in the social realm than in the political and military realm. In terms of the economy or gender relations, the impact was slight. In terms of ethnicity and identity, the impact was much greater but lasted only for the medium term. That the Normans should influence social and economic developments less than political and military ones should not be surprising, given that the immigrants were largely a military elite. Predictably, some of the major social shifts that the Norman Conquest *did* bring had to do with the aristocracy. Still, the Normans did have some wider social influence: they lowered the status of some peasants and, above all, they hastened the end of slavery. Thus, even for the peasantry, the Norman Conquest did not simply represent the replacement of one military elite by another. The Norman Conquest had a highly variable influence on social and economic structures, but in some cases, its impact reached surprisingly far.

NOTES

1. For instance, Orderic Vitalis, *The Ecclesiastical History of Orderic Vitalis*, ed. Marjorie Chibnall (Oxford, 1969–1980), 2:228–33, 268–69; William of Malmesbury, *Gesta Regum Anglorum*, ed. Roger A. B. Mynors, Rodney M. Thomson, and Michael Winterbottom (Oxford, 1998), 1:414–17.

2. George Duby, *Rural Economy and Country Life in the Medieval West*, trans. Cynthia Postan (Columbia, 1968); Reginald Lennard, *Rural England, 1086–1135: A Study of Agrarian Conditions* (Oxford, 1959); Edward Miller, "England in the Twelfth and Thirteenth Centuries: An Economic Contrast?" *Economic History Review*, 2nd ser., 24 (1971), 1–14; Edward Miller and John Hatcher, *Medieval England: Rural Society and Economic Change, 1086–1348* (London, 1978); Edward Miller and John Hatcher, *Medieval England: Towns, Commerce and Crafts, 1086–1348* (Harlow, 1995); Richard H. Britnell, *The Commercialisation of English Society, 1000–1500*, 2nd ed. (Manchester, 1996); Richard H. Britnell and Bruce M. S. Campbell, eds., *A Commercialising Economy: England, 1086 to c. 1300* (Manchester: 1995); John Langdon and James Masschaele, "Commercial Activity and Population Growth in Medieval England," *Past and Present* 190 (2006), 35–81; Marjorie Chibnall, *Anglo-Norman England, 1066–1166* (Oxford, 1986), 135–57; Marjorie Chibnall, *The Debate on the Norman Conquest* (Manchester, 1999), 146–51; Robert Bartlett, *England under the Norman and Angevin Kings, 1075–1225* (Oxford, 2000), 287–376; Christopher Daniell, *From Norman Conquest to Magna Carta: England, 1066–1215* (London, 2003), 162–80; David Carpenter, *The Struggle for Mastery: Britain 1066–1284* (Oxford, 2003), 26–60; Michael T. Clanchy, *England and Its Rulers, 1066–1307*, 3rd ed. (Oxford, 2006), 81–95.

3. R. Welldon Finn, *The Norman Conquest and Its Effects on the Economy* (n.p., 1970).

4. For chronicle accounts, see P. McGurk, ed., *The Chronicle of John of Worcester*, vol. 3 (Oxford, 1998), 10–11; Orderic Vitalis, *Ecclesiastical History*, 2:230–33; Hugh the Chanter, *The History of the Church of York, 1066–1127*, ed. and trans. Charles Johnson, rev. M. Brett, C. N. L. Brooke, and M. Winterbottom (Oxford, 1990), 2–3; William of Malmesbury, *Gesta Regum Anglorum*, 1:82–83, 464–65.

5. Ann Williams and Geoffrey H. Martin, eds., *Domesday Book: A Complete Translation* (London, 2002), 3, 5, 135, 198, 422, 445, 519, 551, 650, 688, 717, 757, 785, 883–84, 1058–59, 1193–94.

6. Finn, *Norman Conquest and Its Effects*, 35.

7. Wilfred E. Wightman, "The Significance of 'Waste' in the Yorkshire Domesday," *Northern History* 10 (1975), 55–71; David M. Palliser, "*Domesday Book* and the 'Harrying of the North,'" *Northern History* 29 (1993), 1–23; and Ann Williams, *The English and the Norman Conquest* (Woodbridge, 1995), 41–44.

8. Much of the material on the fall of the Western Roman Empire is critically assessed in Bryan Ward-Perkins, *The Fall of Rome and the End of Civilization* (Oxford, 2005). For the post-Carolingian debate, see Thomas Bisson, "The 'Feudal Revolution,'" *Past and Present* 142 (1994), 6–42; Dominique Barthélemy and Stephen D. White, "The 'Feudal Revolution,'" *Past and Present* 152 (1996), 196–223; Timothy Reuter, Chris Wickham, and Thomas Bisson, "The 'Feudal Revolution,'" *Past and Present* 155 (1997), 177–225.

9. John Palmer, "War and Domesday Waste," in *Armies, Chivalry and Warfare in Medieval Britain and France*, ed. Matthew Strickland (Stamford, 1998), 256–75. For Stephen's reign, see my forthcoming article, "Violent Disorder in King Stephen's England: A Maximum Argument," in Paul Dalton and Graeme J. White, eds., *King Stephen's Reign (1135–1154)* (Woodbridge, 2008).

10. *Anglo-Saxon Chronicle* DE, 1069.

11. John Gillingham, "Richard I and the Science of War in the Middle Ages," in *War and Government in the Middle Ages*, ed. John Gillingham and James C. Holt (Cambridge, 1984), 78–91; John Gillingham, "William the Bastard at War," in *The Battle of Hastings*, ed. Stephen Morillo (Woodbridge, 1996), 102–4, 107; Stephen Morillo, *Warfare under the Anglo-Norman Kings, 1066–1135* (Woodbridge, 1994), 98–102; Matthew Strickland, *War and Chivalry: The Conduct and Perception of War in England and Normandy, 1066–1217* (Cambridge, 1996), 268–81.

12. Finn, *Norman Conquest and Its Effects*, 35.

13. William of Malmesbury, *The Deeds of the Bishops of England*, trans. David Preest (Woodbridge, 2002), 139–40.

14. Maurice Beresford, *New Towns of the Middle Ages: Town Plantation in England, Wales and Gascony*, 2nd ed. (Gloucester, 1988), 327.

15. Miller and Hatcher, *Medieval England: Rural Society*, 40–42.

16. James C. Holt, *Colonial England, 1066–1215* (London, 1997), 10–12; Christopher Dyer, *Making a Living in the Middle Ages: The People of Britain, 850–1520* (New Haven, 2002), 91.

17. Thomas of Marlborough, *History of the Abbey of Evesham*, ed. Jane Sayers and Leslie Watkiss (Oxford, 2003), 166–67.

18. Dyer, *Making a Living*, 87–89; Rosamond Faith, *The English Peasantry and the Growth of Lordship* (London, 1997), 180; Finn, *Norman Conquest and Its Effects*, 5–6, 12; Lennard, *Rural England*, 155–57.

19. *Anglo-Saxon Chronicle* E, 1087; Williams and Martin, *Domesday Book*, 6, 91–92, 997, 1194; Finn, *Norman Conquest and Its Effects*, 12.

20. William E. Kapelle, *The Norman Conquest of the North: The Region and Its Transformation, 1000–1135* (Chapel Hill, 1979), 158–90; Robin Fleming, *Kings and*

Lords in Conquest England (Cambridge, 1991), 120–25; Faith, *English Peasantry*, 185–200, 214–18, 224–44.

21. Henry C. Darby, *Domesday England* (Cambridge, 1977), 62–63.

22. David A. E. Pelteret, *Slavery in Early Mediaeval England: From the Reign of Alfred until the Twelfth Century* (Woodbridge, 1995), 205.

23. William of Malmesbury, *Gesta Regum Anglorum*, 1:496–99. See, however, David Wyatt, "The Significance of Slavery: Alternative Approaches to Anglo-Saxon Slavery," *Anglo-Norman Studies* 23 (2001), 327–47.

24. Pelteret, *Slavery in Early Mediaeval England*, 234, 253–54.

25. Faith, *English Peasantry*, 245–65.

26. This view is most fully given in Paul Hyams, *Kings, Lords, and Peasants in Medieval England: The Common Law of Villeinage in the Twelfth and Thirteenth Centuries* (Oxford, 1980).

27. David C. Douglas and George W. Greenaway, eds., *English Historical Documents*, 2nd ed. (London, 1981), 2:1012.

28. John Horace Round, *Feudal England* (London, 1895), 552–62; John Horace Round, *The Commune of London and Other Studies* (Westminster, 1899), 219–60.

29. For the early history of the Jewish community, see Robert C. Stacey, "Jewish Lending and the Medieval English Economy," in *A Commercialising Economy: England 1086 to c. 1300*, ed. Richard H. Britnell and Bruce M. S. Campbell (Manchester, 1995), 78–88; H. G. Richardson, *The English Jewry under Angevin Kings* (London, 1960).

30. William of Malmesbury, *Gesta Regum Anglorum*, 1:562–63.

31. For the nobility after the conquest, see Charlotte A. Newman, *The Anglo-Norman Nobility in the Reign of Henry I: The Second Generation* (Philadelphia, 1988); Judith A. Green, *The Aristocracy of Norman England* (Cambridge, 1997); Bartlett, *England under the Norman and Angevin Kings*, 202–51.

32. The surviving Anglo-Saxon wills are collected in Dorothy Whitelock, *Anglo-Saxon Wills* (Cambridge, 1930), 2–97.

33. John Hudson, *Land, Law, and Lordship in Anglo-Norman England* (Oxford, 1994), 109–11.

34. Frank Stenton, *The First Century of English Feudalism, 1066–1166*, 2nd ed. (Oxford, 1961), 38–41; Holt, *Colonial England*, 252–55.

35. Hugh M. Thomas, *Vassals, Heiresses, Crusaders, and Thugs: The Gentry of Angevin Yorkshire, 1154–1216* (Philadelphia, 1993), 115–28.

36. The best recent overviews of the Continental and English literature on the subject in English, though from a sharply critical stance, are David Crouch, *The Birth of the Nobility: Constructing Aristocracy in England and France, 900–1300* (Harlow, 2005), 101–23; Constance Brittain Bouchard, *"Those of My Blood": Constructing Noble Families in Medieval Francia* (Philadelphia, 2001), 59–73, 155–80.

37. Holt, *Colonial England*, 161–78.

38. Holt, *Colonial England*, 179–96.

39. This family held ten knight's fees in 1166; Hubert Hall, ed., *The Red Book of the Exchequer* (London, 1896) 1:288.

40. See Lewis C. Loyd, *The Origins of Some Anglo-Norman Families* (Leeds, 1951), throughout, for the many aristocratic families in England who took their names from Norman places.

41. Crouch, *Birth of the Nobility*, 99–170; Bouchard, *Those of My Blood*, 59–73, 155–80; Pauline Stafford, "La Mutation Familiale: A Suitable Case for Caution," in *The Community, the Family and the Saint: Patterns of Power in Early Medieval Europe*, ed. Joyce Hill and Mary Swan (Turnhouts, 1998), 103–25.

42. Andrew Wareham, *Lords and Communities in Early Medieval East Anglia* (Woodbridge, 2005), 61–77, 95–124, 156.

43. Matthew Strickland, "Slaughter, Slavery or Ransom: The Impact of the Conquest on Conduct in Warfare," in *England in the Eleventh Century*, ed. Carola Hicks (Stamford, 1992), 41–59, and John Gillingham, *The English in the Twelfth Century: Imperialism, National History and Political Values* (Woodbridge, 2000), 56–57, 209–29.

44. Robert Liddiard, *Landscapes of Lordship: Norman Castles and the Countryside in Medieval Norfolk, 1066–1200* (Oxford, 2000), 51–66.

45. Naomi Sykes, "Zooarchaeology of the Norman Conquest," *Anglo-Norman Studies* 27 (2005), 185–97; Naomi Sykes, "The Impact of the Normans on Hunting Practices in England," in *Food in Medieval England: Diet and Nutrition*, ed. Christopher M. Woolgar, D. Serjeantson, and T. Waldron (Oxford, 2006), 162–75.

46. In this paragraph, I draw heavily on Pauline Stafford, "Women and the Norman Conquest," *Transactions of the Royal Historical Society*, 6th ser. 4 (1994), 221–49.

47. For example, Florence G. Buckstaff, who later became the first woman trustee of the University of Wisconsin, used an article on women, property rights, and the conquest to speak about the property rights of women in the United States and Britain in her own time; see her "Married Women's Property in Anglo-Saxon and Anglo-Norman Law and the Origin of Common-Law Dower," *Annals of the American Academy of Political and Social Science* 4 (1893), 233–64.

48. Whitelock, *Anglo-Saxon Wills*, 38–43, 76–79, 84–87, 92–97.

49. In this section, I draw heavily from my book *The English and the Normans: Ethnic Hostility, Assimilation, and Identity, 1066–c. 1220* (Oxford, 2003), and from Williams, *English and the Norman Conquest*, and Gillingham, *English in the Twelfth Century*, 113–60, among other works.

50. Walter W. Skeat, ed., *Aelfric's Lives of Saints, Being a Set of Sermons on Saints' Days Formerly Observed by the English Church* (London, 1881), 1:2; Edward Edwards, *Liber Monasterii de Hyda* (London, 1866), 324.

51. Bryan Ward-Perkins, "Why Did the Anglo-Saxons Not Become More British?" *English Historical Review* 115 (2000), 513–33.

52. For this subject, see Eric John, *Orbis Britanniae and Other Studies* (Leicester, 1966), 1–63; Patrick Wormald, "*Engla Lond*: The Making of an Allegiance," *Journal*

of Historical Sociology 7 (1994), 1–24; James Campbell, "The United Kingdom of England: The Anglo-Saxon Achievement," in *Uniting the Kingdom? The Making of British History*, ed. Alexander Grant and Keith J. Stringer (London, 1995), 31–47; Sarah Foot, "The Making of *Angelcynn*: English Identity before the Norman Conquest," *Transactions of the Royal Historical Society*, 6th ser., 6 (1996), 25–49.

53. Elliot van Kirk Dobbie, *The Anglo-Saxon Minor Poems* (New York, 1942), 8. The term used was *eard*, which was sometimes used to translate the Latin term for homeland, *patria*.

54. Frank Barlow, ed., *The Life of King Edward Who Rests at Westminster*, 2nd ed. (Oxford, 1992), 40–41; *Anglo-Saxon Chronicle* CDE, 1052.

55. R. H. C. Davis, *The Normans and Their Myth* (London, 1976); G. A. Loud, "The *Gens Normannorum*—Myth or Reality?" *Proceedings of the Battle Conference on Anglo-Norman Studies* 4 (1982), 104–16, 204–9; Cassandra Potts, "*Atque unum ex diversis gentibus populum effecit*: Historical Tradition and the Norman Identity," *Anglo-Norman Studies* 18 (1996), 139–52; and Emily Albu, *The Normans in Their Histories: Propaganda, Myth and Subversion* (Woodbridge, 2001).

56. David Bates, *Regesta Regum Anglo-Normannorum: The Acta of William I (1066–1087)* (Oxford, 1998), 846.

57. William of Poitiers, *Gesta Guilelmi*, ed. R. H. C. Davis and Marjorie Chibnall (Oxford, 1998), 124–25.

58. William of Poitiers, *Gesta Guilelmi*, 182–85.

59. Orderic Vitalis, *Ecclesiastical History*, 2:344–45.

60. Susan Ridyard, "*Condigna Veneratio*: Post-Conquest Attitudes to the Saints of the Anglo-Saxons," *Anglo-Norman Studies* 9 (1987), 179–206; Paul Antony Hayward, "Translation-Narratives in Post-Conquest Hagiography and English Resistance to the Norman Conquest," *Anglo-Norman Studies* 21 (1999), 67–93; Jay Rubenstein, "Liturgy against History: The Competing Visions of Lanfranc and Eadmer of Canterbury," *Speculum* 74 (1999), 279–309; Thomas, *English and the Normans*, 48–49, 290–93.

61. *Anglo-Saxon Chronicle* E, 1083. For a good discussion of this incident and its liturgical background, see David Hiley, "Thurstan of Caen and Plainchant at Glastonbury: Musicological Reflections on the Norman Conquest," *Proceedings of the British Academy* 72 (1986), 57–90.

62. William of Malmesbury, *Gesta Regum Anglorum*, 1:414–17; Marc Bloch, ed., "La Vie de S. Édouard le Confesseur par Osbert de Clare," *Analecta Bollandiana* 41 (1923), 107–9; Aelred of Rievaulx, "Vita S. Edwardi Regis et Confessoris," *Patrologia Latina* 195:773–74.

63. For the development of greater distinctions, see David Crouch, *The Image of Aristocracy in Britain, 1000–1300* (London, 1992), 106–73; Peter Coss, "Knights, Esquires and the Origins of Social Gradation in England," *Transactions of the Royal Historical Society*, 6th ser., 5 (1995), 155–78.

64. For good works on identity, see the works noted in notes 49, 52, and 55 above, and Ian Short, "*Tam Angli quam Franci*: Self-definition in Anglo-Norman England," *Anglo-Norman Studies* 18 (1996), 153–75.

65. Henry, Archdeacon of Huntingdon, *Historia Anglorum*, ed. Diana Greenway (Oxford, 1996), 402–3, 412–13.

66. For language use, see chapter 5. For the relative lack of importance of language to identity, see Thomas, *English and the Normans*, 385–90, though the comments of reviewers indicate that this is a controversial claim.

67. George Neilson, *Caudatus Anglicus: A Mediæval Slander* (Edinburgh, 1896).

68. Elizabeth Revell, ed., *The Later Letters of Peter of Blois* (Oxford, 1993), 162–64.

69. George Lacombe, "An Unpublished Document on the Great Interdict (1207–1213)," *Catholic Historical Review*, n. s. 9 (1930), 408–20.

5

CULTURAL CONSEQUENCES

William the Conqueror and his followers set out to gain power and wealth, not to transform English culture. Those with political and economic power, however, often have the ability to reshape culture, so this chapter explores the Norman impact on English civilization. How did the Normans influence religion in England, beyond their introduction of a Jewish community? Did they transform intellectual life, which in this period was closely linked to religion? What changes did the conquest bring in art and architecture? How did it influence language and literature? The Norman impact on culture, like its impact on social structures, varied. In some areas, the Norman Conquest brought only limited change, especially in the long term. In other areas, particularly language, it had profound effects, the consequences of which remain important even in the twenty-first century.

RELIGION AND INTELLECTUAL LIFE

William viewed the English church partly as a source of power.[1] Because bishoprics and monasteries held so much land and influence, William acted carefully and deliberately to make sure that loyal foreigners came to dominate the leadership of the English church.[2] As noted in chapter 2, by William's death there was only one native English bishop. William's sons continued to appoint only foreigners or immigrants, though Henry I may have made a native Englishman bishop of Carlisle late in his reign. Carlisle, however, was a new bishopric and on the northwestern periphery of the kingdom. William and his sons did appoint a few English abbots, but the vast majority of their appointees were foreigners. English monks complained about the bias of Norman kings against natives in church appointments, and their complaints were clearly justified.[3] The Normans replaced the top ec-clesiastical leadership of the English, just as they had created an almost com-pletely new aristocracy.

The Norman purge of church leadership did not extend as far down the ranks as the Norman purge of the Anglo-Saxon nobility, however. Though many Normans and other foreigners took positions in the middle ranks of the church, the Normans did not claim a complete monopoly, for natives were also found in these positions. At the level of ordinary monks and nuns, the English remained very important numerically. At the parish level, English priests probably remained the majority. In practical terms, the Normans could afford to be less thorough in their purge of the English church than of the English aristocracy. Even a fairly minor thane like Here-ward the Wake could lead a rebellion, and collectively minor Anglo-Saxon aristocrats represented a significant military threat. In contrast, Anglo-Saxon priests, monks, and nuns did not pose a military danger, though Anglo-Saxon bishops, abbots, and abbesses might have through their control of land and patronage.

As long as continental leadership dominated the highest levels of the church hierarchy, William and his followers could leave lesser figures in place. However, even minor officials in the church were influential social fig-ures and could be intellectual leaders as well. A few English churchmen had a good deal of influence. For instance, Archbishop Anselm's native student, Elmer, became an author and the prior of Canterbury Cathedral. As prior, he was the highest official other than the archbishop at the most important church in England.[4] Because of the admixture of natives and immigrants be-low the highest level of the hierarchy, the church became simultaneously a conduit for continental cultural influence, a bastion of English culture, and an institution in which Norman and English culture could intermingle.

The Normans not only seized control of many church offices but they also seized land and plunder from the English church. In the short term, the Norman Conquest siphoned wealth away from English churches, and Eng-lish churchmen lamented the theft of rich treasures, including books and sacred art fashioned from precious metals and gems. For instance, at the monastery of Abingdon, a Norman monk melted down a chandelier for £40 (or 9,600 silver coins) worth of gold and silver and carried off precious dishes to Normandy.[5] At Ely, various statues, including one of the virgin and child, were stripped of the gold, silver, and gems that had decorated them.[6] A chronicler of Waltham, Harold Godwineson's favorite church, claimed that William II seized treasures worth 10,000 marks (1,600,000 sil-ver coins) from that church and used them to enrich the churches in Normandy that his parents had built and in which they were buried. The amount is likely an exaggeration, but it is not surprising that Harold's church would contain rich treasures or that William II would seize them.[7] Church officials sometimes had to melt down treasures themselves to meet Norman taxes and other demands. Church chroniclers also filled their works with stories of avaricious Norman nobles and sheriffs seizing church lands.[8] Occasionally, these stories showed the plunderers coming to a nasty end, which, of course, the chroniclers attributed to the wrath of God or a saint. One writer claimed that a Norman oppressor of his monastery died after the patron saint of the monastery, **Æthelthryth**, along with her two equally saintly sisters, appeared in a vision and thrust the tips of their staffs into the oppressor's heart. Saints, according to the beliefs of the time, dealt harshly and summarily with those who crossed them.[9]

Church chroniclers, of course, were not exactly neutral writers. Sometimes the Normans were robbing Peter to pay Paul; more precisely, they were robbing English churches to enrich Norman ones. William's imposition of military quotas on religious houses also forced bishops and abbots to grant out lands; in 1086, about 20 percent of the church's lands were held by the laity.[10] However, much church land had been held by Anglo-Saxon nobles on lease from the church. In addition, Anglo-Saxon bishops and abbots had also had military obligations, which undoubtedly tied up some of their resources. It is therefore hard to know how much of this 20 percent represented a reduction in the resources of English churches after 1066. Despite these caveats, the English church certainly lost much wealth and many estates as a result of the conquest. Moreover, one important difference from the Anglo-Saxon period is that many of the church lands held by knights soon became permanent and hereditary tenures rather than leases, reducing ecclesiastical control over them.[11] Thus, the Norman Conquest diminished ecclesiastical wealth and landholding both directly and indirectly.

The Normans, however, like their Anglo-Saxon predecessors, were generous patrons. William may have seen the English church as an instrument of power, but he and his more pious followers also saw the church as their guide along the difficult path to heaven. Believers were also understandably wary of tangling with vengeful saints. They therefore avoided plundering the English church too thoroughly and sought by their generosity to gain the favor of religious men and women, the saints, and God. At first, admittedly, much of the Normans' patronage went to religious houses in France. They gave to such houses lands worth about £1,000 per year by the end of William's reign, at a time when all of the estates in England recorded in *Domesday Book* produced approximately £72,000 per year.[12] However, some immigrant nobles gave lands to English churches from the beginning, and this patronage increased in the second generation after the conquest and beyond.[13] In addition, the Normans founded or patronized new monasteries, including in northern England, where the Vikings had wiped out monasticism.[14] Overall, generosity by William I, his nobles, and their descendants soon compensated for the initial losses of the English church.

Furthermore, William and some of his followers tried to strengthen the church spiritually. Though English chroniclers often bitterly attacked the Normans for their depredations against church property, they nonetheless admitted that the Normans brought reform and new vigor to the church. The view of the Normans as reformers came partly from Norman propaganda, it is true. It also arose from a belief that God would not have punished England so badly if religious failings had not aroused His anger in the generation before the conquest, and once medieval writers began looking for religious shortcomings, they never had much trouble finding them.[15] However, there was also truth to the idea of Norman reform.[16]

The Middle Ages saw periodic waves of church reform, some local, some international. England had experienced such a wave in the decades on either side of the year 1000. Monastic life had been revived, learning had been revitalized, and strenuous efforts had been made to more thoroughly Christianize society. For a couple of generations, the English church had blossomed, though the new Viking invasions and Canute's conquest seem to have sapped the movement's vitality.[17] In Normandy, much of the eleventh century was a time of reform. William, as noted in the first chapter, helped foster improvement by promoting able churchmen, including foreigners. Meanwhile, in the middle of the eleventh century, a reform movement began in Rome that radically changed the entire Western church.[18] This reform began in a relatively old-fashioned way, with popes and their officials trying to enforce longstanding but widely ignored rules against the marriage of priests and the buying and selling of church offices. As time went on, papal reform became more radical, as the reformers sought to combat widespread secular control of the church. By the end of his reign, William was having polite but tense exchanges with the most vigorous of the reformers, Pope Gregory VII, over the latter's claims of overlordship of England.[19] In 1066, however, papal reform had not gone so far, and the Norman church under William was more in tune with Rome than was the English church. Under Edward the Confessor, even one of the most pious English churchmen, Archbishop Ealdred of York, earned papal anger for trying to hold two bishoprics at once.[20] William's reputation as a reformer helped him gain papal support for his invasion, and according to his biographer, William of Poitiers, he even received a papal banner signifying that support to the world.[21]

The difference between the English and Norman churches should not be exaggerated. One could argue that England was at most a decade or two behind the times and that in the inevitable rise and fall of enthusiasm for reform, it happened to be at a low point in 1066, whereas Normandy was in a reforming phase. Moreover, much depended on individuals; in both Normandy and England some church leaders were more pious than others. But William did in fact appoint a reformer to head the English church. In 1070, with the help of papal representatives, he replaced Archbishop Stigand with Lanfranc, the Italian immigrant who, as I noted in chapter 1, was one of the leading scholars of the age. Lanfranc, who had close ties with the reforming papacy, introduced a collection of church law that soon became widely disseminated throughout England. He also held several church councils in an attempt to foster church reform. One issue he tried to tackle was clerical marriage, though in England, as in Normandy and the rest of Europe, it would be many years before the reformers won on this issue.[22] Other bishops also began introducing regular synods, meetings of the clergy in their bishoprics, to promote reform. Generally speaking, the Norman Conquest brought England into line with the early stages of the papal reform movement.

The embrace of reform in England was inevitable sooner or later, however, given the strength of the reform movement throughout Europe. Intriguingly, Earl Harold had brought a cleric to England from Lotharingia, an area on the borderlands of France and Germany associated with church reform, to help improve his own showcase church at Waltham.[23] One wonders what direction the church might have taken with him as king. Moreover, William and his sons, like most other rulers in Europe, resisted later aspects of the papal reform movement, thus moving from supporting to impeding church reform. Indeed, William II and Henry I fought fiercely with Lanfranc's successor, Anselm, over issues of reform.[24] On a technical level, William's new demand that bishops and abbots swear fealty for their lands sharpened the division between the English kings and papal reformers who were trying to remove abbeys and bishoprics from the control of rulers. Such oaths simply highlighted the power English kings had always possessed over bishops and abbots, but the formal symbolism of the oaths openly contradicted the independence that reformers sought for church officials and made the necessary compromises between church and state more difficult. Nonetheless, the Normans had at least *introduced* the papal reform movement into England.

Overlapping with Norman reforms were organizational changes. Again, a wider perspective is needed. Throughout Europe, the institutions of the church were growing more complex and more defined. Indeed, a major part of the papal reform effort was to more sharply define and enhance the role of the papacy. Ironically, Lanfranc, who resisted enhancement of papal power when it came at his expense, sought to more sharply define and enhance the status of the archbishop of Canterbury in England, Wales, Scotland, and Ireland.[25] Essentially, Lanfranc claimed formal leadership of the church throughout the isles. Not surprisingly, his claims met a mixed reception in Wales, Scotland, and Ireland. Within England, they sparked a major fight with the only other archbishopric in the country, the archbishopric of York. In theory, archbishops were normally equals. In the late Anglo-Saxon period, the archbishops of Canterbury had clearly been more important than the archbishops of York because of Canterbury's wealth and prestige. Nonetheless, the Norman archbishops of York did not appreciate having Canterbury's practical superiority turned into formal supremacy. A remarkably fierce dispute followed, one that lasted a couple of generations and included appeals to various popes, the exile of one archbishop of York, and the manufacture of some blatant forgeries of papal documents at Canterbury. Canterbury did not achieve its final triumph during the Norman period, but it remained the chief bishopric in England and Wales for all practical purposes.[26]

Two other organizational reforms by the Normans had more profound effects. As noted in chapter 3, the Normans advanced the development of church courts in England, again following a European trend. William I issued a decree that attempted to shift certain cases to synods, or to the courts of the bishops, though the exact nature and impact of this change is debated.[27] The Normans also greatly expanded the use of the office of **archdeacon**. Archdeacons increasingly oversaw church courts in subdivisions of bishoprics, and came to be the local overseers of the church's attempt to force an often resentful populace to follow Christian laws and morals.[28] However, Normandy was not that far ahead of England in the use of archdeacons, yet another practice spreading throughout Europe, and thus probably only accelerated changes that would have come anyway.

In two other aspects of organization, however, the Anglo-Saxon church was seriously out of step with much of the rest of the western European church. First, bishoprics were normally in urban centers, but a number of English bishoprics were at rural sites. Second, most European cathedrals were staffed by canons, part of the secular clergy, so called because these clerics lived in the *saecula*, or world, instead of being set apart from society in a monastery. In England, however, several cathedrals were staffed by monks.

The Normans did not tolerate the first aberration, and moved several bishoprics to urban centers. Lanfranc, however, was a monk and embraced the idea of monks staffing cathedrals, as did some other Norman bishops.[29] Overall, the Normans sought to make the English church conform to the latest ways of thinking on the continent, but were willing to make exceptions for practices they favored.

The Normans brought a variety of other changes to the English church that were not so closely linked to broader contemporary efforts at reform and reorganization in the Western church. **William of Warenne**, a powerful Norman noble and one of the greatest beneficiaries of the Norman Conquest, used part of his wealth to introduce to England a new monastic order, the order of **Cluny**, which was noted for the complexity and beauty of its performance of church rituals.[30] For a time, the Normans brought a skeptical attitude to English cults of saints. Prejudice was likely to have been a factor. Some skepticism also arose because the English seem to have been fairly indiscriminate (by continental standards) in treating holy people as saints and because some reformers like Lanfranc desired a narrower focus on the great international saints of the church. One Norman abbot went so far as to test English relics by fire. According to the thinking of the time, no real saint would allow his or her relics to get burned, so no genuine relics would be affected.[31] The major English saints' cults survived the conquest intact and chroniclers probably exaggerated the extent of the skepticism, but English exaggeration and anger illustrates how sensitive the issue was.[32] Norman abbots and bishops also altered parts of the liturgy, the round of chants, prayers, and masses regularly performed by the clergy. Because performance of the liturgy was judged one of the crucial tasks of the church in this period, these changes sometimes provoked deep and (to modern people) surprising hostility, as in the case of the riot and massacre at Glastonbury described in the previous chapter.

Despite the emotions aroused by some of the modifications, most were minor in the greater scheme of things and brought few alterations to religious life in England that would not have happened anyway. One change, however, had serious consequences for English religion in the medium term, namely, the gradual but widespread abandonment of English as a language of religious writing.[33] The use of English for religious purposes had always caused some concern among religious thinkers; to western European intellectuals, Latin was the "real" language of Christianity. Even the late Anglo-Saxon reformer **Aelfric**, who was one of the most prolific writers of religious material in English, expressed serious reservations about translating the Bible.[34] Nonetheless, King Alfred and his circle, faced with a serious decline in learning due to the Viking invasions, had translated a number of religious works into English. The use of English had only grown with the reform movement around 1000, when Aelfric and others produced sermons, translations of Latin works, and collections of religious laws in English. The use of English did not entirely disappear in the postconquest period, a point to which I will return later, but religious writing in English steadily declined in the generations following the conquest, both in absolute terms and relative to writing in Latin and later in French. The new church leadership did not immediately substitute French for English; before the twelfth century, very little was written in French anywhere. Instead, they emphasized the sole use of Latin, the "proper" language for religion and one that both English and Norman intellectuals could understand.

Normally, the decline of written English is treated under the heading of language, and indeed I will return to it in that context later in the chapter. However, I would argue that it also had important religious consequences. From the late twelfth century on, the church made a concerted effort to provide the laity with greater religious education, and a major tool was writing in the **vernacular** (languages other than Latin). The English reformers of the decades around 1000 anticipated this movement to a surprising degree, partly because the goal of teaching the laity was not new in the late twelfth century, even if it received renewed impetus then. But one of the major ways in which the earlier English reformers anticipated later developments was by writing in the local vernacular, which potentially made Christian teachings much more widely available. Poorly educated parish priests were more likely to learn to read in English than in Latin, and even illiterate people could benefit when books or sermons in their own language were read out loud. One of the few works composed in Old English after the conquest praised Anglo-Saxon figures for translating and teaching in English. It finished by blasting the new (continental) church leaders for ending the practice, saying they were leading the English to damnation.[35] Had Harold won at Hastings, England might have been a greater pioneer in spreading religious teachings through the vernacular, and the history of Christianity there and perhaps elsewhere in the twelfth century might have been quite different.

The subject of English and Latin brings us to intellectual history. As with reform, Normandy (or at least some religious centers there) was slightly ahead of England. This was partly because the Norman dukes had imported and nurtured intellectual talent over the course of the eleventh century, and partly, as noted in chapter 1, because Lanfranc and his pupil Anselm were such brilliant thinkers.[36] Simply by making Lanfranc archbishop of Canterbury, William ensured that learning would receive renewed attention in the English church. William II, though less pious than his father, did the same by appointing Anselm as Lanfranc's successor. Their presence alone advanced English intellectual life, particularly at Canterbury, but they also served as role models throughout the English church.

Books are something we take for granted, but they were rare in eleventh-century Europe. Throughout the Catholic world, however, great churches started building up their libraries by copying and otherwise obtaining manuscripts. In particular, intellectuals were striving to build up collections of works of the "church fathers," theologians such as St. **Augustine of Hippo** or St. Jerome who had written in the early centuries of the church. Greater distribution of theological and other works helped fuel an intellectual revival in western Europe in the late eleventh and twelfth centuries.[37] The process of building up libraries had begun in Normandy not long before 1066 but not in England. As a result, it was Norman churchmen who started the process in many great English churches. For instance, one writer described how **Osmund**, the first Norman bishop of Salisbury, took pleasure in copying and binding books himself, and surviving manuscripts attest to the remarkable growth of the cathedral library under his leadership and afterward.[38] The growth in English religious libraries would have happened at some point anyway, and often enough, native English scribes were involved in the effort. Even so, the Normans almost certainly made it happen sooner than it would have otherwise.

The Normans also raised the level of Latinity in England, partly by substantially reducing the English option for reading and writing. Indeed, one of the great intellectual efforts in the postconquest period was the translation of English materials into Latin. Indirectly, the Norman Conquest also created an upsurge in the study of history and law.[39] As we have seen, the conquerors maintained much English law, so they had to translate and learn it. The desire of the conquerors to celebrate and justify the conquest and the need for the conquered to understand it and defend their people fostered a mass of historical writing in the two generations following the conquest. Finally, the Norman Conquest helped cement scholarly ties between England and northern France, including Paris, which would be Europe's leading intellectual center in the twelfth century.[40]

In the main, the Norman Conquest simply sped up reforms and intellectual developments that would have come to England sooner or later anyway. Because of the conquest, more of these developments came via Normandy and other parts of northern France and fewer via Germany and the Low Countries. They also came about in more contentious circumstances.

Perhaps the chief religious result of the conquest, however, was negative: the gradual but nearly complete elimination of written Old English as an effective instrument of religious revival. Eventually, Anglo-Norman French and Middle English took its place, but the history of lay piety in England would have been quite different without the conquest.

ART AND ARCHITECTURE

Though England was slightly backward in intellectual pursuits, according to contemporary views, it had a flourishing artistic tradition that the Normans admired. William the Conqueror's biographer, William of Poitiers, praised the textiles created by English women as well as the craftsmanship of English men and German immigrants who had settled in England.[41] Norman painted manuscripts from before 1066 reveal influences from the English artistic tradition.[42] After the conquest, as already noted, the Normans showed their appreciation of English works of art (along with the gold and silver bullion and the gems they contained), by plundering various pieces, often presenting them as gifts to churches in Normandy. William the Conqueror's wife, Queen **Matilda I of Flanders**, employed at least one English woman for her embroidery skills.[43] According to most scholars, even the Bayeux Tapestry, the great celebration of the Norman Conquest, was embroidered by English women and demonstrates much influence from Canterbury artistic traditions. In art, the Normans, with their usual pragmatism, embraced what they liked and what suited their purposes with open arms.

Therefore, 1066 represented no sharp break in most artistic fields.[44] Instead, for a time, Anglo-Saxon and Norman traditions existed side by side. The greatest surviving corpus of artwork comes from manuscript painting, also known as illumination. This corpus indicates that Norman styles became predominant at some centers, Anglo-Saxon styles dominated at others, and some artistic workshops adopted both styles or created a mixture of the two. The Normans probably weakened English artistic traditions somewhat by shifting some of the funds available for artistic patronage to continental artists or, as we shall see, to architecture. However, neither the Norman nor the English style pushed out the other. Instead, new influences from as far away as the Byzantine Empire came into play during the twelfth century. These influences, along with internal artistic development, eventually made the question of English versus Norman artistic traditions meaningless as art in England simply moved beyond eleventh-century English and Norman styles.

In architecture, however, the Norman Conquest did bring a revolution.[45] The Norman introduction of castle building has already been noted. Norman churchmen also brought massive change to ecclesiastical architecture. Within fifty years of the conquest, and in most cases within thirty years, the Normans began rebuilding every major church in England except Westminster Abbey, which Edward the Confessor had rebuilt in a Norman style shortly before the conquest. According to Eric Fernie, a leading authority on Anglo-Norman architecture, the rebuilding was so thorough that not one indisputable piece of standing Anglo-Saxon masonry survives in a major English church.[46] England may have previously fallen behind European trends in architecture, though the drastic Norman "makeover" makes judgments about monumental Anglo-Saxon architecture risky. A major rebuilding of churches throughout western Europe had begun in the early eleventh century, which led to the creation of what modern scholars call the Romanesque style. Canute's conquest and the resulting economic pressures on England may have made England an exception by creating a recession in church building up until shortly before the conquest.[47] When the Normans took over, they clearly sought to correct any recession, putting up churches in the latest style, not only drawing on Norman models but also borrowing from architectural developments elsewhere in Europe and making innovations of their own. They also thought big—when it came to architecture, the Normans in England were the Texans of their day. Some of the English churches they knocked down were fairly large, but the Normans built on an astonishing scale (see figure 5.1). In 1066, the largest church in Western Christendom was Old Saint Peter's Basilica in Rome (the current church on the site was built in the Renaissance); in the twelfth century, the continental monastery of Cluny surpassed it. During the generations following the Norman Conquest, only two continental churches are known to have approached the size of these structures. By the time the Normans were done, however, no fewer than nine English cathedrals or monasteries were close in scale.[48] One scholar has estimated that England saw a greater per capita investment in architecture during the period following the Norman Conquest than at any other point in history before the Industrial Revolution.[49]

Why did the Normans go on a building frenzy? Castles served as both a military and psychological tool of domination. Some scholars have argued that large churches, too, acted as symbols of domination—signs of Norman power and of the vigor of the new leadership of the church.[50] Certainly, the building of glorious and up-to-date churches fit in with the Norman image of reformers whipping into shape a backward national church. One

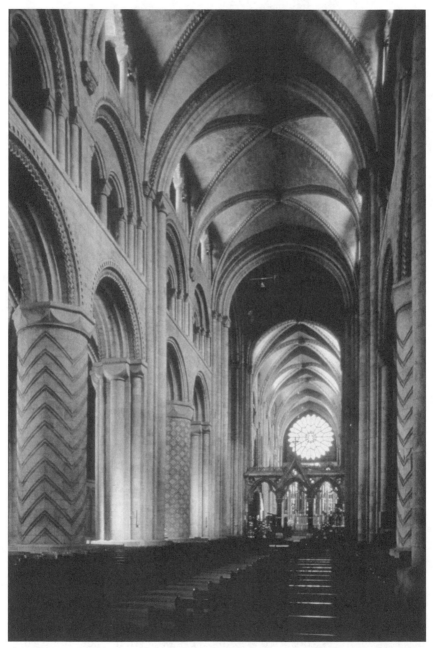

Figure 5.1.   The interior of Durham Cathedral. Anthony Sciblia/Art Resource, NY

chronicler's comments on the Normans and building suggest that cultural preferences, individual Norman ambition, and the contest between immigrant churchmen for glory created a competitive cycle within England.[51] In some cases, the move of bishoprics from one site to another necessitated a new cathedral. Elsewhere, the Norman Conquest created enough of a rupture in individual churches that new abbots and bishops, unimpeded by local traditions and tastes, could divert resources to huge building programs. Finally, the conquest brought remarkable amounts of wealth to the new Norman bishops and abbots, and construction was certainly one noteworthy way to spend all that money.

Even in architecture, however, the revolution was not complete. Both Anglo-Saxon and Norman architecture drew on long traditions of Christian architecture in western Europe, such as the cruciform shape of churches. Therefore, the new churches, even if somewhat newfangled, would not have been alien enough to seriously offend religious sensibilities in England.[52] For parish churches, architectural historians speak of an overlap period in which churches continued to be built in traditional forms or with a mixture of Anglo-Saxon and Norman styles and techniques. In the second generation after the Norman Conquest, some traditional English elements began to creep back, even into the great churches.[53] Nonetheless, the Norman Conquest created a decisive revolution in English architecture even though it did not do so in other areas of art. The architectural revolution shows that where the Normans wished to bring artistic change, they were perfectly capable of doing so.

LANGUAGE AND LITERATURE

The Norman Conquest had some of its most durable and significant consequences in the areas of language and literature. We have seen that the Anglo-Saxons had used writing extensively, especially for administrative and religious purposes. They even created a remarkable standardization in grammar and spelling in the late Anglo-Saxon period. As is well-known, they also built up an extensive body of written poetry, much of it religious but some of it more secular in nature, such as the epic *Beowulf*. The Normans had nothing against the English language or English literature. William the Conqueror even tried to learn English, though he failed.[54] William's failure, however, suggests the low priority the Normans placed on speaking and writing in English. As previously noted, immigrant churchmen considered Latin preferable. We do not know how many Norman nobles learned English in the first generation or two after the conquest, but it is unlikely that many gained enough fluency to appreciate the finer points of Old English poetic technique. Few Normans would have been interested in hearing the heroic poetry of the people they had defeated anyway; they had their own minstrels and their own heroes. Even churchmen of English ancestry or allegiance put little effort into saving written English.[55] Many did work hard to preserve Anglo-Saxon culture, but when they did so, they were more interested in the contents of written works than the language and relied heavily on translation. For literary snobs of the period, what mattered was literature in Latin, mainly by classical writers such as Ovid and Virgil; works in other languages were, almost by definition, barbaric. Those writers who celebrated Anglo-Saxon learning usually celebrated past learning in Latin, not in English. Thus, even writers who were deeply concerned with Anglo-Saxon culture did not consider it a priority to save Old English works simply for their literary merit. The Normans did not set out to destroy written Old English, but their indifference, along with the general preference for Latin in the period, led to the near extinction of written English.

Writing in Old English died with a whimper, not a bang. English religious works continued to be copied for a time (indeed, some Anglo-Saxon religious works survive only in copies from after 1066). Aelfric's work continued to be comparatively popular. A tiny number of new works were even written after the Norman Conquest. One version of the *Anglo-Saxon Chronicle* continued for nearly a century after the conquest, though its final sections showed characteristics of Middle English, the form of English used in the later Middle Ages.[56] Recent work that focuses on the use of Old English in the twelfth century for its own sake rather than as an adjunct to the Anglo-Saxon period shows that there was some vitality in the postconquest religious tradition.[57] Moreover, writing in English never quite disappeared; a handful of Middle English works took up where Old English left off.[58]

Nonetheless, even as the use of writing in general expanded enormously in the late eleventh and the twelfth centuries, the use of written English shriveled.[59] Because of the scarcity of writing in English, standardization was lost. This can be seen most easily in spelling but also appears in grammar.[60] Only in the fourteenth century did English writing become common again (in Middle English), and only then did English literature come roaring back, most notably in the work of Geoffrey Chaucer. By that time, English had changed radically. Modern students naturally struggle with Chaucer or even Shakespeare on their first introduction to the works of these writers, unless the writing has been modernized, but learning to read Old English is far harder. Indeed, it is not very different from learning to read a foreign language. Strikingly, it is not only modern English speakers who have trouble with Old English; even twelfth- and thirteenth-century readers found it hard to understand. The author of a brief and highly fictionalized Latin biography of the English rebel Hereward the Wake, written between 1109 and 1174, complained about the difficulty of reading an English account written by Hereward's priest.[61] An anonymous thirteenth-century monk at Worcester, known to scholars as the "Tremulous Hand" because of his handwriting, carefully studied Old English manuscripts but made many errors of interpretation and sometimes attempted to update the writing.[62] By the time English literature really revived in the fourteenth century, Old English would have been virtually incomprehensible to speakers of Middle English.

As a result, the Norman Conquest brought a literary revolution even greater than its architectural revolution. Some traditional elements did survive. One example is **alliteration**, or front rhyme. In alliterative poetry, the emphasis is placed on holding poetic lines together through the opening sounds of words. Alliterative poetry survived in scattered writings and in oral tradition, and was temporarily revived in the later Middle Ages. Various scholars have also demonstrated or made a case for other continuities as well, particularly with some early Middle English writings. What strikes me most as an outsider to literary studies, however, is how little continuity scholars have found between Old English literature and the Middle English literature of the fourteenth and fifteenth centuries. Scholars, particularly in earlier generations, devoted great efforts to tracing connections with remarkably few results.[63]

Twelfth-century English literature was written largely in Latin and French, often in a dialect of the latter language called Anglo-Norman.[64] One of the great ironies in the history of English literature was that the Normans stifled vernacular writing in English not long before vernacular writing in French began to take off. An oddity of literary history is that England was a key area in the development of French literature and of writing in French more generally. The first examples of works in French in many genres, including drama, science, history, and perhaps romance, were probably written in England.[65] It is possible that the surviving examples of Old English documents and manuscripts made the new French-speaking elites more aware of the possibilities and uses of vernacular writing. The desire of the upper classes to preserve French cultural ties almost certainly contributed to the prominent role England had in the rise of written French. Thus, if the Norman Conquest stifled English literature for a time, it indirectly but significantly fostered the rise of French literature.

French and Latin continued to dominate the English literary scene into the fourteenth century. Therefore, cross-germination between literary works written there and elsewhere in those languages continued to be very easy.[66] When Middle English literature began to emerge, and especially when it began to flourish in the fourteenth century, it owed far more to French and Latin literature than to Old English. No one in the later Middle Ages had heard of Beowulf. The great heroes of that time were King Arthur and his knights, first popularized in a Latin pseudo-history by **Geoffrey of Monmouth**, a Welsh scholar active in England, and then in French versions of that history and in scores of French romances. Many Middle English works were simply translations or reworkings of pieces originally written in French. Chaucer drew on a variety of sources and influences, but none of them was Old English. One can easily trace a continuity in English literature back to Middle English, but from there the path goes back to Latin and French. Despite scholarly efforts to show further continuity, the Norman Conquest brought a deep rupture in the history of writing in English.

One reason Chaucer and other Middle English writers were able to develop such a rich literary tradition so quickly is that they drew on so many different languages and literary influences. Latin and French literary works from England have been unjustifiably neglected because they do not fit into the normal categories of English, French, and classical literature. Classicists once considered medieval Latin works as automatically inferior, while Anglo-Norman works remained excluded from the French canon because they were written in England and from the English canon because they were written in French. In the nineteenth and early twentieth centuries, a nationalistic desire to understand and promote "national" literature was an important justification for studying language and literature (which is probably one reason why members of some earlier generations were so intent on describing a continuous history of English literature stretching back to Old English). One of the most important and promising current developments in literary studies is the growing interest in Anglo-Latin and Anglo-Norman works and their influence on Middle English. Even now, however, despite the vigorous efforts of a few specialists in medieval French and Latin, works not in English remain scandalously neglected. Greater study of Anglo-Norman and Anglo-Latin works promises to greatly increase our understanding of Middle English and to open up a neglected period in the literary history of England.

Even while celebrating the study of Latin and Anglo-Norman works, however, I cannot help but treat the death of the Old English tradition as a tragedy. English literature would have certainly changed over time even had Harold won at Hastings, but doubtlessly it would have been shaped more strongly by Old English traditions. Instead, Old English literature disappeared as an influence until modern times. In the twentieth century, it inspired writers as diverse as Jorge Luis Borges and J. R. R. Tolkien, the latter of whom did much as a scholar to establish *Beowulf*'s literary merit. Even with this period of rediscovery, Old English is not particularly central to modern English literature, certainly not in the way the later historical periods of English literature are. Moreover, the death of the Old English literary tradition doubtlessly meant that many manuscripts with Old English literature in them disappeared simply due to neglect. The bulk of remaining Old English poetry survives in only five manuscripts. How many other great epics like *Beowulf* might have survived had the Norman Conquest not led to the neglect and the careless disposal of manuscripts containing Old English? How many small gems like such surviving poems as "The Battle of Maldon" or "The Wanderer" might have been available to modern scholars and students? Such sentiments are, of course, a matter of taste. *Beowulf* has an aesthetic that is alien to us, and some students reading this book who have worked their way through *Beowulf*, perhaps as an assigned reading, may wish the Normans had actively burned Old English manuscripts rather than simply neglecting them. Nonetheless, for those of us who love Old English literature, the Norman Conquest had its tragic cultural consequences.

The history of spoken English was naturally different from written English, since English remained the first language of the overwhelming majority of the population and never suffered any serious threat of being replaced by French.[67] Even by my calculations of immigration after the conquest, which are more generous than those of many historians, the Normans and their allies never constituted more than a small minority of the population in England.[68] Yet spoken English changed radically in the period following the Norman Conquest.[69] The question of determining the extent to which these changes resulted directly from the conquest remains a thorny one, however, since languages change constantly even without the impact of a conquest. The reason that so many words in English are spelled quite differently from how they are pronounced is that when they were first written, they sounded different. In words beginning with *kn*, such as knife, knight, or knee, the *k* was pronounced until the seventeenth century. The loss of the *kn* compound in spoken English resulted from ordinary linguistic change rather than from any political upheaval.[70] To what degree, then, was the Norman Conquest responsible for the massive changes that separated Old from Middle English?

Before addressing that question, I must indicate what some of those changes were. First, Old English was an inflected language, meaning that one could often tell the grammatical function of a noun or adjective by its ending. In the modern English sentence "The tall boy throws the ball to the short boy," we know that the tall boy is the subject, the ball is the direct object, and the short boy is the indirect object because of word order and the preposition *to*. In an inflected language, one would know this by word endings, and thus might rearrange the sentence and drop the preposition. Latin and German are examples of inflected languages, and anyone who has studied these languages knows what a difference inflection makes. In Latin, the word order of the sentence above might go something like "The tall boy the short boy the ball throws," with the reader using word endings to determine what is going on. Elements of the system survive in modern English with pronouns (*I* as subject, *me* as object) and with the use of an apostrophe and an *s* to indicate possessive ("the man's hat" being more common than "the hat of the man"). By and large, however, inflection disappeared during the later Middle Ages.

A second shift was the loss of gender. In Old English, as in most western European languages, nouns and related words are divided into masculine, feminine, and sometimes neuter categories. Thus, in Spanish, cup (*la taza*) is feminine but plate (*el plato*) is masculine, and any native English speaker who studies one of these languages must memorize the gender of each noun to become fluent. Linguistic gender has only a tenuous relation to biological gender; in modern German, *Mädchen*, or girl, is grammatically neuter, and in Old English, *wifmann*, or woman, was grammatically masculine.[71] Nonetheless, gender is crucial to knowledge of these languages. Happily for those of us who find gender a headache, this aspect of Old English went into the trash bin of linguistic history during the shift from Old to Middle English (of course, if it had remained part of the language, native English speakers would learn genders just as effortlessly as they learn other aspects of the language that nonnative learners find illogical and baffling).[72] Third, the shift to Middle English saw many sound changes in both vowels and consonants. Fourth, the shift brought extensive additions in vocabulary.

The Norman Conquest was certainly not the cause of all these transformations. Some of them began even before 1066. Moreover, a parallel loss of inflection (though not of gender) happened in the transition from Latin to many of the romance languages, including French and Spanish, without the impetus of any comparable conquest. Changes in language, as in literature, would have occurred even if Harold had won at Hastings. But William's successful conquest did make some differences. First, a standardized written language can slow down linguistic shifts. The postconquest loss of standardized written English, however, allowed changes in spoken English to advance unimpeded. The contact between a powerful French-speaking elite and the majority of native English speakers may also have led to certain simplifications in the latter language for ease of understanding. Finally, contact with the French language probably influenced some sound changes. Overall, however, the current consensus seems to be that French had a limited impact on English grammar and pronunciation.

One reason for this is that the elites seem to have picked up English within a few generations. For practical purposes, bilingualism, with varying amounts of fluency in the second language, must have become reasonably common fairly quickly in the upper reaches of society. By the late twelfth century, at least some members of the elite already had to learn French as a second language. The current consensus that French was a second language for most at that point is probably correct.[73] Nonetheless, French had a very long history as a second language in England, and this helped it to have a major impact on one aspect of the English language: vocabulary. Though French grammar had a relatively limited impact on English, in terms of vocabulary, every English speaker today actually speaks Franglais.

Until the fourteenth century, French remained the second language of writing after Latin, not only for literature but also for many government and business documents. Not until the early fifteenth century did French really disappear from frequent use in writing in England. French also continued to be spoken by many people as a second language for several centuries, and not just by aristocrats, but by priests, monks, nuns, townspeople, and lawyers. Indeed, French remained the language of some legal courts well past the Middle Ages, though the French spoken there would have been incomprehensible to most French speakers. Law French, as it was called, had long since evolved into a jargon-laden mishmash of French and English, as the following example will show. In 1631, a man in court picked up a piece of a brick and threw it at the justice who had just convicted him. Even the reader who has absolutely no knowledge of French can tell from the following "French" record of the event whether he hit the judge: "il ject un brickbat a le dit justice, que narrowly missed."[74] The approximately 350-year span in which French was much used by the elites in England, and the even longer span in which Law French was spoken in courts, gave French ample opportunity to influence English vocabulary.

These days, English vocabulary is spreading throughout the world, partly because so many people speak English as a second language. So powerful is this spread that the prestigious Académie Français has tried to make itself a bulwark against the flood of English and American words spilling into French, and the French government even established a law in 1994 to try to stem the onslaught of English and American vocabulary. In the Middle Ages, the flow went the other way as a result of the Norman Conquest. Between 1066 and 1485, some ten thousand French loanwords entered into English, of which about seven thousand survive in common English usage.[75] Ironically, at least one of the modern English loanwords offensive to French language purists first came from France. The term *fouaille*, originally meaning "firewood," came to England after the Norman Conquest, subsequently dropped out of French usage, transformed into *fuel* in English, and reentered France in that guise in modern times.[76] Whatever the ultimate impact of English on French vocabulary, the impact of French on English vocabulary has been remarkably strong. Consider the following paraphrase from the work of the Anglo-Norman specialist Ian Short, with words of Anglo-Norman origin in italics: "There is *scarcely* a *sentence* in current English that does not *indicate* the *profound* and *enduring* imprint from Anglo-Norman that has *remained* a *feature* of our *language* since the end of the twelfth century."[77] One of the glories of the English language is its unusually large vocabulary. Much of this vocabulary entered English in the later Middle Ages, but the influx of so many French words would never have happened without the Norman Conquest. As a result, we English speakers can scarcely open our mouths without unconsciously demonstrating the linguistic impact of William's successful conquest of England.

NOTES

1. For general overviews of the church in the Anglo-Norman period, see Frank Barlow, *The English Church, 1066–1154* (New York, 1979), and Martin Brett, *The English Church under Henry I* (London, 1975).

2. For this paragraph and the ones following, see Hugh M. Thomas, *The English and the Normans: Ethnic Hostility, Assimilation, and Identity, 1066–c. 1220* (Oxford, 2003), 200–235.

3. P. McGurk, ed., *The Chronicle of John of Worcester*, vol. 3 (Oxford, 1998), 12–13; Eadmer, *Historia Novorum in Anglia*, ed. Martin Rule (London, 1884), 191–92, 224.

4. Richard W. Southern, *Saint Anselm and His Biographer: A Study in Monastic Life and Thought, 1059–c. 1139* (Cambridge, 1963), 271–73.

5. Joseph Stevenson, ed., *Chronicon Monasterii de Abingdon* (London, 1858), 2:278.

6. Janet Fairweather, trans., *Liber Eliensis: A History of the Isle of Ely from the Seventh Century to the Twelfth* (Woodbridge, 2005), 102–3, 231.

7. Leslie Watkiss and Marjorie Chibnall, eds., *The Waltham Chronicle* (Oxford, 1994), 58–59.

8. Ann Williams, *The English and the Norman Conquest* (Woodbridge, 1995), 140–45.

9. Fairweather, *Liber Eliensis*, 251–53.

10. Andrew Ayton and Virginia Davis, "Ecclesiastical Wealth in England in 1086," in *The Church and Wealth*, ed. William J. Sheils and Diana Wood; Studies in Church History 24 (Oxford, 1987), 50.

11. Williams, *English and the Norman Conquest*, 141, 194.

12. Donald Matthew, *The Norman Monasteries and Their English Possessions* (London, 1962; reprint Westport, Ct., 1979), 13–14.

13. Emma Cownie, *Religious Patronage in Anglo-Norman England, 1066–1135* (Woodbridge, 1998), 185–201.

14. Janet Burton, *Monastic and Religious Orders in Britain, 1000–1300* (Cambridge, 1994), 31–33.

15. See Antonia Gransden, "Traditionalism and Continuity during the Last Century of Anglo-Saxon Monasticism," *Journal of Ecclesiastical History* 40 (1989), 159–207, which includes a discussion of some of the ways in which postconquest writers schematized the process of monastic reform and change. For the contemporary view that God was punishing the English, see Thomas, *English and the Normans*, 243–44.

16. Barlow, *English Church*, 54–75, 122–29, 177–93; R. Allen Brown, *The Normans and the Norman Conquest* (New York, 1968), 101–6, 253–60; Burton, *Monastic and Religious Orders*, 7–42; David C. Douglas, *William the Conqueror: The Norman Impact upon England* (Berkeley, 1964), 317–45.

17. There has been much work on this reform movement but no good recent overview. The best place to start is Catherine Cubitt, "Review Article: The Tenth-Century Benedictine Reform in England," *Early Medieval Europe* 6 (1997), 77–94.

18. Uta-Renate Blumenthal, *The Investiture Controversy: Church and Monarchy from the Ninth to the Twelfth Century* (Philadelphia, 1988); Colin Morris, *The Papal Monarchy: The Western Church from 1050 to 1250* (Oxford, 1989), 11–173.

19. David C. Douglas and George W. Greenaway, eds., *English Historical Documents*, 2nd ed. (London, 1981), 2:692–94.

20. Barlow, *English Church*, 86–90.

21. William of Poitiers, *Gesta Guillelmi*, ed. R. H. C. Davis and Marjorie Chibnall (Oxford, 1998), 104–5.

22. H. E. J. Cowdrey, *Lanfranc: Scholar, Monk, and Archbishop* (Oxford, 2003), 78–225.

23. Watkiss and Chibnall, *Waltham Chronicle*, 28–29.

24. Richard W. Southern, *Saint Anselm: A Portrait in a Landscape* (Cambridge, 1990), 277–307.

25. Cowdrey, *Lanfranc*, 87–103, 197–205.

26. For an overview of the struggle during the Norman period, see Barlow, *English Church*, 39–44.

27. Douglas and Greenaway, *English Historical Documents*, 2:647–48.

28. Christopher Brooke, "The Archdeacon and the Norman Conquest," in *Tradition and Change: Essays in Honour of Marjorie Chibnall*, ed. Diana Greenway, Christopher Holdsworth, and Jane Sayers (Cambridge, 1985), 1–19.

29. Barlow, *English Church*, 47–48; Burton, *Monastic and Religious Orders*, 28–29.

30. Burton, *Monastic and Religious Orders*, 36–37.

31. William Dunn MacRay, ed., *Chronicon Abbatiae de Evesham* (London, 1863), appendix 1, 323–24, 335–37.

32. See chapter 4, n. 60.

33. I discuss this issue in my article, "Lay Piety in England from 1066 to 1215," *Anglo-Norman Studies* 29 (2007), 179–92.

34. Samuel J. Crawford, ed., *The Old English Version of the Heptateuch* (Oxford, 1922; reprinted 1969), 76–80.

35. Bruce Dickens and Richard M. Wilson, eds., *Early Middle English Texts* (New York, 1951), 1–2.

36. Cowdrey, *Lanfranc*, 46–74; Southern, *Saint Anselm: A Portrait*, 91–137, 197–227.

37. Rodney M. Thomson, "The Norman Conquest and English Libraries," in *The Role of the Book in Medieval Culture*, vol. 2, ed. Peter Ganz (Turnhout, 1986), 27–40.

38. William of Malmesbury, *The Deeds of the Bishops of England*, trans. David Preest (Woodbridge, 2002), 122. For the growth of the library at Salisbury, see Teresa Webber, *Scribes and Scholars at Salisbury Cathedral, c. 1075–c. 1125* (Oxford, 1992).

39. Richard W. Southern, "Aspects of the European Tradition of Historical Writing: 4. The Sense of the Past," *Transactions of the Royal Historical Society*, 5th ser., 23 (1973), 243–63; Williams, *English and the Norman Conquest*, 155–86.

40. Rodney Thomson, "England and the Twelfth-Century Renaissance," *Past and Present* 101 (1983), 3–21.

41. William of Poitiers, *Gesta Guillelmi*, 176–77.

42. Charles R. Dodwell, *The Pictorial Arts of the West* (New Haven, 1993), 191–93.

43. David Bates, *Regesta Regum Anglo-Normannorum: The Acta of William I (1066–1087)* (Oxford, 1998), 296.

44. For overviews of English art in the period, see Dodwell, *Pictorial Arts*, 120–22, 321–73; Thomas S. R. Boase, *English Art: 1100–1216* (Oxford, 1953); Claus M. Kauffmann, *Romanesque Manuscripts, 1066–1190* (London, 1975); George Zarnecki, *English Romanesque Sculpture, 1066–1140* (London, 1951); George Zarnecki, Janet Holt, and Tristram Holland, *English Romanesque Art, 1066–1200* (London, 1984); Christopher Daniell, *From Norman Conquest to Magna Carta: England, 1066–1215* (London, 2003), 200–216. For works which focus on the impact of the conquest, see Richard Gameson, "English Manuscript Art in the Late Eleventh Century: Canterbury and Its Context," in *Canterbury and the Norman Conquest: Churches, Saints and Scholars, 1066–1109*, ed. Richard Eales and Richard Sharpe, 95–144 (London, 1995); George Zarnecki, "1066 and Architectural Sculpture," in *Studies in Romanesque Sculpture*, 173–84 (London, 1979).

45. Alfred W. Clapham, *English Romanesque Architecture after the Conquest* (Oxford, 1934), 1–50; Eric Fernie, *The Architecture of Norman England* (Oxford, 2000). For the impact of the Norman Conquest on Architecture, see Eric Fernie, "The Effect of the Conquest on Norman Architectural Patronage," *Anglo-Norman Studies* 9 (1987), 71–85, and "Architecture and the Effects of the Norman Conquest," in *England and Normandy in the Middle Ages*, ed. David Bates and Anne Curry (London, 1994), 105–16.

46. Fernie, *Architecture of Norman England*, 24.

47. Richard Gem, "A Recession in English Architecture during the Early Eleventh Century and its Effect on the Development of the Romanesque Style," *The Journal of the British Archaeological Association*, 3rd ser., 38 (1975), 28–49.

48. Fernie, *Architecture of Norman England*, 299.

49. James C. Holt, *Colonial England, 1066–1215* (London, 1997), 6.

50. Fernie, "Architecture and the Effects," 106; Charles R. Dodwell, *Anglo-Saxon Art: A New Perspective* (Ithaca, 1982), 234.

51. William of Malmesbury, *Gesta Regum Anglorum*, ed. Roger A. B. Mynors, Rodney M. Thomson, and Michael Winterbottom (Oxford, 1998), 1:460–61; William of Malmesbury, *Deeds of the Bishops*, 98.

52. For the way in which some new churches may even have been designed to incorporate traditional liturgy, see Arnold Klukas, "The Continuity of Anglo-Saxon Liturgical Traditions as Evident in the Architecture of Winchester, Ely and Canterbury Cathedrals," in *Les mutations socio-culturelles au tournant des XIe-XIIe siècles: Études Anselmiennes* (Paris, 1984), 111–23.

53. Fernie, *Architecture of Norman England*, 20, 34, 208–9; Lisa A. Reilly, "The Emergence of Anglo-Norman Architecture: Durham Cathedral," *Anglo-Norman Studies* 19 (1997), 335–51; Lisa A. Reilly, *An Architectural History of Peterborough Cathedral* (Oxford, 1997), 41–42, 77, 85–86, 126.

54. Orderic Vitalis, *The Ecclesiastical History of Orderic Vitalis*, ed. Marjorie Chibnall (Oxford, 1969–1980), 2:256–57.

55. Thomas, *English and the Normans*, 256.

56. Cecily Clark, ed., *The Peterborough Chronicle, 1070–1154* (Oxford, 1958), xlix–lxvi.

57. See in particular the articles in Mary Swan and Elaine M. Treharne, eds., *Rewriting Old English in the Twelfth Century* (Cambridge, 2000).

58. For early Middle English, see Richard M. Wilson, *Early Middle English Literature*, 3rd ed. (London, 1968).

59. For the rise of writing in general, see Michael T. Clanchy, *From Memory to Written Record: England, 1066–1307*, 2nd ed. (Oxford, 1993).

60. Donald G. Scragg, *A History of English Spelling* (New York, 1974), 15–21. See n. 69 for grammatical change.

61. Michael Swanton, *Three Lives of the Last Englishmen* (New York, 1984), 45. The source may be fictional, but the writer clearly thought that difficulties reading eleventh-century English would be believable.

62. Christine Franzen, *The Tremulous Hand of Worcester: A Study of Old English in the Thirteenth Century* (Oxford, 1991), 94–95, 101–2, 173–82.

63. See Thomas, *English and the Normans*, 379–80, and the works cited there.

64. M. Dominica Legge, *Anglo-Norman Literature and Its Background* (Oxford, 1963); Ian Short, "Patrons and Polyglots: French Literature in Twelfth-Century England," *Anglo-Norman Studies* 14 (1992), 229–49; Susan Crane, "Anglo-Norman Cultures in England, 1066–1460," in *The Cambridge History of Medieval English Literature*, ed. David Wallace (Cambridge, 1999), 35–60; A. G. Rigg, *A History of Anglo-Latin Literature, 1066–1422* (Cambridge, 1992), 9–156.

65. Short, "Patrons and Polyglots," 229; David R. Howlett, *The English Origins of Old French Literature* (Dublin, 1996), 162.

66. Elizabeth Salter, *English and International: Studies in Literature, Art, and Patronage of Medieval England*, ed. Derek Pearsall and Nicolette Zeeman, 1–100 (Cambridge, 1988); Derek Pearsall, *Old English and Middle English Poetry* (London, 1977), 85–102; Susan Crane, *Insular Romance: Politics, Faith, and Culture in Anglo-Norman and Middle English Literature* (Berkeley, 1986).

67. Useful discussions of the relative roles of French and English are William Rothwell, "The Role of French in Thirteenth-Century England," *Bulletin of the John Rylands Society* 58 (1976), 445–66; Ian Short, "On Bilingualism in Anglo-Norman England," *Romance Philology* 33 (1980), 467–79; Richard M. Wilson, "English and French in England, 1100–1300," *History* 28 (1943), 37–60; M. Dominica Legge, "Anglo-Norman as a Spoken Language," *Proceedings of the Battle Conference on Anglo-Norman Studies* 2 (1980), 108–17, 188–90.

68. Thomas, *English and the Normans*, 162–65.

69. Georges Bourcier, *An Introduction to the History of the English Language*, trans. Cecily Clark (Cheltenham, 1981), 40–41, 119–59; Barbara A. Fennell, *A History of English: A Sociolinguistic Approach* (Oxford, 2001), 94–134.

70. Fennell, *History of English*, 139.

71. Fennell, *History of English*, 64.

72. For instance, to people whose languages lack articles, the distinctions between the proper use of *the* and *a* are as trivial as they are confusing and annoying.

73. For bilingualism, see particularly Short, "On Bilingualism," 467–79; Short, "Patrons and Polyglots," 245–49.

74. M. Dominica Legge, "Anglo-Norman and the Historian," *History* 26 (1941), 163.

75. Bourcier, *Introduction*, 40.

76. William Rothwell, "Anglo-French Lexical Contacts, Old and New," *Modern Language Review* 74 (1979), 296.

77. Ian Short, "Language and Literature," in *A Companion to the Anglo-Norman World*, ed. Christopher Harper-Bill and Elisabeth van Houts (Woodbridge, 2003), 213.

CONCLUSION: THE IMPACT OF
THE NORMAN CONQUEST

The Norman Conquest was far from inevitable. Had William died in one of his many earlier campaigns or at Hastings, it surely would not have happened. Had Edward the Confessor successfully exiled Earl Godwine's family, Harold Godwineson would never have become king. What would have happened then? What if Harald Hardrada had chosen not to invade? What if Harold had won at Hastings? Above all, as I have stressed, William might simply have decided that the risk was not worth taking. The Norman Conquest occurred and succeeded because of the decisions and calculations of a few powerful people, mainly men, and because of successes and failures in the field of war. To what extent did the powerful men and the battles of the Norman Conquest alter English society and change English history? The answer is, "It depends." It depends on what aspects of English society and English history one is discussing, for one gets a variety of answers for various facets of society and history.

The varying outcome depended partly on choices, mainly the choices of the victors. William and his followers could have completely reorganized English government, but they chose not to. They could have conceivably changed the landholding structure to a greater extent than they did, creating more of the blocks of estates common on the continent, but they did not do so. Choice, however, was only one factor. It is a fairly safe bet that William and his followers did not have increasing the vocabulary of the English language as one of their key goals when they prepared to cross the English Channel. The conquest set in motion changes that the conquerors did not care about and in some cases could not have foreseen. At the same time, their choices were also limited. The Normans did not have the institutional structures and technological and economic base to make the kinds of changes European colonialists so often did in the early modern and modern periods (and it is worth noting that European colonialists were often frustrated in many of their aims by local resistance, their own incompetence and miscalculations, or simple insufficiency of means). The Normans succeeded so well in the changes they sought partly because they sought only limited changes.

Nonetheless, the Normans intentionally or unintentionally brought a substantial transformation to English society. The introduction of castles and mounted warfare, along with the decline in emphasis upon naval warfare, markedly affected the nature of combat in England and therefore in Britain and Ireland for some time to come. The new system of military quotas on tenants-in-chief had social consequences for many decades and fiscal consequences for many centuries. Though the Normans sought to maintain the "Law of Edward," they ended up undermining it and thereby opened the way for a new legal system, the English common law, which is the basis for modern law in Britain and many former British colonies, including the United States. The Normans also shifted England's place in geopolitics, especially by tying England so closely to France, a shift with ramifications throughout the Middles Ages and beyond.

The Norman Conquest had a good deal of influence beyond the concerns of the elites. Most important, the Normans reshuffled the divisions within peasant status, particularly by speeding up the end of slavery and, indirectly, by helping to set a new line between free and unfree with the defining of serfdom in the common law. They introduced into medieval England a Jewish minority that endured for some two centuries. They hastened religious and intellectual reforms while retarding the use of English writing for religious purposes. They created an architectural revolution while suffocating a rich tradition of English literature. They introduced French into England, which reshaped the subsequent history of English literature and altered and enhanced the English language. In short, the Norman Conquest did far more than replace one elite with another.

Nonetheless, there were also many key aspects of English society that the Normans left virtually untouched. Despite the drastic short-term economic impact of the conquest, the long-term influence was negligible. Outside of the military arena, the Norman Conquest brought little or no technological change. The Normans had no wish to bring fundamental religious change, and so they mainly accelerated or decelerated changes that would have taken place anyway. Likewise, the Norman impact on political structures was surprisingly limited.

Moreover, though William was the individual most crucial to the Norman Conquest, he clearly could not have accomplished it without thousands of soldiers, many of them nobles but many others commoners. This is an obvious point, but it is a reminder that one must look beyond military leadership, even for an understanding of conquest. Similarly, the changes brought by the Norman Conquest were not the work of one man alone, or even of the elites. English law changed not because William or anyone else decreed major transformations but because the legal consequences of the conquest and the interactions between Norman and English law worked themselves out in countless legal discussions and disputes in the generations after 1066. The elites may have had the upper hand in most of these discussions, but most levels of society were involved in some way with legal change. Similarly, French came to have so much influence on the English language not just because the Normans brought it to England but also because so many English speakers at all levels of society slowly began adopting useful or prestigious French words into their language over the course of some three or four centuries.

A "great man" approach to the history of the Norman Conquest and its impact obviously has limitations. To say this to an audience of professional historians would be akin to beating a dead horse, though pointing out the limitations to a more general audience is probably a more useful exercise. The same goes for an approach that focuses solely on military history. However, a study of the Norman Conquest shows that battles and unusual individuals can have a profound impact on history. Old-fashioned approaches to history cannot be ignored simply because they are old-fashioned. Fortunately, though individual historians generally have to specialize, historians as a group do not have to choose one approach or one method at the expense of all others. Indeed, the complexity of historical change can be grasped only if historians adopt various approaches and methods. Therefore, we can profitably revisit traditional historical topics (and few are more traditional than the impact of the Norman Conquest), while we simultaneously look at historical change in new and innovative ways. Study of the Norman Conquest may not explain everything about English history, even in the period immediately following 1066, but it can certainly explain a lot.

TIMELINE

871–899	Alfred the Great is king
899–924	Edward the Elder is king
919	Edward seizes Mercia from his niece
925–939	Athelstan is king
978	Æthelræd Unræd becomes ruler after the murder of his brother
1002	Æthelræd Unræd marries Emma of Normandy
1013–1014	King Swein of Denmark drives Æthelræd Unræd from England, but dies shortly thereafter, allowing Æthelræd to return
1016	Canute takes control of England after the deaths of Æthelræd Unræd and Edmund Ironside
1017	Canute marries Emma of Normandy
1028	Canute takes control of Norway
1030	King Olaf is killed trying to recover Norway
c. 1034	Magnus, son of Olaf, drives Canute's forces from Norway
1035	Canute dies; Duke Robert of Normandy dies on pilgrimage to Jerusalem
1036	Alfred, son of Æthelræd Unræd and Emma, travels to England, where he is betrayed by Earl Godwine and killed by Harold Harefoot
1037	After much jockeying for power, Harold I Harefoot becomes king
1040	Harold Harefoot dies, and Harthacanute becomes king

1042	Harthacanute dies, and Edward the Confessor becomes king
1045	Edward the Confessor marries Edith, daughter of Godwine and Gytha
1051	Edward the Confessor drives Godwine and his family into exile; Queen Edith is sent to a nunnery
1052	Godwine and his family return to England and reclaim their former position
1053	Earl Godwine dies and is succeeded in Wessex by his son Harold
1065	Revolt against Tosti
1066	
January 4 or 5	King Edward dies
January 6	Harold is crowned king
late spring	Tosti raids England but is defeated by Edwin and Morcar
September 8	Harold disbands the forces defending the southern coast
September 20	Harald Hardrada and Tosti defeat the forces of Edwin and Morcar at Fulford, outside of York
September 25	Harold Godwineson defeats Harald Hardrada and Tosti at the Battle of Stamford Bridge
September 27–28	William the Conqueror's fleet crosses overnight to England
October 14	Battle of Hastings
December 25	William is crowned king at Westminster
1067	William returns to Normandy; Count Eustace and English rebels fail to seize Dover; Eadric the Wild rises in rebellion
1068	William suppresses a revolt at Exeter; King Harold's sons make their first attack; Edwin and Morcar revolt for a short time; the northern revolt begins; William leads his first campaign in the north
1069	Rebels in the north defeat two Norman contingents; Harold's sons invade again and are defeated; a Danish fleet arrives and begins raiding; William marches north twice

1069–1070	In a decisive campaign, William defeats the main rebellions and devastates large sections of northern and northeastern England
1070	The Danes eventually return home; rebellion around Ely occurs
1071	Edwin and Morcar rebel and are crushed; William captures Ely
1073	William reestablishes control of Maine with English support
1075	Waltheof is implicated in a rebellion with two other earls
1076	Waltheof is executed
1085	Domesday survey is commissioned
1086	Information is gathered for *Domesday Book*
1087	William dies; Robert Curthose succeeds in Normandy and William II Rufus succeeds in England
1096	Robert Curthose mortgages Normandy to William Rufus and departs on the First Crusade
1100	William Rufus dies; Henry I seizes England and Robert Curthose recovers Normandy
1106	Henry I captures Robert Curthose and takes control of Normandy
1120	Henry I's son, William, dies in a shipwreck
1135	Henry I dies; Stephen seizes England and Normandy
1139	Matilda arrives in England; civil war begins there in earnest
1153	Peace is made between Stephen and the future Henry II
1154	Stephen dies and Henry II succeeds

INDIVIDUALS MENTIONED
IN THE TEXT

Individuals are listed alphabetically by their first names.

Aegelric. Anglo-Saxon bishop, deposed after the Norman Conquest, who was known for his expertise in the law and who testified in a case between Archbishop Lanfranc and Bishop Odo of Baycux.

Aelfric. Abbot of Eynsham from 1005 to his death at an unknown date. One of the key intellectuals and authors of the late Anglo-Saxon reform movement.

Æthelflæd. Daughter of Alfred the Great. Along with her brother, Edward the Elder, she began the unification of England by capturing areas that had been seized by the Vikings.

Æthelræd Unræd. King of England (978–1016) and father of Edward the Confessor. During his reign, England suffered from a second wave of Viking invasions that culminated in the conquest of England by Canute.

Æthelthryth. Anglo-Saxon queen who embraced the religious life in the seventh century and founded the nunnery of Ely. After the nunnery disappeared during the Viking invasions, it was refounded as a monastery in the tenth century, but Æthelthryth remained its patron saint.

Ailred of Rievaulx. Important monk and abbot of native English descent in the middle of the twelfth century. He was most important for his religious writings but also wrote several historical works.

Alfred. Son of Æthelræd Unræd and Emma and brother of Edward the Confessor. He was betrayed by Earl Godwine and killed by Harold Harefoot in 1036.

Alfred the Great. King of Wessex (871–899) and ancestor of Edward the Confessor. Alfred the Great defended Wessex against the Vikings and paved the way for the unification of England.

Anselm. Burgundian scholar who became abbot of Bec in Normandy and archbishop of Canterbury in 1093. He was a leading intellectual of the Middle Ages.

Athelstan. Son of Edward the Elder and King of Wessex (925–939). He began the process of incorporating into the country much of what is now northern England.

Augustine of Canterbury. Missionary sent by Pope Gregory the Great to convert England at the end of the sixth century. He founded the archbishopric of Canterbury.

Augustine of Hippo. Greatest western theologian of the late Roman period.

Bede. One of the greatest historians of the early medieval period and the most important source for information on the early Germanic kingdoms in England.

Beorn. Son of Estrith, sister of Canute, and of Ulf, brother of Countess Gytha. Earl Beorn was murdered by his cousin, Earl Swein, in 1049.

Canute. Son of King Swein of Denmark. Canute was king of England and Denmark.

David. King of Scotland, youngest son of King Malcolm, and a close ally of Henry I. During Stephen's reign, David seized a large part of northern England. He died in 1153.

Eadnoth the Staller. Powerful English noble who supported William and died fighting Harold's sons in 1068. His son Harding became a minor noble, and one of Harding's younger sons founded a powerful noble family, the Berkeleys.

Eadric the Wild. Powerful English noble who led an early revolt against William in alliance with the Welsh.

Ealdred of York. Bishop of Worcester from 1046 to 1062 and archbishop of York from 1061 to 1069. Like many earlier archbishops of York, including one key reformer, Ealdred tried to retain the bishopric of Worcester but was prevented from doing so by the pope. He crowned William in 1066 since Archbishop Stigand of Canterbury suffered from papal displeasure.

Edgar Atheling. Grandson of Edmund Ironside and great-nephew of Edward the Confessor. Although he had the best claim to the throne in 1066 in terms of descent, Edgar was passed over for Harold. Despite playing an important role in the early resistance to William the Conqueror, Edgar eventually made his peace with the new ruling family and died in obscurity in England during the reign of Henry I.

Edith. Daughter of Earl Godwine and Gytha. She became queen as wife of Edward the Confessor in 1045. She survived the conquest and held an honorable position as Edward's widow until her death in 1075.

Edith. Sister of Earls Edwin and Morcar and wife of Harold II Godwineson.

Edith. See Matilda II.

Edith Swansneck. Mistress or unofficial wife of Harold II Godwineson and mother of his older sons.

Edmund Ironside. Son of Æthelræd Unræd and grandfather of Edgar Atheling. After his father died in 1016, Edmund fought Canute to a standstill and split the country with him, but died shortly thereafter.

Edward the Confessor. Last king of the West Saxon line (1042–1066). He was succeeded by his brother-in-law, Harold Godwineson.

Edward the Elder. Son and heir of Alfred the Great and king of Wessex (925–939). Along with his sister Æthelflæd, Edward the Elder began the unification of England by capturing areas that had been seized by the Vikings.

Edward I. King of England from 1272 to 1307. Edward I expelled the Jews from England, completed the English conquest of Wales, and embroiled England in a disastrous war with Scotland.

Edwin. Earl of Mercia, grandson of Earl Leofric and Godgifu, and brother-in-law of Harold Godwineson. Edwin rebelled in 1068 and 1071 and was killed by his own men in 1071.

Eleanor. Wife of Henry II and heiress of Poitou and Aquitaine.

Emma of Normandy. Daughter of Duke Richard I of Normandy; wife of Æthelræd Unræd and then Canute; and mother of Edward the Confessor, Alfred, and Harthacanute.

Eustace of Boulogne. Ruler of a small region near Normandy. Eustace joined William's invasion and fought in the Battle of Hastings. In 1067, he tried to seize Dover from William in alliance with the local English. Later he became reconciled with William and received extensive lands in England from him.

Geoffrey. Count of Anjou from 1129 to 1151 who married Matilda, daughter of Henry I. While she sought to recover England from Stephen, Geoffrey conquered Normandy, which along with Anjou passed to his son Henry II when he died.

Geoffrey Martel. Count of Anjou. Geoffrey Martel was a powerful rival of William the Conqueror who died in 1060.

Geoffrey of Monmouth. Author of the *History of the Kings of the Britons*, which purported to tell the story of the British people from the arrival of their fictional Trojan founder, Brutus, to the Germanic invasions of Britain. His work popularized the figure of King Arthur.

Gilbert of Brionne. Norman nobleman and guardian of William the Conqueror who was killed during William's minority.

Godgifu. Daughter of King Æthelræd and mother of Earl Ralph the Timid.

Godgifu. Wife of Earl Leofric of Mercia and grandmother of Earls Edwin and Morcar. She was the historical original of the legendary Lady Godiva.

Godwine, son of Wulfnoth. Powerful thane in the time of Æthelræd Unræd. Godwine became earl of Wessex under Canute and married Gytha, Canute's relative by marriage. He was the father of King Harold; Queen Edith; and Earls Swein, Tosti, Gyrth, and Leofric. Earl Godwine died in 1053.

Godwines, or **Godwinesons**. The family of Earl Godwine.

Goscelin of St. Bertin. Flemish monk who immigrated to England and wrote many saints' biographies in the late eleventh century.

Gyrth. Younger brother of Harold Godwineson. Earl Gyrth died at Hastings.

Gytha. Sister-in-law of Canute's sister Estrith and wife of Earl Godwine. She was the mother of King Harold; Queen Edith; and Earls Swein, Tosti, Gyrth, and Leofric.

Harald Hardrada. King of Norway who invaded England in 1066 and was defeated by Harold Godwineson at Stamford Bridge, where he died.

Harold Godwineson. Son of Godwine and Gytha, earl of Wessex from 1053 to 1066, and king of England in 1066. Harold died at Hastings.

Harold I Harefoot. Son of Canute and Ælfgifu of Northampton. He was formally crowned in 1037 and ruled England until 1040.

Harold, son of Earl Ralph the Timid. Great-nephew of Edward the Confessor but never treated as a serious candidate to the throne. He became a minor baron after the Norman Conquest.

Harthacanute. Son of Canute and Emma of Normandy and king of England from 1040 to 1042. He was succeeded by his half brother, Edward the Confessor, whom he had brought back to England from Normandy.

Henry. King of France. Henry was an early supporter and later bitter enemy of William the Conqueror. He died in 1060.

Henry I. Youngest son of William the Conqueror. After his brother William II died in 1100, Henry seized control of England. He later took over

Normandy from his brother Robert, whom he captured in 1106. He died in 1135.

Henry II. King of England from 1154 to 1189. He was the son of Empress Matilda and grandson of Henry I.

Henry III. King of England from 1216 to 1272.

Hereward the Wake. A minor English thane who led an uprising in eastern England from 1070 to 1071.

Humphrey de Vieilles. Powerful Norman noble in the time of William the Conqueror's father, Duke Robert.

John. King of England from 1199 to 1216. During John's reign, the king of France conquered most of the French territories held by the king of England. John was also the king forced to issue the Magna Carta when many of his barons rebelled.

Lanfranc. Italian scholar who became abbot of Caen in Normandy and archbishop of Canterbury in 1070. He was a leading intellectual and reformer.

Leofric. Earl of Mercia, husband of Godgifu, and grandfather of Earls Edwin and Morcar.

Leofwine. Younger brother of Harold Godwineson. Earl Leofwine died at Hastings.

Malcolm III Canmore. King of Scotland who overthrew Macbeth in 1054 with the help of Earl Siward. He died in northern England in 1093 in a Norman ambush.

Matilda I of Flanders. Wife of William the Conqueror and daughter of the count of Flanders. She was crowned queen of England in 1068 and died in 1083.

Matilda II. Originally named Edith. Daughter of King Malcolm of Scotland and niece of Edgar Atheling, Matilda became queen when she married Henry I. She was the mother of William Atheling and Empress Matilda and died in 1118.

Matilda III. Daughter of Henry I and Edith-Matilda (Matilda II). Matilda III was married first to Emperor Henry V (for which reason she was often called empress) and second to Geoffrey of Anjou. She spent much of Stephen's reign locked in civil war with him but passed her claim to her son Henry II, who succeeded to the English throne when Stephen died.

Mauger. Archbishop of Rouen and uncle of William the Conqueror. William deprived him of his office.

Morcar. Grandson of Earl Leofric and Godgifu and brother-in-law of Harold Godwineson. He became earl of Northumbria after rebels drove

Tosti out. Earl Morcar rebelled in 1068 and 1071, and he remained imprisoned after 1071 except for a brief time in 1087.

Odo. Bishop of Bayeux, half brother of William the Conqueror, and a leading supporter until William broke with him and broke his power in 1082.

Orderic Vitalis. Important twelfth-century historian. His father was French but his mother was almost certainly English. Orderic grew up in England until the age of ten, when his father sent him to become a monk in a Norman monastery.

Osbern. William the Conqueror's steward, murdered during William's minority.

Osmund. Bishop of Salisbury from 1078 to 1099. He was later canonized as a saint.

Ralph the Timid. Earl of Hereford. Ralph was the son of the count of Mantes and of Godgifu, daughter of Æthelræd Unræd and sister of Edward the Confessor.

Regenbald. Immigrant cleric who played an important role in Edward the Confessor's government and continued to serve under William I.

Robert. Duke of Normandy from 1027 to 1035. He was the father of William the Conqueror and nephew of Queen Emma.

Robert Curthose. Eldest son of William the Conqueror. He was in rebellion when his father died and succeeded to Normandy but not to England. Robert participated in the First Crusade. He was captured by his brother Henry in 1106 and imprisoned until his death in 1134.

Robert of Mortain. Half brother of William the Conqueror and a leading supporter. He was count of Mortain.

Roger of Montgomery. Powerful Norman noble and leading follower of William the Conqueror.

Siward. Earl of Northumbria and father of Earl Waltheof. He helped Malcolm of Scotland defeat Macbeth in 1054 and died in 1055.

Stephen. King of England, 1135–1154. He was the younger son of Count Stephen of Blois and of Countess Adela, daughter of William the Conqueror. He was a favorite of his uncle, Henry I, and seized England and Normandy after Henry died. Thereafter, he spent much of his reign in a civil war with Henry's daughter, Matilda. Stephen died in 1154.

Stephen Langton. Archbishop of Canterbury from 1206 to 1228. He was an influential intellectual and reformer appointed by the pope against the wishes of King John.

Stigand. Archbishop of York and bishop of Winchester. The most powerful figure in the English church in 1066, he was condemned by the papacy for holding two bishoprics and supporting an antipope. He submitted to William after Hastings, but William deposed him in 1070.

Swein. Eldest son of Godwine and Gytha. Earl Swein died in 1052.

Swein I Forkbeard. King of Denmark. He temporarily drove Æthelræd Unræd from England and died in 1014.

Tosti. Son of Godwine and Gytha who married Judith, a member of the ruling family of Flanders. He was earl of Northumbria until he was driven out by a rebellion in 1065. In 1066 Tosti unsuccessfully attacked England and then went to the court of Harald Hardrada. After he returned with Harald to England, Tosti was killed at the Battle of Stamford Bridge.

Turold. Guardian of William the Conqueror who was killed during William's minority.

Waltheof. Son of Earl Siward. Despite participating in the rebellions after 1066, Earl Waltheof married Judith, a relative of King William, and prospered until 1075, when he was implicated in another revolt. He was executed in 1076.

William of Arques. Uncle of William the Conqueror, who drove him from power.

William Atheling. Only legitimate son of Henry I. He died in a shipwreck in 1120.

William of Malmesbury. An important twelfth-century historian who was of mixed English and Norman background.

William of Montgomery. Norman nobleman. He killed William the Conqueror's steward, Osbern, and was killed in turn by Osbern's followers.

William of Norwich. A young Christian boy who disappeared around the time of Passover in 1144. His death was blamed on Jews, which sparked the widespread medieval view that Jews sacrificed innocents.

William of Poitiers. Norman churchman who was trained at Poitiers and writer of William the Conqueror's biography.

William of Warenne. One of William the Conqueror's chief followers, who became one of the six richest landholders in England after the Norman Conquest. He founded a religious house at Lewes with monks from Cluny before 1077.

William II Rufus. Succeeded his father, William I, in England in 1087. He died in a hunting accident in 1100.

William, son of Osbern. Powerful Norman noble and leading follower of William the Conqueror.

William the Conqueror. Duke of Normandy and conqueror of England in 1066.

Woden. Anglo-Saxon god who was equivalent to the Norse Odin.

Wulfnoth. Father of Earl Godwine and grandfather of King Harold.

GLOSSARY

alliteration. A poetic technique in which words are connected through having the same initial sound. Anglo-Saxon poetry, and some Middle English poetry, was constructed around alliteration in much the same way that most later English poetry came to be constructed around end rhymes.

Angli. One of the Germanic peoples who invaded Britain after the Romans withdrew their troops. The term *English* comes from the Angli.

archdeacon. A church official under the bishop who carried out some of the bishop's tasks, especially in the judicial sphere. Archdeaconries came to be territorial subdivisions of a bishopric, each run by a single archdeacon.

Bayeux Tapestry. Technically, a piece of embroidery rather than a woven tapestry. Almost certainly commissioned by Odo of Bayeux, it depicts Harold's trip to Normandy, the Norman expedition to England, and the Battle of Hastings.

blood feud. A system, somewhat formalized in Anglo-Saxon law, in which relatives and friends avenged those who were murdered or injured.

carucate. See *hide*.

chivalry. A code of behavior and a set of practices idealized by nobles of the central and late Middle Ages.

Cluny. One of the largest and most influential monasteries of the central Middle Ages. Cluny was noted for the elaborateness of its daily round of worship services.

common law. The law, common to all of England, that began emerging under royal guidance in the twelfth century.

danegeld. Originally money paid to buy off Danish Vikings, it became a regular tax in the late Anglo-Saxon period.

demesne. The part of the manor held directly by a lord and farmed by slaves, through the labor rents of peasants or by paid labor. The term can also refer to those parts of an honor that lords did not grant out to their followers.

Domesday Book. The written version of a survey commissioned by William the Conqueror in 1085 and largely carried out in 1086.

earl. The highest noble in English society. After the Norman Conquest, earls came to be considered equivalent to counts in France.

enfeoffment. The granting of a fief.

exchequer. The accounting office founded under Henry I. It was based on a form of the abacus.

fief. Land granted in return for service, generally of a military nature.

forest law. Laws originally intended to preserve wild animals and their habitat for royal hunting. These laws came to cover many areas that were not forest in the modern sense, and the related fines became an important source of royal revenue.

heraldry. The practice of assigning coats of arms, a type of symbolic design, to individual noble families.

hide. An administrative unit of land used for allotting taxation and for other purposes, nominally equivalent to 120 acres of farmland with attached pastureland, meadow, and woodland. In some parts of the country the term *carucate* was used instead.

honor. The estates granted to a powerful noble, including both the manors the lord kept in his own possession and those he granted out to followers.

hundred. An administrative subdivision of a county or shire.

Magna Carta. The "great charter" that rebelling barons forced King John to issue in 1215. It was a significant document in the history of medieval English political development.

motte–and–bailey castle. A castle consisting of two main elements. The motte was a large mound of dirt topped by a tower, usually made of wood. A bailey was a large courtyard below, protected by fences and ditches.

murdrum. A fine introduced by Canute and revived by William the Conqueror to protect foreigners. Under William, if a Norman or other French follower was found dead, the surrounding villages would be fined heavily unless the murderer was captured or revealed. Started as a tactic against guerrilla warfare, the murdrum fine soon became an important source of royal revenue.

Normanitas. Norman identity.

numismatics. The study of coinage.

ordeals. A variety of judicial and religious processes in which the determination of guilt or innocence was theoretically left to God.

ploughland. A fairly mysterious measurement of land in *Domesday Book*, perhaps intended for a new tax assessment.

primogeniture. Inheritance system in which lands automatically passed to the oldest son of the previous owner upon the death of the latter.

Romano-British. The inhabitants of Roman Britain and their descendants after the withdrawal of Roman troops.

Rus. Vikings who established a loosely united set of city-states in parts of what is now the Ukraine and Russia. Our term *Russian* comes from them.

scutage. Monetary payments made by knights and lords in place of military service.

serf. An unfree peasant. Serfs were generally different from slaves in that they held and farmed specific pieces of land and usually lived in the normal family units of the period.

shire. Another term for county.

shire reeve. The chief royal official in a county, other than the earl. The term *shire reeve* later evolved into *sheriff*.

sokemen. One type of English peasant. Though their precise status remains unclear, sokemen were fairly close in level to free peasants.

squire. Initially an assistant to a knight. In England the squires also became a social class just below the level of knight.

subinfeudation. The process by which lords who had received fiefs granted out part of their lands as fiefs to others.

tenant-in-chief. A lord (or lady) who held his (or her) land directly from the king.

thane. A noble in Anglo-Saxon society.

Varangian guard. Scandinavian and later English troops employed in the Byzantine Empire, often as bodyguards of the emperors.

vernacular. In a medieval context, the languages spoken by ordinary people, in contrast to Latin.

villani. The largest category of peasants in *Domesday Book*. Though they were above slaves, villani were below free peasants and therefore were only partially free.

villein. An alternative term for serf.

wapentake. An administrative subdivision of a county or shire. Wapentakes were found in some of the areas once controlled by the Danes and were equivalent to hundreds elsewhere in England.

wardship. Guardianship of minors and their land by their lords.

wasting. A medieval military tactic to undermine enemies by deliberate devastation of their land.

Welsh Marches. The borderlands between England and Wales, often highly militarized.

Wessex. The kingdom of the West Saxons. One of a number of kingdoms founded by the Germanic invaders in Britain after the withdrawal of Roman troops, Wessex came to dominate what is now southern England and then, under Alfred's descendants, formed the nucleus of the English kingdom.

FURTHER READING

OVERVIEW OF SOURCES

Here and in the chapter notes I provide references to English translations where possible. Fortunately, most of the sources are translated, in some cases in facing page editions, which also include the original language. Many important sources for the Anglo-Saxon and Norman periods are found in Dorothy Whitelock, ed., *English Historical Documents*, vol. 1 (New York, 1955), and David C. Douglas and George W. Greenaway, eds., *English Historical Documents*, vol. 2, 2nd ed. (London, 1981). A good collection of sources specifically on the Norman Conquest is R. Allen Brown, *The Norman Conquest* (London, 1984). For sources about the Battle of Hastings, see Stephen Morillo, ed., *The Battle of Hastings: Sources and Interpretations* (Woodbridge, 1996).

For England before, during, and after the conquest, the best source of historical narrative is the *Anglo-Saxon Chronicle*, actually a series of related chronicles. This work is available in a variety of translations from the Old English. An early biography of Edward the Confessor, commissioned by his wife, Edith, daughter of Earl Godwine, is Frank Barlow, ed., *The Life of King Edward Who Rests at Westminster*, 2nd ed. (Oxford, 1992). The most important medieval work on William the Conqueror is a contemporary biography: William of Poitiers, *Gesta Guillelmi*, ed. R. H. C. Davis and Marjorie Chibnall (Oxford, 1998). A key source for Norman history is *The* Gesta Normannorum Ducum *of William of Jumièges, Orderic Vitalis and Robert of Torigni*, ed. Elisabeth M. C. van Houts, 2 vols. (Oxford, 1992–1995). An important work for the Battle of Hastings is Frank Barlow, ed., *The* Carmen de Hastingae Proelio *of Guy, Bishop of Amiens* (Oxford, 1999). For sources on the Normans more generally, see Elisabeth M. C. van Houts, *The Normans in Europe* (New York, 2000).

One twelfth-century work that incorporated lost portions of the *Anglo-Saxon Chronicle* is Reginald R. Darlington and P. McGurk, eds., Jennifer Bray and P. McGurk, trans., *The Chronicle of John of Worcester*, vols. 2–3 (Oxford, 1995–1998). Other twelfth-century works that shed light on the Norman Conquest are William of Malmesbury, *Gesta Regum Anglorum*, ed. Roger A. B. Mynors, Rodney M. Thomson, and Michael Winterbottom, vol. 1 (Oxford, 1998); William of Malmesbury, *The Deeds of the Bishops of England*, trans. David Preest (Woodbridge, 2002); Henry, Archdeacon of Huntingdon, *Historia Anglorum*, ed. Diana Greenway (Oxford, 1996); and Orderic Vitalis, *The Ecclesiastical History of Orderic Vitalis*, ed. Marjorie Chibnall, 6 vols. (Oxford, 1969–1980). A later twelfth-century work that probably contains some useful oral history is translated in Glyn S. Burgess, *The History of the Norman People: Wace's* Roman de Rou (Woodbridge, 2004). Eadmer's *The Life of St Anselm Archbishop of Canterbury*, ed. Richard W. Southern (Oxford, 1972) is an English monk's biography of the second archbishop of Canterbury under the Normans. William of Malmesbury, *Saints' Lives: Lives of SS. Wulfstan, Dunstan, Patrick, Benignus and Indract*, ed. Michael Winterbottom and Rodney M. Thomson (Oxford, 2002), includes a biography of Bishop Wulfstan, the one native bishop to survive William the Conqueror's purge of the church. Local monastic chronicles with useful information on the conquest include Eleanor Searle, ed., *The Chronicle of Battle Abbey* (Oxford, 1980); John Hudson, ed., *Historia Ecclesie Abbendonensis: The History of the Church of Abingdon*, vol. 2 (Oxford, 2002); Thomas of Marlborough, *History of the Abbey of Evesham*, ed. Jane Sayers and Leslie Watkiss (Oxford, 2003); Symeon of Durham, *Libellus de Exordio atque Procursu istius hoc est Dunhelmensis Ecclesie*, ed. David Rollason (Oxford, 2000); Janet Fairweather, trans., *Liber Eliensis: A History of the Isle of Ely from the Seventh Century to the Twelfth* (Woodbridge, 2005); and Leslie Watkiss and Marjorie Chibnall, eds., *The Waltham Chronicle* (Oxford, 1994).

For discussions of some of the key sources, see Antonia Gransden, *Historical Writing in England c. 550 to c. 1307* (Ithaca, 1974); Leah Shopkow, *History and Community: Norman Historical Writing in the Eleventh and Twelfth Centuries* (Washington, 1997); Emily Albu, *The Normans in Their Histories: Propaganda, Myth and Subversion* (Woodbridge, 2001); Nancy F. Partner, *Serious Entertainments: The Writing of History in Twelfth-Century England* (Chicago, 1977); Elisabeth M. C. van Houts, *History and Family Traditions in England and the Continent, 1000–1200* (Aldershot, 1999); and Rodney M. Thomson, *William of Malmesbury*, rev. ed. (Woodbridge, 2003).

Detailed photographs of the Bayeux Tapestry may be found in David M. Wilson, *The Bayeux Tapestry: The Complete Tapestry in Color* (New York, 1985); Wolfgang Grape, *The Bayeux Tapestry: Monument to a Norman Triumph* (Munich, 1994); and Lucien Musset, *The Bayeux Tapestry*, trans. Richard Rex (Woodbridge, 2005). Digital versions of the tapestry are also available. Important recent works on the tapestry include David J. Bernstein, *The Mystery of the Bayeux Tapestry* (Chicago, 1987); Richard Gameson, ed., *The Study of the Bayeux Tapestry* (Woodbridge, 1997); Pierre Bouet, Brian Levy, and François Neveux, eds., *The Bayeux Tapestry: Embroidering the Facts of History* (Caen, 2004); Gale R. Owen-Crocker, ed., *King Harold II and the Bayeux Tapestry* (Woodbridge, 2005); and George Beech, *Was the Bayeux Tapestry Made in France? The Case for Saint-Florent of Saumur* (New York, 2005).

The most convenient translation of *Domesday Book* is Ann Williams and Geoffrey H. Martin, eds., *Domesday Book: A Complete Translation* (London, 2002). Information on many of the people there can be found in Katherine S. B. Keats-Rohan, *Domesday People: A Prosopography of Persons Occurring in English Documents, 1066–1166* (Woodbridge, 1999). The literature on *Domesday Book* is voluminous and not for the faint of heart. Two relatively accessible but out-of-date discussions of the work are R. Welldon Finn, *An Introduction to* Domesday Book (London, 1963), and R. Welldon Finn, Domesday Book: *A Guide* (New York, 1973).

GENERAL READING

The most detailed history of the Norman Conquest, though now dated, is Edward A. Freeman, *The History of the Norman Conquest of England*, 6 vols., 3rd ed. (Oxford, 1877). Also important is R. Allen Brown, *The Normans and the Norman Conquest* (New York, 1968). Important recent discussions of the conquest and the period following, which naturally include some discussion of the impact of the Normans, include Brian Golding, *Conquest and Colonisation: The Normans in Britain, 1066–1100*, 2nd ed. (New York, 2001); Marjorie Chibnall, *The World of Orderic Vitalis* (Oxford, 1984); and Marjorie Chibnall, *Anglo-Norman England, 1066–1166* (Oxford, 1986). Various aspects of the Norman period in England are studied in Christopher Harper-Bill and Elisabeth van Houts, eds., *A Companion to the Anglo-Norman World* (Woodbridge, 2003). A comprehensive view of various debates over the conquest and its consequences, going back to the immediate aftermath of 1066, is Marjorie Chibnall, *The Debate on the Norman Conquest* (Manchester, 1999). Although Ann Williams, *The English and the Norman Conquest*

(Woodbridge, 1995), focuses on relations between the English and Normans, she includes valuable information about a range of subjects. Many of the articles in Richard Eales and Richard Sharpe, eds., *Canterbury and the Norman Conquest: Churches, Saints and Scholars, 1066–1109* (London, 1995), shed light on broader issues than the title of the book would suggest. The collection edited by David Bates and Anne Curry, *England and Normandy in the Middle Ages* (London, 1994), also contains many useful articles. For Norman expansion both in England and elsewhere, see David C. Douglas, *The Norman Achievement, 1050–1100* (Berkeley, 1969), and John Le Patourel, *The Norman Empire* (Oxford, 1976). For the Normans as a people, see Marjorie Chibnall, *The Normans* (Oxford, 2000). The journals *Anglo-Norman Studies* and the *Haskins Society Journal* include many important articles on the Norman Conquest and its aftermath.

CHAPTER 1

An excellent overview of Anglo-Saxon England is James Campbell, Eric John, and Patrick Wormald, *The Anglo-Saxons* (London, 1982). An older but more detailed and still valuable work is Frank M. Stenton, *Anglo-Saxon England*, 3rd ed. (Oxford, 1971). Another useful survey is Henry R. Loyn, *Anglo-Saxon England and the Norman Conquest* (London, 1962). Excellent overviews of the late Anglo-Saxon period, which also cover the Norman Conquest, are Pauline Stafford, *Unification and Conquest: A Political and Social History of England in the Tenth and Eleventh Centuries* (London, 1989), and Nicholas J. Higham, *The Death of Anglo-Saxon England* (Stroud, 1997). The most recent overview is Wendy Davies, ed., *From the Vikings to the Normans* (Oxford, 2003). A general overview of Anglo-Saxon government is Ann Williams, *Kingship and Government in Pre-Conquest England, c. 500–1066* (New York, 1999). For the late Anglo-Saxon church, see Frank Barlow, *The English Church, 1000–1066: A Constitutional History* (Hamden, 1963), and John Blair, *The Church in Anglo-Saxon Society* (Oxford, 2005). For military organization, see Richard P. Abels, *Lordship and Military Obligation in Anglo-Saxon England* (Berkeley, 1988). For late Anglo-Saxon Art, with some information on its impact after the conquest, see Janet Backhouse, D. H. Turner, and Leslie Webster, *The Golden Age of Anglo-Saxon Art, 966–1066* (Bloomington, 1984); and Charles R. Dodwell, *Anglo-Saxon Art: A New Perspective* (Manchester, 1987). For Harold Godwineson and his family, see Ian W. Walker, *Harold: The Last Anglo-Saxon King* (Stroud, 1997); Frank Barlow, *The Godwins: The Rise and Fall of a Noble Dynasty* (Harlow, 2002);

Emma Mason, *The House of Godwine: The History of a Dynasty* (London, 2004); and Peter Rex, *Harold II* (Stroud, 2005).

For Normandy before the conquest, the best book in English is David Bates, *Normandy before 1066* (Harlow, 1982). Another important book is Eleanor Searle, *Predatory Kinship and the Creation of Norman Power, 840–1066* (Berkeley, 1988). Two important biographies of William the Conqueror are David C. Douglas, *William the Conqueror: The Norman Impact upon England* (Berkeley, 1964), and David Bates, *William the Conqueror* (Stroud, 2001).

CHAPTER 2

The biographies of William and Harold and several of the overall accounts of the Norman Conquest have good accounts of the warfare discussed in this chapter. A good short account, with lavish illustrations and excellent maps, is Matthew Bennett, *Campaigns of the Norman Conquest* (Oxford, 2001). For Harald Hardrada and his invasion, see Kelly Devries, *The Norwegian Invasion of England in 1066* (Woodbridge, 1999). For the Battle of Hastings, see Stephen Morillo, ed., *The Battle of Hastings: Sources and Interpretations* (Woodbridge, 1996); Jim Bradbury, *The Battle of Hastings* (Stroud, 1998); and Michael K. Lawson, *The Battle of Hastings, 1066* (Stroud, 2003).

CHAPTER 3

Important recent overviews of the period after the Norman Conquest include Michael T. Clanchy, *England and Its Rulers, 1066–1307*, 3rd ed. (Oxford, 2006); Robert Bartlett, *England under the Norman and Angevin Kings, 1075–1225* (Oxford, 2000); Barbara Harvey, ed., *The Short Oxford History of the British Isles: The Twelfth and Thirteenth Centuries, 1066–c. 1280* (Oxford, 2001); David Carpenter, *The Struggle for Mastery: Britain 1066–1284* (Oxford, 2003); and Christopher Daniell, *From Norman Conquest to Magna Carta: England, 1066–1215* (London, 2003).

Changes in government are discussed in many of the overviews of the conquest and biographies of William noted earlier. Two works argue that the Normans undermined rather than built on the existing government: Henry G. Richardson and George O. Sayles, *The Governance of Mediaeval England from the Conquest to Magna Carta* (Edinburgh, 1963), and Wilfred L. Warren, "The Myth of Norman Administrative Efficiency," *Transactions of the Royal Historical Society*, 5th ser., 34 (1984), 113–32. Though they make interesting points, I believe their arguments go too far. For coinage, see Michael Dolley, *The Norman Conquest and the English Coinage* (London, 1966). For the history of the royal forests, see Charles R. Young, *The Royal Forests of Medieval England* (Philadelphia, 1979). For developments in government in the early twelfth century, see Judith A. Green, *The Government of England under Henry I* (Cambridge, 1986).

The securing of northern England by the Normans is studied in William E. Kapelle, *The Norman Conquest of the North: The Region and Its Transformation, 1000–1135* (Chapel Hill, 1979); William M. Aird, *St Cuthbert and the Normans: The Church of Durham, 1071–1153* (Woodbridge, 1998); and Paul Dalton, *Conquest, Anarchy, and Lordship: Yorkshire, 1066–1154* (Cambridge, 1994). A good overview of the English Conquest of Wales from Harold's time on is R. R. Davies, *The Age of Conquest: Wales, 1063–1415* (Oxford, 1991). For relations between England and Scotland in the aftermath of the conquest, see G. W. S. Barrow, *Kingship and Unity: Scotland, 1000–1306*, 2nd ed. (Edinburgh, 2003). Relations between England and France during the Middle Ages are discussed in all general histories of the two countries in that period. A recent work that is particularly devoted to this subject is Donald Matthew, *Britain and the Continent, 1000–1300* (London, 2005).

The best recent introductions to the military changes brought by the Normans are Matthew Strickland, "Military Technology and Conquest: The Anomaly of England," *Anglo-Norman Studies* 19 (1997), 353–82, and Stephen Morillo, *Warfare under the Anglo-Norman Kings, 1066–1135* (Woodbridge, 1994). For good overviews of the history of medieval English castles, see R. Allen Brown, *English Castles* (London, 1970), and Norman J. G. Pounds, *The Medieval Castle in England and Wales: A Social and Political History* (Cambridge, 1990).

Robin Fleming, *Kings and Lords in Conquest England* (Cambridge, 1991) is the most important work for the history of landholding in the immediate aftermath of the Norman Conquest. More work needs to be done on long-term alienation of property by lords, but a start has been made in my own article, Hugh M. Thomas, "Subinfeudation and Alienation of Land, Economic Development, and the Wealth of Nobles on the Honor of Richmond, 1066 to c. 1300," *Albion* 26 (1994), 397–417.

I developed some of my arguments on feudalism in my first book, Thomas, *Vassals, Heiresses, Crusaders, and Thugs: The Gentry of Angevin Yorkshire, 1154–1216* (Philadelphia, 1993), especially in the first chapter. The classic work on Anglo-Norman feudalism is Frank Stenton, *The First Century of English Feudalism, 1066–1166*, 2nd ed. (Oxford, 1961). For a traditional view of the Norman introduction of feudalism, see R. Allen Brown,

Origins of English Feudalism (London, 1973), which also contains many primary sources. Other important works include David A. Carpenter, "The Second Century of English Feudalism," *Past and Present* 168 (2000), 30–71; S. F. C. Milsom, *The Legal Framework of English Feudalism* (Cambridge, 1976); John Hudson, *Land, Law, and Lordship in Anglo-Norman England* (Oxford, 1994); and David Crouch, *The Birth of the Nobility: Constructing Aristocracy in England and France, 900–1300* (Harlow, 2005).

The classic work on law in the period, which is still useful despite being over a century old, is Frederick Pollock and Frederic William Maitland, *The History of English Law before the Time of Edward I*, 2nd ed., revised by S. F. C. Milsom (Cambridge, 1968). A much shorter and more current overview is John Hudson, *The Formation of the English Common Law: Law and Society in England from the Norman Conquest to Magna Carta* (London, 1996).

CHAPTER 4

For overviews of the English economy after the Norman Conquest, see Reginald Lennard, *Rural England, 1086–1135: A Study of Agrarian Conditions* (Oxford, 1959); Edward Miller and John Hatcher, *Medieval England: Rural Society and Economic Change, 1086–1348* (London, 1978); and Edward Miller and John Hatcher, *Medieval England: Towns, Commerce and Crafts, 1086–1348* (Harlow, 1995). For the growth of the market in England in the period, see Richard H. Britnell, *The Commercialisation of English Society, 1000–1500*, 2nd ed. (Manchester, 1996); John Langdon and James Masschaele, "Commercial Activity and Population Growth in Medieval England," *Past and Present* 190 (2006), 35–81. For the European economy more fully, see George Duby, *Rural Economy and Country Life in the Medieval West*, trans. Cynthia Postan (Columbia, 1968). The best overview of the immediate economic impact of the Norman Conquest is R. Welldon Finn, *The Norman Conquest and Its Effects on the Economy* (n.p., 1970).

Many of the works in the previous paragraph discuss the peasantry. Another important work is Rosamond Faith, *The English Peasantry and the Growth of Lordship* (London, 1997). For slaves and slavery, see David A. E. Pelteret, *Slavery in Early Mediaeval England: From the Reign of Alfred until the Twelfth Century* (Woodbridge, 1995). The crucial work on the shift in inheritance and possibly the family structure after 1066 is James C. Holt, "Feudal Society and the Family in Early Medieval England, I: The Revolution of 1066," in his *Colonial England, 1066–1215* (London, 1997), 161–78. For recent criticism of the idea of a shift from kin group to lineage that discusses both England and France, see David Crouch, *The Birth of the Nobility: Constructing Aristocracy in England and France, 900–1300* (Harlow, 2005), 99–170. For a broad discussion of chivalry and rules of war in the 150 years after the Norman Conquest, see Matthew Strickland, *War and Chivalry: The Conduct and Perception of War in England and Normandy, 1066–1217* (Cambridge, 1996). For the nobility after the conquest more generally, see Charlotte A. Newman, *The Anglo-Norman Nobility in the Reign of Henry I: The Second Generation* (Philadelphia, 1988), and Judith A. Green, *The Aristocracy of Norman England* (Cambridge, 1997). For the best recent discussion of the Norman Conquest and women, see Pauline Stafford, "Women and the Norman Conquest," *Transactions of the Royal Historical Society*, 6th ser., 4 (1994), 221–49.

Much of the thinking in the last section of the chapter is from my own book, Thomas, *The English and the Normans: Ethnic Hostility, Assimilation, and Identity, 1066–c. 1220* (Oxford, 2003). Other important work on the subject can be found in Ann Williams, *The English and the Norman Conquest* (Woodbridge, 1995); John Gillingham, *The English in the Twelfth Century*; and Ian Short, "*Tam Angli quam Franci*: Self-definition in Anglo-Norman England," *Anglo-Norman Studies* 18 (1996), 153–75. Among the most important works on Englishness before the conquest are Patrick Wormald, "*Engla Lond*: The Making of an Allegiance," *Journal of Historical Sociology* 7 (1994), 10–18; James Campbell, "The United Kingdom of England: The Anglo-Saxon Achievement," in *Uniting the Kingdom? The Making of British History*, ed. Alexander Grant and Keith J. Stringer, 31–47 (London, 1995); and Sarah Foot, "The Making of *Angelcynn*: English Identity before the Norman Conquest," *Transactions of the Royal Historical Society*, 6th ser., 6 (1996), 25–49. For Norman Identity, see R. H. C. Davis, *The Normans and Their Myth* (London, 1976); G. A. Loud, "The *Gens Normannorum*—Myth or Reality?" *Proceedings of the Battle Conference on Anglo-Norman Studies* 4 (1982), 104–16, 204–9; Cassandra Potts, "*Atque unum ex diversis gentibus populum effecit*: Historical Tradition and the Norman Identity," *Anglo-Norman Studies* 18 (1996), 139–52; and Emily Albu, *The Normans in Their Histories: Propaganda, Myth and Subversion* (Woodbridge, 2001).

CHAPTER 5

For the church in the period, see Frank Barlow, *The English Church, 1066–1154* (New York, 1979), and Martin Brett, *The English Church under Henry I* (London, 1975). For Lanfranc, see H. E. J. Cowdrey, *Lanfranc: Scholar, Monk, and Archbishop* (Oxford, 2003). The most important biography of

Anselm is Richard W. Southern, *Saint Anselm: A Portrait in a Landscape* (Cambridge, 1990). For a different view of Anselm, see Sally N. Vaughn, *Anselm of Bec and Robert of Meulan: The Innocence of the Dove and the Wisdom of the Serpent* (Berkeley, 1987). All of these biographies deal fruitfully with England's relationship with the papacy. For this issue, see also Zachary N. Brooke, *The English Church and the Papacy from the Conquest to the Reign of John*, 2nd ed. (Cambridge, 1989). For overviews of monasteries and patronage of religious houses after the conquest, see Janet Burton, *Monastic and Religious Orders in Britain, 1000–1300* (Cambridge, 1994), and Emma Cownie, *Religious Patronage in Anglo-Norman England, 1066–1135* (Woodbridge, 1998).

For overviews of English art in the period, see Charles R. Dodwell, *The Pictorial Arts of the West, 800–1200* (New Haven, 1993); T. S. R. Boase, *English Art: 1100–1216* (Oxford, 1953); Claus M. Kauffmann, *Romanesque Manuscripts, 1066–1190* (London, 1975); George Zarnecki, *English Romanesque Sculpture, 1066–1140* (London, 1951); George Zarnecki, "1066 and Architectural Sculpture," in *Studies in Romanesque Sculpture*, 173–84 (London, 1979); and George Zarnecki, Janet Holt, and Tristram Holland, *English Romanesque Art, 1066–1200* (London, 1984). For a recent overview of architecture after the Norman Conquest, see Eric Fernie, *The Architecture of Norman England* (Oxford, 2000). For the impact of the Norman Conquest on architecture, see Eric Fernie, "The Effect of the Conquest on Norman Architectural Patronage," *Anglo-Norman Studies* 9 (1987), 71–85, and "Architecture and the Effects of the Norman Conquest," in *England and Normandy in the Middle Ages*, ed. David Bates and Anne Curry, 105–16 (London, 1994).

For the general rise of the use of writing in the central Middle Ages, see Michael T. Clanchy, *From Memory to Written Record: England, 1066–1307*, 2nd ed. (Oxford, 1993). For an accessible overview of Old and Middle English poetry, see Derek Pearsall, *Old English and Middle English Poetry* (London, 1977). For Anglo-Norman literature generally, see M. Dominica Legge, *Anglo-Norman Literature and Its Background* (Oxford, 1963), and Susan Crane, "Anglo-Norman Cultures in England, 1066–1460," in *The Cambridge History of Medieval English Literature*, ed. David Wallace, 35–60 (Cambridge, 1999). For Latin literature from Medieval England, see A. G. Rigg, *A History of Anglo-Latin Literature, 1066–1422* (Cambridge, 1992). For histories of the English language that discuss the impact of the Norman Conquest, see Georges Bourcier, *An Introduction to the History of the English Language*, trans. Cecily Clark (Cheltenham, 1981), and Barbara A. Fennell, *A History of English: A Sociolinguistic Approach* (Oxford, 2001).

INDEX

Notes: *All medieval individuals are indexed by their forenames. Page numbers in italics indicate figures.*

173

ABOUT THE AUTHOR

Hugh M. Thomas received his PhD from Yale University and has taught at the University of Miami ever since. He specializes in the history of England from the late eleventh through the early thirteenth century. He has written *Vassals, Heiresses, Crusaders, and Thugs: The Gentry of Angevin Yorkshire, 1154–1216* and *The English and The Normans: Ethnic Hostility, Assimilation, and Identity, 1066–c. 1220*. Currently, he is working on a book on the clergy in twelfth-century England.